C++ Template Metaprogramming

The C++ In-Depth Series

Bjarne Stroustrup, Editor

"I have made this letter longer than usual, because I lack the time to make it short."
—BLAISE PASCAL

The advent of the ISO/ANSI C++ standard marked the beginning of a new era for C++ programmers. The standard offers many new facilities and opportunities, but how can a real-world programmer find the time to discover the key nuggets of wisdom within this mass of information? **The C++ In-Depth Series** minimizes learning time and confusion by giving programmers concise, focused guides to specific topics.

Each book in this series presents a single topic, at a technical level appropriate to that topic. The Series' practical approach is designed to lift professionals to their next level of programming skills. Written by experts in the field, these short, in-depth monographs can be read and referenced without the distraction of unrelated material. The books are cross-referenced within the Series, and also reference *The C++ Programming Language* by Bjarne Stroustrup.

As you develop your skills in C++, it becomes increasingly important to separate essential information from hype and glitz, and to find the in-depth content you need in order to grow. The C++ In-Depth Series provides the tools, concepts, techniques, and new approaches to C++ that will give you a critical edge.

Titles in the Series

Accelerated C++: Practical Programming by Example, Andrew Koenig and Barbara E. Moo

Applied C++: Practical Techniques for Building Better Software, Philip Romanik and Amy Muntz

The Boost Graph Library: User Guide and Reference Manual, Jeremy G. Siek, Lie-Quan Lee, and Andrew Lumsdaine

C++ Coding Standards: 101 Rules, Guidelines, and Best Practices, Herb Sutter and Andrei Alexandrescu

C++ In-Depth Box Set, Bjarne Stroustrup, Andrei Alexandrescu, Andrew Koenig, Barbara E. Moo, Stanley B. Lippman, and Herb Sutter

C++ Network Programming, Volume 1: Mastering Complexity with ACE and Patterns, Douglas C. Schmidt and Stephen D. Huston

C++ Network Programming, Volume 2: Systematic Reuse with ACE and Frameworks, Douglas C. Schmidt and Stephen D. Huston

C++ Template Metaprogramming: Concepts, Tools, and Techniques from Boost and Beyond, David Abrahams and Aleksey Gurtovoy

Essential C++, Stanley B. Lippman

Exceptional C++: 47 Engineering Puzzles, Programming Problems, and Solutions, Herb Sutter

Exceptional C++ Style: 40 New Engineering Puzzles, Programming Problems, and Solutions, Herb Sutter

Modern C++ Design: Generic Programming and Design Patterns Applied, Andrei Alexandrescu

More Exceptional C++: 40 New Engineering Puzzles, Programming Problems, and Solutions, Herb Sutter

C++ Template Metaprogramming
Concepts, Tools, and Techniques
from Boost and Beyond

David Abrahams
Aleksey Gurtovoy

✦✦Addison-Wesley

Boston

The publisher offers discounts on this book when ordered in quantity for bulk purchases and special sales. For more information, please contact:

U.S. Corporate and Government Sales
(800) 382-3419
corpsales@pearsontechgroup.com

For sales outside the U.S., please contact:

International Sales
international@pearsoned.com

Visit Addison-Wesley on the Web: www.awprofessional.com

Library of Congress Cataloging-in-Publication Data

Abrahams, David.
    C++ template metaprogramming : concepts, tools, and
techniques from Boost and beyond / David Abrahams, Aleksey
Gurtovoy.
       p. cm.
    ISBN 0-321-22725-5 (pbk. : alk. paper)
    1. C++ (Computer program language) 2. Computer
programming. I. Gurtovoy, Aleksey. II. Title.

QA 76.73.C153A325 2004
005.13'3—dc22

                          2004017580

ISBN: 0-321-22725-5
Text printed on recycled paper
1 2 3 4 5 6 7 8 9 10—CRS—0807060504
First printing, November 2004

Contents

Preface

In 1998 Dave had the privilege of attending a workshop in Generic Programming at Dagstuhl Castle in Germany. Near the end of the workshop, a very enthusiastic Kristof Czarnecki and Ullrich Eisenecker (of *Generative Programming* fame) passed out a few pages of C++ source code that they billed as a complete Lisp implementation built out of C++ templates. At the time it appeared to Dave to be nothing more than a curiosity, a charming but impractical hijacking of the template system to prove that you can write programs that execute at compile time. He never suspected that one day he would see a role for metaprogramming in most of his day-to-day programming jobs. In many ways, that collection of templates was the precursor to the Boost Metaprogramming Library (MPL): It may have been the first library designed to turn compile-time C++ from an ad hoc collection of "template tricks" into an example of disciplined and readable software engineering. With the availability of tools to write and understand metaprograms at a high level, we've since found that using these techniques is not only practical, but easy, fun, and often astoundingly powerful.

Despite the existence of numerous real systems built with template metaprogramming and the MPL, many people still consider metaprogramming to be other-worldly magic, and often as something to be avoided in day-to-day production code. If you've never done any metaprogramming, it may not even have an obvious relationship to the work you do. With this book, we hope to lift the veil of mystery, so that you get an understanding not only of *how* metaprogramming is done, but also *why* and *when*. The best part is that while much of the mystery will have dissolved, we think you'll still find enough magic left in the subject to stay as inspired about it as we are.

— Dave and Aleksey

Acknowledgments

We thank our reviewers, Douglas Gregor, Joel de Guzman, Maxim Khesin, Mat Marcus, Jeremy Siek, Jaap Suter, Tommy Svensson, Daniel Wallin, and Leor Zolman, for keeping us honest. Special thanks go to Luann Abrahams, Brian McNamara, and Eric Niebler, who read and commented on every page, often when the material was still *very* rough. We also thank Vesa Karvonen and Paul Mensonides for reviewing Appendix A in detail. For their faith that we'd write something of value, we thank our editors, Peter Gordon and Bjarne Stroustrup. David Goodger and Englebert Gruber built the ReStructuredText markup language in which this book was written. Finally, we thank the Boost community for creating the environment that made our collaboration possible.

Dave's Acknowledgments

In February of 2004 I used an early version of this book to give a course for a brave group of engineers at Oerlikon Contraves, Inc. Thanks to all my students for struggling through the tough parts and giving the material a good shakedown. Special thanks go to Rejean Senecal for making that investment high-performance code with a long future, against the tide of a no-investment mentality.

Chuck Allison, Scott Meyers, and Herb Sutter have all encouraged me to get more of my work in print—thanks guys, I hope this is a good start.

I am grateful to my colleagues on the C++ standards committee and at Boost for demonstrating that even with egos and reputations at stake, technical people can accomplish great things in collaboration. It's hard to imagine where my career would be today without these communities. I know this book would not have been possible without them.

Finally, for taking me to see the penguins, and for reminding me to think about them at least once per chapter, my fondest thanks go to Luann.

Aleksey's Acknowledgments

My special thanks go to my teammates at Meta for being my "extended family" for the past five years, and for creating and maintaining the most rewarding work environment ever. A fair amount of knowledge, concepts, and ideas reflected in this book were shaped during the pair programming sessions, seminars, and casual insightful discussions that we held here.

I also would like to thank all the people who in one or another way contributed to the development of the Boost Metaprogramming Library—the tool that in some sense this book is centered around. There are many of them, but in particular, John R. Bandela, Fernando Cacciola, Peter Dimov, Hugo Duncan, Eric Friedman, Douglas Gregor, David B. Held, Vesa Karvonen, Mat Marcus, Paul Mensonides, Jaap Suter, and Emily Winch all deserve a special thank you.

My friends and family provided me with continued encouragement and support, and it has made a big difference in this journey—thank you all so much!

Last but not least, I thank Julia for being herself, for believing in me, and for everything she has done for me. Thank you for everything.

Making the Most of This Book

The first few chapters of this book lay the conceptual foundation you'll need for most everything else we cover, and chapters generally build on material that has come before. That said, feel free to skip ahead for any reason—we've tried to make that possible by providing cross-references when we use terms introduced earlier on.

Chapter 10, Domain-Specific Embedded Languages, is an exception to the rule that later chapters depend on earlier ones. It focuses mostly on concepts, and only appears late in the book because at that point you'll have learned the tools and techniques to put Domain-Specific Embedded Languages into play in real code. If you only remember one chapter by the time you're done, make it that one.

Near the end of many chapters, you'll find a Details section that summarizes key ideas. These sections usually add new material that deepens the earlier discussion,[1] so even if you are inclined to skim them the first time through, we suggest you refer back to them later.

We conclude most chapters with exercises designed to help you develop both your programming and conceptual muscles. Those marked with asterisks are expected to be more of a workout than the others. Not all exercises involve writing code—some could be considered "essay questions"—and you don't have to complete them in order to move on to later chapters. We *do* suggest you look through them, give a little thought to how you'd answer each one, and try your hand at one or two; it's a great way to gain confidence with what you've just read.

Supplementary Material

This book comes with a companion CD that supplies the following items in electronic form

- Sample code from the book.

- A release of the Boost C++ libraries. Boost has become known for high-quality, peer-reviewed, portable, generic, and freely reusable C++ libraries. We make extensive use of one Boost library

---

1. We borrowed this idea from Andrew Koenig and Barbara Moo's *Accelerated C++: Practical Programming By Example* [KM00].

throughout the book—the Boost Metaprogramming Library (MPL)—and we discuss several others.

- A complete MPL reference manual, in HTML and PDF form.
- Boost libraries discussed in this book that are not yet part of an official release.

The `index.html` file at the top level of the CD will provide you with a convenient guide to all of its contents. Additional and updated material, including the inevitable errata, will appear on the book's Web site: http://www.boost-consulting.com/mplbook. You'll also find a place there to report any mistakes you might find.

Trying It Out

To compile any of the examples, just put the CD's `boost_1_32_0/` directory into your compiler's `#include` path.

The libraries we present in this book go to great lengths to hide the problems of less-than-perfect compilers, so it's unlikely that you'll have trouble with the examples we present here. That said, we divide C++ compilers roughly into three categories.

A. Those with mostly conforming template implementations. On these compilers, the examples and libraries "just work." Almost anything released since 2001, and a few compilers released before then, fall into this category.

B. Those that can be made to work, but require some workarounds in user code.

C. Those that are too broken to use effectively for template metaprogramming.

Appendix D lists the compilers that are known to fall into each of these categories. For those in category B, Appendix D refers to a list of portability idioms. These idioms have been applied to the copies of the book's examples that appear on the accompanying CD, but to avoid distracting the majority of readers they don't appear in the main text.

The CD also contains a portability table with a detailed report of how various compilers are doing with our examples. GCC is available free for most platforms, and recent versions have no problems handling the code we present here.

Even if you have a relatively modern compiler from category A, it might be a good idea to grab a copy of GCC with which to cross-check your code. Often the easiest way to decipher an inscrutable error message is to see what some other compiler has to say about your program. If you find yourself struggling with error messages as you try to do the exercises, you might want to skip ahead and read the first two sections of Chapter 8, which discusses how to read and manage diagnostics.

And now, on to *C++ Template Metaprogramming*!

1

Introduction

You can think of this chapter as a warm-up for the rest of the book. You'll get a chance to exercise your tools a little and go through a short briefing on basic concepts and terminology. By the end you should have at least a vague picture of what the book is about, and (we hope) you'll be eager to move on to bigger ideas.

1.1 Getting Started

One of the nice things about template metaprograms is a property they share with good old traditional systems: Once a metaprogram is written, it can be used without knowing what's under the hood—as long as it works, that is.

To build your confidence in that, let us begin by presenting a tiny C++ program that simply *uses* a facility implemented with template metaprogramming:

```
#include "libs/mpl/book/chapter1/binary.hpp"
#include <iostream>

int main()
{
    std::cout << binary<101010>::value << std::endl;
    return 0;
}
```

Even if you were always good at binary arithmetic and can tell what the output of the program will be without actually running it, we still suggest that you go to the trouble of trying to compile and run the example. Besides contributing to building your confidence, it's a good test of whether your compiler is able to handle the code we present in this book. The program should write the decimal value of the binary number 101010:

```
42
```

to the standard output.

1.2   So What's a Metaprogram?

If you dissect the word **metaprogram** literally, it means "a program about a program."[1] A little less poetically, a metaprogram is a program that manipulates code. It may be an odd-sounding concept, but you're probably already familiar with several such beasts. Your C++ compiler is one example: it manipulates your C++ code to produce assembly language or machine code.

Parser generators such as YACC [Joh79] are another kind of program-manipulating program. The input to YACC is a high-level parser description written in terms of grammar rules and attached actions brace-enclosed. For instance, to parse and evaluate arithmetic expressions with the usual precedence rules, we might feed YACC the following grammar description:

```
expression : term
           | expression '+' term { $$ = $1 + $3; }
           | expression '-' term { $$ = $1 - $3; }
           ;

term : factor
     | term '*' factor { $$ = $1 * $3; }
     | term '/' factor { $$ = $1 / $3; }
     ;

factor : INTEGER
       | group
       ;

group : '(' expression ')'
      ;
```

In response, YACC would generate a C/C++ source file containing (among other things), a yyparse function that we can call to parse text against the grammar and execute the appropriate actions:[2]

```
int main()
{
  extern int yyparse();
  return yyparse();
}
```

---

1. In philosophy and, as it happens, programming, the prefix "meta" is used to mean "about" or "one level of description higher," as derived from the original Greek meaning "beyond" or "behind."

2. This is provided that we also implemented an appropriate yylex function to tokenize the text. See Chapter 10 for a complete example or, better yet, pick up a YACC manual.

The user of YACC is operating mostly in the domain of parser design, so we'll call YACC's input language the **domain language** of this system. Because the rest of the user's program typically requires a general-purpose programming system and must interact with the generated parser, YACC translates the domain language into the **host language**, C, which the user then compiles and links together with her other code. The domain language thus undergoes two translation steps, and the user is always very conscious of the boundary between it and the rest of her program.

1.3   Metaprogramming in the Host Language

YACC is an example of a **translator**—a metaprogram whose domain language differs from its host language. A more interesting form of metaprogramming is available in languages such as Scheme [SS75]. The Scheme metaprogrammer defines her domain language as a subset of the legal programs in Scheme itself, and the metaprogram executes in the same translation step used to process the rest of the user's program. Programmers move between ordinary programming, metaprogramming, and writing in the domain language, often without being aware of the transition, and they are able to seamlessly combine multiple domains in the same system.

Amazingly, if you have a C++ compiler, this is precisely the kind of metaprogramming power you hold in your fingertips. The rest of this book is about unlocking that power and showing how and when to use it.

1.4   Metaprogramming in C++

In C++, it was discovered almost by accident [Unruh94], [Veld95b] that the template mechanism provides a rich facility for native language metaprogramming. In this section we'll explore the basic mechanisms and some common idioms used for metaprogramming in C++.

1.4.1   Numeric Computations

The earliest C++ metaprograms performed integer computations at compile time. One of the very first metaprograms was shown at a C++ committee meeting by Erwin Unruh; it was actually an illegal code fragment whose error messages contained a sequence of computed prime numbers!

Since illegal code is hard to use effectively in a larger system, let's examine a slightly more practical application. The following metaprogram (which lies at the heart of our little compiler test above) transliterates unsigned decimal numerals into their binary equivalents, allowing us to express binary constants in a recognizable form.

```
template <unsigned long N>
struct binary
{
    static unsigned const value
        = binary<N/10>::value << 1    // prepend higher bits
          | N%10;                      // to lowest bit
};

template <>                           // specialization
struct binary<0>                      // terminates recursion
{
    static unsigned const value = 0;
};

unsigned const one   =    binary<1>::value;
unsigned const three =    binary<11>::value;
unsigned const five  =   binary<101>::value;
unsigned const seven =   binary<111>::value;
unsigned const nine  =  binary<1001>::value;
```

If you're wondering "Where's the program?" we ask you to consider what happens when we access the nested ::value member of binary<N>. The binary template is instantiated again with a smaller N, until N reaches zero and the specialization is used as a termination condition. That process should have the familiar flavor of a recursive function call—and what is a program, after all, but a function? Essentially, the compiler is being used to *interpret* our little metaprogram.

Error Checking

There's nothing to prevent a user from passing binary a number such as 678, whose decimal representation is not also valid binary. The result would make a strange sort of sense (it would be $6 \times 2^2 + 7 \times 2^1 + 8 \times 2^0$), but nonetheless an input like 678 probably indicates a bug in the user's logic. In Chapter 3 we'll show you how to ensure that binary<N>::value only compiles when N's decimal representation is composed solely of 0s and 1s.

Because the C++ language imposes a distinction between the expression of compile-time and runtime computation, metaprograms look different from their runtime counterparts. As in Scheme, the C++ metaprogrammer writes her code in the same language as the ordinary program, but in C++ only the compile-time subset of the full language is available to her. Compare the previous example with this straightforward runtime version of binary:

```
unsigned binary(unsigned long N)
{
    return N == 0 ? 0 : N%10 + 2 * binary(N/10);
}
```

A key difference between the runtime and compile time versions is the way termination conditions are handled: our meta-binary uses **template specialization** to describe what happens when N is zero. Terminating specializations are a common characteristic of nearly all C++ metaprograms, though in some cases they will be hidden behind the interface of a metaprogramming library.

Another important difference between runtime and compile time C++ is highlighted by this version of `binary`, which uses a `for` loop in lieu of recursion.

```
unsigned binary(unsigned long N)
{
    unsigned result = 0;
    for (unsigned bit = 0x1; N; N /= 10, bit <<= 1)
    {
        if (N%10)
            result += bit;
    }
    return result;
}
```

Though more verbose than the recursive version, many C++ programmers will be more comfortable with this one, not least because at runtime iteration is sometimes more efficient than recursion.

The compile-time part of C++ is often referred to as a "pure functional language" because of a property it shares with languages such as Haskell: (meta)data is immutable and (meta)functions can have no side effects. As a result, compile-time C++ has nothing corresponding to the non-const variables used in runtime C++. Since you can't write a (non-infinite) loop without examining some mutable state in its termination condition, iteration is simply beyond reach at compile time. Therefore, recursion is idiomatic for C++ metaprograms.

1.4.2 Type Computations

Much more important than its ability to do compile time numeric computations is C++'s ability to compute with **types**. As a matter of fact, type computation will dominate the rest of this book, and we'll cover examples of it in the very first section of the next chapter. By the time we're through, you'll probably think of template metaprogramming as "computing with types."

Although you may have to read Chapter 2 to understand the specifics of type computation, we'd like to give you a sense of its power. Remember our YACC expression evaluator? It turns out we don't need to use a translator to get that kind of power and convenience. With appropriate surrounding code from the Boost Spirit library, the following legal C++ code has equivalent functionality.

```
expr =
    ( term[expr.val = _1] >> '+' >> expr[expr.val += _1] )
    | ( term[expr.val = _1] >> '-' >> expr[expr.val -= _1] )
    | term[expr.val = _1]
    ;

term =
    ( factor[term.val = _1] >> '*' >> term[term.val *= _1] )
    | ( factor[term.val = _1] >> '/' >> term[term.val /= _1] )
    | factor[term.val = _1]
    ;

factor =
    integer[factor.val = _1]
    | ( '(' >> expr[factor.val = _1] >> ')' )
    ;
```

Each assignment stores a function object that parses and evaluates the bit of grammar on its right hand side. The behavior of each stored function object, when invoked, is determined entirely by the *type* of the expression used to construct it, and the type of each expression is *computed by a metaprogram* associated with the various operators used.

Just like YACC, the Spirit library is a metaprogram that generates parsers from grammar specifications. Unlike YACC, Spirit defines its domain language as a subset of C++ itself. If you don't see how that's possible at this point, don't worry. By the time you finish this book, you will.

1.5   Why Metaprogramming?

So, what are the benefits of metaprogramming? There are definitely simpler ways to address the same kinds of problems we've been discussing here. Let's take a look at two other approaches and see how they stack up when applied to the interpretation of binary numerals and parser construction.

1.5.1   Alternative 1: Runtime Computation

Most straightforwardly, we could do the computation at runtime instead of compile time. For example, we might use one of the binary *function* implementations shown earlier, or a parsing system could be designed to interpret the input grammar at runtime the first time we ask it to parse.

The most obvious reason to rely on a metaprogram is that by doing as much work as possible before the resulting program starts, we get **faster programs**. When a grammar is compiled, YACC performs substantial parse table generation and optimization steps that, if done at runtime, could noticeably degrade a program's overall performance. Similarly, because binary does its work at compile time, its ::value is available as a compile-time constant, and the compiler can encode it directly in the object code, saving a memory lookup when it is used.

A subtler but perhaps more important argument for using a metaprogram is that the result of the computation can **interact more deeply with the target language**. For example, the size of a C++ array can only be legally specified by a compile-time constant like binary<N>::value—not by a runtime function's return value. The brace-enclosed actions in a YACC grammar can contain arbitrary C/C++ code to be executed as part of the generated parser. That's only possible because the actions are processed during grammar *compilation* and passed on to the target C/C++ compiler.

1.5.2 Alternative 2: User Analysis

Instead of doing computation at runtime or compile time, we could just do it by hand. After all, it's common practice to translate binary numbers to hexadecimal so that they can be used directly as C++ literals, and the translation steps performed by YACC and Boost.Spirit to convert the grammar description into a parser are well-known.

If the alternative is writing a metaprogram that will only be used once, one could argue that user analysis is more convenient: It certainly is easier to translate one binary number than to write a correct metaprogram to do so. It only takes a few such instances to tip the balance of **convenience** in the opposite direction, though. Furthermore, once the metaprogram is written, its benefits of convenience can be spread across a community of other programmers.

Regardless of how many times it's used, a metaprogram enables its user to write **more expressive code**, because she can specify the result in a form that corresponds to her mental model. In a context where the values of individual bits are meaningful, it makes much more sense to write binary<101010>::value than 42 or the traditional 0x2a. Similarly, the C source to a handwritten parser usually obscures the logical relationships among its grammar elements.

Finally, because humans are fallible, and because the logic of a metaprogram only needs to be written once, the resulting program is more likely to be **correct and maintainable**. Translating binary numbers is such a mundane task that it's easy to pay too little attention and get it wrong. By contrast—as anyone who's done it can attest—writing parse tables by hand requires *too much* attention, and preventing mistakes is reason enough to use a parser generator such as YACC.

1.5.3 Why C++ Metaprogramming?

In a language such as C++, where the domain language is just a subset of the language used in the rest of the program, metaprogramming is even more powerful and convenient.

- The user can enter the domain language directly, without learning a foreign syntax or interrupting the flow of her code.

- Interfacing metaprograms with other code, especially other metaprograms, becomes much smoother.

- No additional build step (like the one imposed by YACC) is required.

In traditional programming it is very common to find oneself trying to achieve the right balance of expressivity, correctness, and efficiency. Metaprogramming often allows us to interrupt that classic tension by moving the computation required for expressivity and correctness from runtime to compile time.

1.6   When Metaprogramming?

You've just seen some examples of the *why* of template metaprogramming, and you've had a tiny glimpse of the *how*, but we haven't discussed *when* metaprogramming is appropriate. However, we've touched on most of the relevant criteria for using template metaprogramming already. As a guideline, if any three of the following conditions apply to you, a metaprogrammed solution may be appropriate.

- You want the code to be expressed in terms of the abstractions of the problem domain. For example, you might want a parser to be expressed by something that looks like a formal grammar rather than as tables full of numbers or as a collection of subroutines; you might want array math to be written using operator notation on matrix and vector objects rather than as loops over sequences of numbers.

- You would otherwise have to write a great deal of boilerplate implementation code.

- You need to choose component implementations based on the properties of their type parameters.

- You want to take advantage of valuable properties of generic programming in C++ such as static type checking and behavioral customization, without loss of efficiency.

- You want to do it all within the C++ language, without an external tool or custom source code generator.

1.7 Why a Metaprogramming Library?

Rather than building up metaprograms from scratch, we'll be working with the high-level facilities of the Boost Metaprogramming Library (MPL). Even if you didn't pick up this book to explore the MPL, we think you'll find your investment in learning it to be well worthwhile because of the benefits the MPL can bring to your day-to-day work.

1. **Quality**. Most programmers who use template metaprogramming components see them—quite properly—as implementation details to be applied toward some greater purpose. By contrast, the MPL authors saw the job of developing useful, high-quality tools and idioms as their central mission. On average, the components in the Boost Metaprogramming Library are more flexible and better implemented than what one would produce along the way to some other goal, and you can expect more optimizations and improvements in the future as updates are released.

2. **Reuse**. All libraries encapsulate code in reusable components. More importantly, a well-designed generic library establishes a framework of concepts and idioms that provides a *reusable mental model* for approaching problems. Just as the C++ Standard Template Library gave us iterators and a function object protocol, the Boost Metaprogramming Library provides type iterators and a metafunction protocol. A well-considered framework of idioms focuses the metaprogrammer's design decisions and enables her to concentrate on the task at hand.

3. **Portability**. A good library can smooth over the ugly realities of platform differences. While in theory no C++ metaprogram should be concerned with these issues, in practice support for templates remains inconsistent even six years after standardization. No surprises here: C++ templates are the language's furthest-reaching and most complicated feature, a fact that also accounts for the power of metaprogramming in C++.

4. **Fun**. Repeating the same boilerplate code over and over is tedious. Quickly assembling high-level components into readable, elegant designs is fun! The MPL reduces boredom by eliminating the need for the most commonly repeated metaprogramming patterns. In particular, terminating specializations and explicit recursion are often easily and elegantly avoided.

5. **Productivity**. Aside from personal gratification, the health of our projects depends on having fun programming. When we stop having fun we get tired, slow, and sloppy—and buggy code is even more costly than slowly written code.

As you can see, the Boost Metaprogramming Library is motivated by the same practical considerations that underlie the development of any other library. We think its emergence is a sign that template metaprogramming is finally ready to leave the realm of the esoteric and find a home in the everyday repertoire of working C++ programmers.

Finally, we'd like to emphasize the fourth item above: The MPL not only makes metaprogramming practical and easy, but it's also a great pleasure to work with. We hope that you'll enjoy learning about it as much as we have enjoyed using and developing it.

2

Traits and Type Manipulation

We hope the numerical bias of Chapter 1 didn't leave you with the impression that most metaprograms are arithmetic in nature. In fact, numeric computation at compile time is comparatively rare. In this chapter you'll learn the basics of what is going to be a recurring theme: metaprogramming as "type computation."

2.1 Type Associations

In C++, the entities that can be manipulated at compile time, called **metadata**, are divided roughly into two categories: *types* and *non-types*. Not coincidentally, all the kinds of metadata can be used as template parameters. The constant integer *values* used in Chapter 1 are among the non-types, a category that also includes values of nearly everything else that can be known at compile time: the other integral types, enums, pointers and references to functions and "global" objects, and pointers to members.[1]

It's easy to imagine doing calculations on some kinds of non-type metadata, but it may surprise you to learn that there is also a way to do calculations with types. To get a feeling for what that means—and why it matters—we're going to look at one of the simplest algorithms from the C++ standard library: iter_swap. It is iter_swap's humble duty to take two iterators and exchange the values of the objects they refer to. It looks something like this:

```
template <class ForwardIterator1, class ForwardIterator2>
void iter_swap(ForwardIterator1 i1, ForwardIterator2 i2)
{
    T tmp = *i1;
    *i1 = *i2;
    *i2 = tmp;
}
```

---

1. The standard also allows *templates* to be passed as template parameters. If that's not mind-bending enough for you, these parameters are treated in the standard "as types for descriptive purposes." Templates aren't types, though, and can't be passed to another template where a type is expected.

If at this point you're wondering where T came from, you've got a sharp eye. It hasn't been defined, and `iter_swap` can't compile if we write it that way. Informally, of course, T is the type you get when the iterator is dereferenced, what's known in the C++ standard (section 24.1) as the iterator's **value type**. Okay, but how do we name that type?

2.1.1 Using a Direct Approach

In case you already know the answer chosen by the authors of the standard library, we'll ask you to forget it for the time being; we have a couple of deeper points to make. Instead, imagine *we're* implementing the standard library ourselves and choosing its method of handling iterators. We're going to end up writing a lot of algorithms, and many of them will need to make an association between an iterator type and its value type. We could require all iterator implementations to supply a nested type called `value_type`, which we'd access directly:

```
template <class ForwardIterator1, class ForwardIterator2>
void iter_swap(ForwardIterator1 i1, ForwardIterator2 i2)
{
    typename                          // (see Language Note)
      ForwardIterator1::value_type tmp = *i1;
    *i1 = *i2;
    *i2 = tmp;
}
```

C++ Language Note

The C++ standard requires the `typename` keyword when we use a **dependent name** as though it refers to a type. `ForwardIterator1::value_type` may or may not name a type, *depending* on the particular `ForwardIterator1` that is passed. See Appendix B for more information about `typename`.

That's a perfectly good strategy for making type associations, but it's not very general. In particular, iterators in C++ are modeled on the design of pointers, with the intention that plain pointers should themselves *be* valid iterators. Unfortunately, pointers can't have nested types; that privilege is reserved for classes:

```
void f(int* p1, int* p2)
{
    iter_swap(p1,p2); // error: int* has no member 'value_type'
}
```

2.1.2   Taking the Long Way Around

We can solve any problem by introducing an extra level of indirection.

—Butler Lampson

Lampson's idea is so universal in programming that Andrew Koenig[2] is fond of calling it "the Fundamental Theorem of Software Engineering" (FTSE). We may not be able to add a nested `::value_type` to all iterators, but we *can* add it to a template that takes the iterator type as a parameter. In the standard library this template, called `iterator_traits`, has a simple signature:

```
template <class Iterator> struct iterator_traits;
```

Here's how we put it to work in `iter_swap`:

```
template <class ForwardIterator1, class ForwardIterator2>
void iter_swap(ForwardIterator1 i1, ForwardIterator2 i2)
{
    typename
      iterator_traits<ForwardIterator1>::value_type tmp = *i1;
    *i1 = *i2;
    *i2 = tmp;
}
```

`iterator_traits` is so named because it describes properties (or traits) of its argument. In this case, the traits being described are the iterator's five associated types: `value_type`, `reference`, `pointer`, `difference_type`, and `iterator_category`.

The most important feature of traits templates is that they give us a way to associate information with a type *non-intrusively*. In other words, if your ornery coworker Hector gives you some iterator-like type called `hands_off` that refers to an `int`, you can assign it a `value_type` without disturbing the harmony of your workgroup. All you have to do is add an explicit specialization of `iterator_traits`, and `iter_swap` will see the type `int` when it asks about the `value_type` of Hector's iterator:[3]

```
namespace std
{
```

---

2. Andrew Koenig is the co-author of *Accelerated C++* and project editor for the C++ standard. For an acknowledgment that does justice to his many contributions to C++ over the years, see almost any one of Bjarne Stroustrup's C++ books.

3. For a brief review of template specialization and instantiation, see the Details section at the end of this chapter.

```
template <>
struct iterator_traits<Hector::hands_off>
{
    typedef int value_type;
    four more typedefs...
};
}
```

This non-intrusive aspect of traits is precisely what makes `iterator_traits` work for pointers: the standard library contains the following *partial* specialization of `iterator_traits`, which describes the `value_type` of all pointers:

```
template <class T>
struct iterator_traits<T*> {
    typedef T value_type;
    ...four more typedefs
};
```

Thanks to the indirection through `iterator_traits`, generic functions can now access an iterator's associated types uniformly, whether or not it happens to be a pointer.

2.1.3 Finding a Shortcut

While specialization is a perfectly general mechanism, it's not nearly as convenient as adding nested types to classes. Specialization comes with a lot of baggage: You may have to close the namespaces you're working in and open the namespace of the traits template, and then you'll have to write the text of the traits specialization itself. That's not a very efficient use of keystrokes: its nested typedef is the only information that really counts for anything.

Thoughtfully, the standard library provides a shortcut that allows the author of an iterator to control the types nested in its `iterator_traits` just by writing member types in the iterator. The primary `iterator_traits` template[4] reaches into the iterator to grab its member types:

```
template <class Iterator>
struct iterator_traits {
    typedef typename Iterator::value_type value_type;
    ...four more typedefs
};
```

---

4. The C++ standard refers to ordinary template declarations and definitions—as opposed to partial or explicit (full) specializations—as **primary** templates.

Here you can see the "extra level of indirection" at work: Instead of going directly to `Iterator::value_type`, `iter_swap` gets there by asking `iterator_traits` for the iterator's `value_type`. Unless some specialization overrides the primary `iterator_traits` template, `iter_swap` sees the same `value_type` as it would have if it had directly accessed a nested type in the iterator.

2.2   Metafunctions

If at this point you have begun to notice some similarity between traits templates and ordinary functions, that's good. The parameters and nested types of a traits template play similar roles at compile time to those played by function parameters and return values at runtime. The `binary` template from Chapter 1 is certainly function-like. If the "type computation" performed by `iterator_traits` seems a little too banal to be compared to a function, though, we understand; rest assured that things will quickly get more interesting.

Apart from passing and returning types instead of values, traits templates exhibit two significant features that we *don't* see in ordinary functions:

- **Specialization.** We can non-intrusively alter the result of a traits template for particular "values" (types) of its parameters just by adding a specialization. We can even alter the result for a whole range of "values" (e.g., all pointers) by using partial specialization. Specialization would be really strange if you could apply it to regular functions. Imagine being able to add an overload of `std::abs` that is called only when its argument is an odd number!

- **Multiple "return values."** While ordinary functions map their arguments to just one value, traits often have more than one result. For example, `std::iterator_traits` contains five nested types: `value_type`, `reference`, `pointer`, `difference_type`, and `iterator_category`. It's not even uncommon to find traits templates that contain nested constants or static member functions. `std::char_traits` is an example of just such a component in the standard library.

Still, class templates are enough like functions that we can get some serious mileage out of the analogy. To capture the idea of "class templates-as-functions," we'll use the term **metafunctions**. Metafunctions are a central abstraction of the Boost Metaprogramming Library, and formalizing them is an important key to its power. We'll be discussing metafunctions in depth in Chapter 3, but we're going to cover one important difference between metafunctions and classic traits right here.

The traits templates in the standard library all follow the "multiple return values" model. We refer to this kind of traits template as a "blob," because it's as though a handful of separate and loosely related metafunctions were mashed together into a single unit. We will avoid this idiom at all costs, because it creates major problems.

First of all, there's an efficiency issue: The first time we reach inside the `iterator_traits` for its `::value_type`, the template will be **instantiated**. That means a lot of things to the compiler, but to us the important thing is that at that point the compiler has to work out the meaning of *every* declaration in the template body that happens to depend on a template parameter. In the case of `iterator_traits`, that means computing not only the `value_type`, but the four other associated types as well—even if we're not going to use them. The cost of these extra type computations can really add up as a program grows, slowing down the compilation cycle. Remember that we said type computations would get much more interesting? "More interesting" also means more work for your compiler, and more time for you to drum your fingers on the desk waiting to see your program work.

Second, and more importantly, "the blob" interferes with our ability to write metafunctions that take other metafunctions as arguments. To wrap your mind around that, consider a trivial *runtime* function that accepts two function arguments:

```
template <class X, class UnaryOp1, class UnaryOp2>
X apply_fg(X x, UnaryOp1 f, UnaryOp2 g)
{
    return f(g(x));
}
```

That's not the only way we could design `apply_fg`, though. Suppose we collapsed f and g into a single argument called `blob`, as follows:

```
template <class X, class Blob>
X apply_fg(X x, Blob blob)
{
    return blob.f(blob.g(x));
}
```

The protocol used to call f and g here is analogous to the way you access a "traits blob": to get a result of the "function," you reach in and access one of its members. The problem is that there's no single way to get at the result of invoking one of these blobs. Every function like `apply_fg` will use its own set of member function names, and in order to pass f or g on to another such function we might need to repackage it in a wrapper with new names.

"The blob" is an **anti-pattern** (an idiom to be avoided), because it decreases a program's overall **interoperability**, or the ability of its components to work smoothly together. The original choice to write `apply_fg` so that it accepts function arguments is a good one, because it increases interoperability.

When the callable arguments to `apply_fg` use a single protocol, we can easily exchange them:

```
#include <functional>
float log2(float);

int a = apply_fg(5.0f,  std::negate<float>(), log2);
int b = apply_fg(3.14f, log2, std::negate<float>());
```

The property that allows different argument types to be used interchangeably is called **polymorphism**; literally, "the ability to take multiple forms."

> ## Polymorphism
>
> In C++, there are two kinds of polymorphism. **Dynamic polymorphism** allows us to handle objects of multiple derived types through a single base class pointer or reference. **Static polymorphism**, which we've been discussing in this chapter, allows objects of different types to be manipulated in the same way merely by virtue of their support for a common syntax. The words *dynamic* and *static* indicate that the actual type of the object is determined at runtime or compile time, respectively. Dynamic polymorphism, along with "late-binding" or "runtime dispatch" (provided in C++ by virtual functions), is a key feature of object-oriented programming. Static polymorphism (also known as parametric polymorphism) is essential to generic programming.

To achieve polymorphism among metafunctions, we'll need a single way to invoke them. The convention used by the Boost libraries is as follows:

metafunction-name<type-arguments...>`::type`

From now on, when we use the term *metafunction,* we'll be referring to templates that can be "invoked" with this syntax.

2.3   Numerical Metafunctions

You might find it astonishing that even metafunctions that yield numbers are invoked as shown above. No, we're not asking you to give the name `type` to something that is really a number. The result `::type` of a metafunction with a numerical result really *is* a type—a type known as an **integral constant wrapper**, whose nested `::value` member is an integral constant. We'll explore the details of integral constant wrappers in Chapter 4, but in the meantime, the following example should give you a feeling for what we mean:

```
struct five // integral constant wrapper for the value 5
{
    static int const value = 5;
    typedef int value_type;
    ...more declarations...
};
```

So, to get at the value of a numerical metafunction result, we can write:

metafunction-name<*type arguments...*>`::type::value`

Likewise, integral constants are *passed* to metafunctions in similar wrappers. This extra level of indirection might seem inconvenient, but by now you can probably guess the reason for it: Requiring all metafunctions to accept and return types makes them more uniform, more polymorphic, and more interoperable. You'll see lots of examples of how this application of the FTSE pays off in the next few chapters.[5]

All those benefits aside, writing `::type::value` whenever you want to compute an actual integral constant *does* grow somewhat tedious. Purely as a convenience, a numerical metafunction author may decide to provide an identical nested `::value` directly in the metafunction itself. All of the numerical metafunctions from the Boost library we cover in this book do just that. Note that although it's okay to take advantage of `::value` when you know it's supplied by the metafunction you're calling, you can't count on a nested `::value` in general, even when you know the metafunction yields a numerical result.

2.4   Making Choices at Compile Time

If at this point you still find yourself a little nonplussed at the idea of type computations, we can hardly blame you. Admittedly, using a metafunction to find the `value_type` of an iterator is not much more than a kind of glorified table lookup. If this idea of "computation with types" is going to have legs, there's got to be more to it than making type associations.

2.4.1   More `iter_swap`

To see how we can put metafunctions to use in real code, let's go back to playing "C++ standard library implementor." Sorry to say it, but by now we'll have received a flood of bug reports

---

5. You may have noticed that the metafunction protocol seems to prevent us from achieving the very goal that was our reason for making metafunctions polymorphic: we wanted to be able to write metafunctions that take other metafunctions as arguments. Since metafunctions are templates, not types, we can't pass them where types are expected. For now we'll just have to ask you to suspend your disbelief for the rest of this chapter; we promise to deal with that issue in Chapter 3.

from our performance-minded customers, complaining that the way we defined `iter_swap` in section 2.1.3 is horribly inefficient for some iterators. Apparently one guy tried passing in the iterators of `std::list<std::vector<std::string> >`, which iterate over *vectors of strings,* and his profiler told him that `iter_swap` was the performance bottleneck.

In hindsight, it's hard to be very surprised: The first statement in `iter_swap` makes a copy of the value referenced by one of the iterators. Since copying a vector means copying all of its elements, and each string element copied or assigned is likely to require a dynamic memory allocation and a bitwise copy of the string's characters, this starts to look pretty bad for performance.

Fortunately, there's a workaround. Because the standard library provides an efficient version of `swap` for `vectors` that just exchanges a few internal pointers, we can tell our customer to simply dereference the iterators and call `swap` on the results:

```
std::swap(*i1, *i2);
```

That response isn't very satisfying, though. Why shouldn't `iter_swap` be equally efficient? In a flash of inspiration, we remember the fundamental theorem of software engineering: Can't we just add a level of indirection and delegate the responsibility for efficiency to `swap`?

```
template <class ForwardIterator1, class ForwardIterator2>
void iter_swap(ForwardIterator1 i1, ForwardIterator2 i2)
{
    std::swap(*i1,*i2);
}
```

That *looks* good, but running our test suite shows that calling `swap` doesn't always work. Did you notice that `iter_swap` will accept two iterators of different types? It seems one of the tests tries to exchange the value pointed to by an `int*` with the one pointed to by a `long*` using `iter_swap`. The `swap` function, however, only operates on two objects of the *same* type:

```
template <class T> void swap(T& x, T& y);
```

The implementation of `iter_swap` above causes a compilation error when we try to use it on `int*` and `long*`, because no `std::swap` overload matches the argument types (`int`, `long`).

We could try to solve this problem by leaving the slow implementation of `iter_swap` in place, and adding an overload:

```
// Generalized (slow) version
template <class ForwardIterator1, class ForwardIterator2>
void iter_swap(ForwardIterator1 i1, ForwardIterator2 i2)
{
```

```
    typename
      iterator_traits<ForwardIterator1>::value_type
    tmp = *i1;
    *i1 = *i2;
    *i2 = tmp;
}

// A better match when the two iterators are the same type
template <class ForwardIterator>
void iter_swap(ForwardIterator i1, ForwardIterator i2)
{
    std::swap(*i1, *i2); // sometimes faster
}
```

The C++ rules for partial ordering of function templates say that the new overload is a better
match, when it matches. That handles the problem for int* and long* and passes the test suite.
We ship it!

2.4.2   A Fly in the Ointment

Pretty soon, though, someone will notice that we're still missing an important opportunity for optimization. Consider what happens when we call iter_swap on the iterators of std::vector<
std::string> and std::list<std::string>.   The two iterators will have the same
value_type—with its own efficient swap—but since the iterators themselves are different types, the
fast iter_swap overload that uses it won't be called. What's needed here is a way to get iter_swap
to work on two different iterator types that share a single value_type.

Since we're playing "standard library implementor," we can always try rewriting swap so it works
on two different types:

```
template <class T1, class T2>
void swap(T1& a, T2& b)
{
    T1 tmp = a;
    a = b;
    b = tmp;
}
```

This simple fix will handle most of the cases our users encounter.

2.4.3 Another Fly!

Unfortunately, there's a category of iterators for which this *still* won't work: those whose `operator*` yields a **proxy reference**. A proxy reference isn't, in fact, a reference at all, but a class that tries to emulate one: For an iterator that's both readable and writable, a proxy reference is just a class that is both convertible to, and assignable from, the `value_type`.

The best-known example of such an iterator is that of `vector<bool>`,[6] a container that stores each of its elements in a single bit. Since there's no such thing as a real reference to a bit, a proxy is used so the vector behaves almost exactly like any other vector. The proxy's `operator=(bool)` writes into the appropriate bit of the vector, and its `operator bool()` returns `true` if and only if that bit is set in the vector, something like:

```
struct proxy
{
    proxy& operator=(bool x)
    {
        if (x)
            bytes[pos/8] |= (1u << (pos%8));
        else
            bytes[pos/8] &= ~(1u << (pos%8));
        return *this;
    }

    operator bool() const
    {
        return bytes[pos/8] & (1u << (pos%8));
    }

    unsigned char* bytes;
    size_t pos;
};

struct bit_iterator
{
    typedef bool value_type;
```

---

6. The problem might easily have been missed by our regression tests; some people aren't even convinced `vector<bool>::iterator` is a valid iterator. The subject of how `vector<bool>` and its iterators fit into the standard has been the subject of much debate. Herb Sutter even wrote two papers for the C++ standards committee ([n1185], [n1211]), and a Guru of the Week [GotW50] about the problems. Work has begun in the committee on a system of new iterator concepts [n1550] that, we hope, will help to resolve the issues.

```
    typedef proxy reference;
    more typedefs...

    proxy operator*() const;
    more operations...
};
```

Now consider what happens when `iter_swap` dereferences a `bit_iterator` and tries to pass a couple of proxy references off to `std::swap`. Recall that since `swap` modifies its arguments, they are passed by non-const reference. The problem is that the proxies returned by `operator*` are temporaries, and the compiler will issue an error when we try to pass temporaries as non-const reference arguments. Most of the time that's the right decision, because any changes we made to the temporaries would just disappear into the ether. The original implementation of `iter_swap`, though, works fine on the iterators of `vector<bool>`.

2.4.4   The Flyswapper

What's needed, finally, is a way to pick the "fast" implementation of `iter_swap` only when the iterators have the same `value_type` *and* their `reference` types are real references, not proxies. To make these choices, we need some way to ask (and answer!) the questions "Is T a real reference?" and "Are these two `value_type`s the same?"

Boost contains an entire library of metafunctions designed to query and manipulate fundamental traits like type identity and "reference-ness." Given the appropriate type traits, we can decide whether to use `swap` or do the swapping ourselves:

```
#include <boost/type_traits/is_reference.hpp>
#include <boost/type_traits/is_same.hpp>
#include <iterator>  // for iterator_traits
#include <utility>   // for swap

namespace std {

template <bool use_swap> struct iter_swap_impl; // see text

template <class ForwardIterator1, class ForwardIterator2>
void iter_swap(ForwardIterator1 i1, ForwardIterator2 i2)
{
    typedef iterator_traits<ForwardIterator1> traits1;
    typedef typename traits1::value_type v1;
    typedef typename traits1::reference r1;

    typedef iterator_traits<ForwardIterator2> traits2;
```

```
typedef typename traits2::value_type v2;
typedef typename traits2::reference r2;

bool const use_swap = boost::is_same<v1,v2>::value
                   && boost::is_reference<r1>::value
                   && boost::is_reference<r2>::value;
```

We haven't closed the final brace on `iter_swap`, but at this point all we have to do is find a way to pick different behaviors based on the value of `use_swap`. There are actually *lots* of ways to approach that problem, many of which we'll cover in Chapter 9. We've cleverly anticipated the need for dispatching by forward-declaring `iter_swap_impl`.[7]   We can provide the two behaviors in specializations of `iter_swap_impl` (outside the body of `iter_swap`):

```
template <>
struct iter_swap_impl<true>  // the "fast" one
{
    template <class ForwardIterator1, class ForwardIterator2>
    static void do_it(ForwardIterator1 i1, ForwardIterator2 i2)
    {
        std::swap(*i1, *i2);
    }
};

template <>
struct iter_swap_impl<false>  // the one that always works
{
    template <class ForwardIterator1, class ForwardIterator2>
    static void do_it(ForwardIterator1 i1, ForwardIterator2 i2)
    {
        typename
          iterator_traits<ForwardIterator1>::value_type
        tmp = *i1;
        *i1 = *i2;
        *i2 = tmp;
    }
};
```

Now `iter_swap_impl <use_swap>::do_it` provides an appropriate implementation of `iter_swap` for either possible value of `use_swap`. Because `do_it` is a *static* member function, `iter_swap` can call it without constructing an instance of `iter_swap_impl`:

---

7. A little unnatural foresight is the authors' prerogative!

```
iter_swap_impl<use_swap>::do_it(*i1,*i2);
```

Now we can close the brace and breathe a sigh of relief while our regression tests all pass. We ship! There is much rejoicing! Our customers have an `iter_swap` that is both fast *and* correct.

2.5 A Brief Tour of the Boost Type Traits Library

It turns out that almost every serious template metaprogram ends up needing facilities like those provided by the Boost.Type Traits. The library has proven so useful that it has been accepted into the C++ standard committee's first "Technical Report" ([n1424], [n1519]), a harbinger of things to come in the next official standard. For a complete reference, see the documentation in the `libs/type_traits` subdirectory of your Boost distribution, or at http://www.boost.org/libs/type_traits.

2.5.1 General

There are a few things you need to know about the library as a whole: First, as you may have guessed from the `iter_swap` example, all of the library's metafunctions are in `namespace boost`, and there's a simple convention for `#include`-ing the header that defines any of them:

```
#include <boost/type_traits/ metafunction-name.hpp>
```

Second, as we implied earlier, all of Boost's numerical metafunctions, as a convenience, provide a nested `::value` directly in the metafunction. It may be a bit strange to think of `bool`-valued metafunctions like `is_reference` as "numerical," but C++ classifies `bool` as an integral type and the same convention applies to all integral-valued metafunctions.

Third, there are a few type traits (e.g., `has_trivial_destructor`) that require non-standard compiler support in order to be fully functional. A few compilers, notably Metrowerks CodeWarrior and SGI MipsPro, have actually implemented the necessary primitives. On other compilers, these traits generally are correct for some types and degrade "gracefully and safely" for others. By "gracefully" we mean that even when the traits don't have the correct result, their use will still compile.

To understand what we mean by "safely," you have to know that these traits are mostly used to decide whether certain optimizations are possible. For example, the storage for a type with a trivial destructor may be reused without destroying the object it contains. If, however, you can't determine that the type has a trivial destructor, you must destroy the object before reusing its storage. When `has_trivial_destructor<T>` can't determine the correct result value, it returns `false` so that generic code will always take the safe route and invoke T's destructor.

Last, be aware that type categorization metafunctions like `is_enum<T>`, which we describe next, generally ignore *cv-qualification* (`const` and `volatile`), so that `is_enum<T const>` always has the same result as `is_enum<T>`.

Each of the following subsections describes a different group of traits.

2.5.2 Primary Type Categorization

These unary metafunctions determine which of the fundamental type categories described in the C++ standard applies to their argument. For any given type T, one and only one of these metafunctions should yield a `true` result.

Nine traits cover the type categories that most people are familiar with. There's not much to say about `is_void<T>`, `is_pointer<T>`, `is_reference<T>`, `is_array<T>`, and `is_enum<T>`; they do just what you'd expect. `is_integral<T>` identifies `char`, `bool`, and all the varieties of `signed` and `unsigned` integer types. Similarly, `is_float<T>` identifies the floating-point types `float`, `double`, and `long double`. Unfortunately, without compiler support, `is_union<T>` always returns `false`, thus `is_class<T>` is `true` for both classes and unions.[8]

There are two more categories that most programmers encounter less often. Pointers to member functions, which have the form

$R\ (C::*)\ (args...)\ cv$

and pointers to data members, written as

$D\ C::*$

are identified by `is_member_pointer<T>`. Note that `is_pointer` doesn't identify these types, even though they're called pointers.

Lastly, `is_function<T>` identifies function types of the form

$R\ (args...)$

Many people never see an unadorned function type, because of the way function names, when not immediately invoked, automatically become function pointers or references of the form

$R\ (*)\ (args...)$ or $R\ (\&)\ (args...)$

Table 2.1 lists the primary type traits.

---

8. Classes may be declared using the `struct` keyword, but they are still classes according to the C++ standard. In fact, the following two declarations are interchangeable:

```
class X;
struct X;    // declares the same X
```

`struct` is only distinguished from `class` in *definitions,* where `struct` causes bases and members to be `public` by default.

Table 2.1 Primary Type Categorization

Primary Trait	`::type::value` and `::value`
`is_array<T>`	true iff T is an array type.
`is_class<T>`	true iff T is a class type; without compiler support, may also report `true` for unions.
`is_enum<T>`	true iff T is an enumeration type.
`is_float<T>`	true iff T is a floating-point type.
`is_function<T>`	true iff T is a function type.
`is_integral<T>`	true iff T is an integral type.
`is_member_pointer<T>`	true iff T is a pointer to function or data member.
`is_pointer<T>`	true iff T is a pointer type (but not a pointer to member).
`is_reference<T>`	true iff T is a reference type.
`is_union<T>`	true iff T is a union; without compiler support, always reports `false`.
`is_void<T>`	true iff T is of the form *cv* `void`.

2.5.3 Secondary Type Categorization

The traits in Table 2.2 represent useful groupings of, or distinctions within, the primary categories.

Table 2.2 Secondary Type Categorization

Secondary Trait	`::type::value` and `::value`
`is_arithmetic<T>`	`is_integral<T>::value ||` `is_float<T>::value`
`is_compound<T>`	`!is_fundamental<T>::value`
`is_fundamental<T>`	`is_arithmetic<T>::value ||` `is_void<T>::value`
`is_member_function_` `pointer<T>`	true iff T is a pointer to member function.

`is_object<T>`	`!(is_function<T>::value ||`
	`is_reference<T>::value ||`
	`is_void<T>::value)`

`is_scalar<T>`	`is_arithmetic<T>::value`
	`|| is_enum<T>::value ||`
	`is_pointer<T>::value ||`
	`is_member_pointer<T>::value`

2.5.4 Type Properties

The type traits library uses the term *properties* as a kind of catch-all term for traits other than those directly related to the standard type categories. The simplest traits in this group are `is_const` and `is_volatile`, which detect their arguments' cv-qualification. The rest of the type properties are summarized in Tables 2.3 and 2.4.

Table 2.3 Type Properties

Type Property	`::type::value` and `::value`
`alignment_of<T>`	A positive multiple of T's memory alignment requirements (the library tries to minimize that multiple).
`is_empty<T>`	`true` iff the compiler optimizes away space for empty base classes and T is an empty class.
`is_polymorphic<T>`	`true` iff T is a class with at least one virtual member function.

Table 2.4 More Type Properties

Type Property	`::type::value` and `::value`
`has_nothrow_assign<T>`	`true` only if T has a non-throwing assignment operator.
`has_nothrow_constructor<T>`	`true` only if T has a non-throwing default constructor.
`has_nothrow_copy<T>`	`true` only if T has a non-throwing copy constructor.
`has_trivial_assign<T>`	`true` only if T has a trivial assignment operator.
`has_trivial_constructor<T>`	`true` only if T has a trivial default constructor.
`has_trivial_copy<T>`	`true` only if T has a trivial copy constructor.
`is_pod<T>`	`true` only if T is a POD type.[9]
`is_stateless<T>`	`true` only if T is empty and its constructors and destructors are trivial.

---

9. POD stands for "plain old data." Believe it or not, that's a technical term in the C++ standard. The standard gives us license to make all kinds of special assumptions about POD types. For example, PODs always occupy contiguous bytes of storage; other types might not. A POD type is defined to be either a scalar, an array of PODs, or a struct or union that has no user-declared constructors, no user-declared copy assignment, no user-declared destructor, no private or protected non-static data members, no base classes, no non-static data members of non-POD, reference, or pointer to member type, or array of such types, and no virtual functions.

The traits in Table 2.4 are most useful for selecting optimizations. With compiler support they can be implemented more accurately, allowing *only if* to be replaced by *if and only if* (iff) in the table.

2.5.5 Relationships Between Types

The library contains three important metafunctions that indicate relationships between types. We've already seen `is_same<T,U>`, whose `::value` is `true` when T and U are identical types. `is_convertible<T,U>` yields `true` if and only if an object of type T can be implicitly converted to type U. Finally, `is_base_and_derived<B,D>::value` is `true` if and only if B is a base class of D.

2.5.6 Type Transformations

The metafunctions listed in Table 2.5 perform fundamental type manipulations. Note that unlike other type traits metafunctions we've discussed so far, members of this group yield type results rather than Boolean values. You can think of them as being operators in the "arithmetic of types."

At this point you might be wondering why we bothered with the last three transformations in the table. After all, `add_const<T>::type` is just a more verbose way to write `T const`. It turns out that it's important to be able to express even the simplest transformations in metafunction form so they can be passed on to other metafunctions (which, as promised, we'll show you how to do in the next chapter).

Table 2.5 Transformations Types

Transformation	`::type`
`remove_const<T>`	T without any top-level `const`. For example, `const int` becomes `int`, but `const int*` remains unchanged.
`remove_volatile<T>`	T without any top-level `volatile`. For example, `volatile int` becomes `int`.
`remove_cv<T>`	T without any top-level cv-qualifiers. For example, `const volatile int` becomes `int`.
`remove_reference<T>`	T without any top-level reference. For example, `int&` becomes `int` but `int*` remains unchanged.
`remove_bounds<T>`	T without any top-level array brackets. For example, `int[2][3]` becomes `int[3]`.
`remove_pointer<T>`	T without any top-level pointer. For example, `int*` becomes `int`, but `int&` remains unchanged.
`add_reference<T>`	If T is a reference type, then T, otherwise T&.

Table 2.5 Transformations Types (continued)

Transformation	`::type`
add_pointer<T>	`remove_reference<T>::type*`. For example, `int` and `int&` both become `int*`.
add_const<T>	`T const`
add_volatile<T>	`T volatile`
add_cv<T>	`T const volatile`

2.6 Nullary Metafunctions

Probably the most important thing we've done in this chapter has been to describe the "metafunction" concept, but there's one question we still haven't answered: What does a nullary (zero-argument) metafunction look like?

From the requirements standpoint, a **nullary metafunction** is any type, whether it's a plain class or a class template specialization, that provides us with a nested `::type` member. For instance, `add_const<int>` is a nullary metafunction that always returns the same result: `int const`.

The easiest way to *write* a nullary metafunction is to go with a simple `struct`:

```
struct always_int
{
    typedef int type;
};
```

2.7 Metafunction Definition

Finally, we have everything we need to write a complete, formal description of metafunctions.

> **Definition**
>
> A **metafunction** is either
>
> * a class template, all of whose parameters are types
>
> *or*
>
> * a class
>
> with a publicly accessible nested result type called `type`.

2.8   History

The Boost Type Traits library was inspired by a component in SGI's STL implementation that looked something like this:

```
struct true_type {}; struct false_type {};

template <class T> struct type_traits // assume nothing
{
    typedef false_type has_trivial_default_constructor;
    typedef false_type has_trivial_copy_constructor;
    typedef false_type has_trivial_assignment_operator;
    typedef false_type has_trivial_destructor;
    typedef false_type is_POD_type;
};

template<> struct type_traits<char> // specialization for char
{
    typedef true_type has_trivial_default_constructor;
    typedef true_type has_trivial_copy_constructor;
    typedef true_type has_trivial_assignment_operator;
    typedef true_type has_trivial_destructor;
    typedef true_type is_POD_type;
};
more specializations follow...
```

It's interesting to note that although the SGI type traits yielded result *types,* it's still a "blob," which kills polymorphism. The SGI designers must have had other reasons for using nested types instead of **bool** constants.[10]

Boost.Type Traits was the first C++ library that explicitly recognized the importance of using single-valued metafunctions. Boost rejected the "blob" design primarily because it would reserve a very general name, `type_traits`, for a single template. The name seemed to demand that any new traits be assimilated there—a Borg blob! Anyone who wanted to write a similar component would have felt compelled to go in and modify this one template, potentially causing bugs. At the time, the positive impact this choice would have on efficiency and interoperability wasn't well understood.

The designers established a convention that traits with a Boolean result would have a `::value` and those with a type result would have a `::type`, so users didn't have to guess at how to invoke a

---

10. For a clue as to one possible reason, see section 9.2.3.

given trait. That choice indicates that they recognized the value of polymorphism, even if they didn't reach the ultimate conclusion that *all* metafunctions should supply a `::type`.

As a matter of fact, the type traits weren't seen as "metafunctions" until work on the Boost Metaprogramming Library (MPL) was begun. At that point, the convention used in the Type Traits library became the basis for the uniform protocol used by MPL metafunctions, and Boost Type Traits library was updated accordingly.

2.9 Details

We've covered a lot of ground in this chapter; the journey from traits to metafunctions takes us from the ad hoc type associations used in the simplest generic programs, to the fundamentals that allow metaprogramming to be viewed as a first-class coding activity. We also dipped into the mechanics of C++ templates, got an overview of the type traits library, and saw some of its components in action. In such a broad landscape, some important details are bound to be missed; we'll fill them in as we review the chapter's most important points.

Specialization.   The meaning of *specialization* as applied to C++ templates can be tough to get a handle on, because it's used in two different ways. Its first usage refers to a template with specific arguments filled in, as in `iterator_traits<int*>`. In other words, a template specialization names the actual class (or function, in the case of function template specializations) that results from replacing its parameters with specific arguments.

The second use of *specialization* shows up in "explicit specialization" and "partial specialization"; we showed both explicit and partial specializations of `iterator_traits` in this chapter. The name "explicit" is probably not well-chosen, since partial specializations are just as explicit; you can think of "explicit specialization" as meaning "full specialization" without any loss of understanding.

To remember the syntax rules for declaring class template specializations (the second meaning), keep this form in mind:

```
template <variable part>
struct template-name<fixed part>
```

In an explicit (or full) specialization, the *variable part* is empty and the *fixed part* consists of concrete template arguments. In a partial specialization, the *variable part* contains a parameter list, and at least one argument in the *fixed part* depends on those parameters.

Primary template.   The declaration of a template that is not a specialization (second meaning above) is called the primary template. We can think of the primary template as covering the general case, while specializations cover various special cases.

Instantiation.   The moment the compiler needs to know much more about a template than what
its arguments are—the names of its members or the identity of its base classes, for example—
the template will be instantiated. At that point, the compiler fills in the actual values of
all the template parameters, picks the best-matching explicit or partial specialization (if any),
figures out all of the types and constants used in declarations in the template body, and rechecks
those declarations for errors. It does not, however, instantiate *definitions* (such as member
function bodies) until they are actually used. For example:

```
template <class T, class U>
struct X
{
    int f(T* x)  // declaration
    {
       U y[10];  // definition
       return 0;
    }
};

typedef X<int&, char> t1; // OK; no instantiation yet
t1 x1;                    // error: pointer to int& illegal
typedef X<int, char&> t2;
t2 x2;                    // OK; declarations check out
int a = x2.f();          // error: array of char& illegal
```

As you can see, template instantiation can affect not only compilation speed, but whether your
program compiles at all!

The blob.   A class with lots of members (including member functions) is known in the object-
oriented programming literature as a "blob" [BMMM98]. The members of a class are all
"coupled" to one another, because they must be declared together. To avoid coupling and
increase modularity, avoid this anti-pattern. Instead, define separate traits as independent
metafunctions.

Metadata.   A "value" that can be manipulated by the C++ compile-time machinery can be thought
of as metadata. In template metaprogramming, the two most common kinds of metadata are
types and integer (including `bool`) constants. The compile-time part of C++ is often referred
to as a "pure functional language" because metadata is immutable and metafunctions can't
have any side effects.

Polymorphism.   Literally, "having many forms." In computer languages polymorphism has come
to mean the ability to manipulate different types through a common interface. Having a con-
sistent interface is the best way to ensure that code is reusable and components interoperate

naturally. Because C++ templates do not inherently treat the different kinds of metadata poly-
morphically, MPL follows the convention of using type wrappers around non-type metadata.
In particular, **numerical metadata** is represented as a type with a nested numeric constant
member called `::value`.

Metafunction. A "function" that operates on metadata and can be "invoked" at compile time. For
the remainder of this book, a template or class will only be called a metafunction if it has
no non-type parameters and returns a type called `type`. The arguments to the class template
are the inputs to the compile time computation, and the `::type` member is its result. Thus,
expressions like:

```
some_metafunction<Arg1, Arg2>::type
```

are analogous to runtime computations like:

```
some_function(arg1, arg2)
```

Numerical metafunction. A metafunction that returns a wrapper type for a numerical value. As a
convenience, many numerical metafunctions themselves provide a nested `::value` member,
so that you can write:

```
some_numerical_metafunction<Arg>::value
```

instead of the more general:

```
some_numerical_metafunction<Arg>::type::value
```

if you want to access the numerical result directly.

Nullary metafunction. Any class with a publicly accessible `::type` can be used as a metafunction
that accepts no arguments. As a consequence of this definition, any metafunction specialization (first meaning above), such as `boost::remove_pointer<char*>`, is a legal nullary
metafunction.

Traits. A technique for establishing associations between pieces of metadata via class template
specializations. A key feature of the traits idiom is that it's *non-intrusive:* We can establish a
new mapping without modifying the associated items themselves. MPL metafunctions can be
viewed as a special case of traits, where there is only one result value for any input.

Type traits. The Boost Type Traits library is a metafunction library. It contains a few metafunctions
for low-level type manipulation. For example, the result of `add_reference` is always a
reference type:

```
boost::add_reference<char>::type    // char&
boost::add_reference<int&>::type    // int&
```

The Type Traits library is mainly comprised of Boolean-valued metafunctions that can be used to answer questions about the fundamental properties of any type. For example:

```
boost::is_reference<char>::value    // false
boost::is_reference<int&>::value    // true
```

2.10 Exercises

2-0. Write a unary metafunction add_const_ref<T> that returns T if it is a reference type, and otherwise returns T const&. Write a program to test your metafunction. Hint: you can use boost::is_same to test the results.

2-1. Write a ternary metafunction replace_type<c,x,y> that takes an arbitrary compound type c as its first parameter, and replaces all occurrences of a type x within c with y:

```
typedef replace_type< void*, void, int >::type t1; // int*
typedef replace_type<
    int const*[10]
  , int const
  , long
>::type t2; // long* [10]

typedef replace_type<
    char& (*)(char&)
  , char&
  , long&
>::type t3; // long& (*)(long&)
```

You can limit the function types you operate on to those with fewer than two arguments.

2-2. The boost::polymorphic_downcast function template[11] implements a checked version of static_cast intended for downcasting pointers to polymorphic objects:

```
template <class Target, class Source>
inline Target polymorphic_downcast(Source* x)
{
    assert( dynamic_cast<Target>(x) == x );
    return static_cast<Target>(x);
}
```

---

11. See http://www.boost.org/libs/conversion/cast.htm.

In released software, the assertion disappears and `polymorphic_downcast` can be as efficient as a simple `static_cast`. Use the type traits facilities to write an implementation of the template that allows both pointer and reference arguments:

```
struct A {};
struct B : A {};

B b;
A* a_ptr = &b;
B* b_ptr = polymorphic_downcast<B*>(a_ptr);

A& a_ref = b;
B& b_ref = polymorphic_downcast<B&>(b_ref);
```

2-3. Use the type traits facilities to implement a `type_descriptor` class template, whose instances, when streamed, print the type of their template parameters:[12]

```
// prints "int"
std::cout << type_descriptor<int>();

// prints "char*"
std::cout << type_descriptor<char*>();

// prints "long const*& volatile"
std::cout << type_descriptor<long const*& volatile>();
```

You can assume that `type_descriptor`'s template parameter is limited to compound types built from the following four integral types: `char`, `short int`, `int`, and `long int`.

2-4. Write an alternative solution for exercise 2-3 that does not use the Type Traits library. Compare the solutions.

2-5. Change the `type_descriptor` template from exercise 2-3 to output a pseudo-English description of the type, along the lines of the `explain` command of the `cdecl` program:[13]

```
// prints "array of pointer to function returning pointer to "
//         "char"
std::cout << type_descriptor< char *(*[])() >();
```

---

12. We cannot use runtime type information (RTTI) to the same effect since, according to 18.5.1 [lib.type.info] paragraph 7 of the standard, `typeid(T).name()` is not guaranteed to return a meaningful result.
13. http://linuxcommand.org/man_pages/cdecl1.html.

2-6*. While at first sight the type algebra supplied by the Type Traits library might seem complete, it's not. There are at least a few type categories, relationships, and transformations that are not covered by the library's facilities. For example, they don't provide a way to get the corresponding unsigned counterpart of a signed integer type.

Try to identify as many of these missing parts as you can—there is at least one in each traits category, and we can think of at least 11 in all. Design an interface and come up with a motivating use case for each of the missing traits.

2-7*. One of the nice things about touring the Type Traits library is that we also made a mini-tour of the C++ runtime type system. Each of the primary type categories, plus the `const` and `volatile` qualifiers, is a fundamental building block that can be used in constructing arbitrarily rich types.

All possible C++ types are possible "values" of type metadata, which leads to the question, "What does C++'s compile-time type system look like?" Write a short description of the static type system of compile time C++. Hint: a static type system restricts the values that can be passed to particular functions.

2-8*. Describe the effect of making all metadata polymorphic in terms of static and dynamic type checking.

3

A Deeper Look at Metafunctions

With the foundation laid so far, we're ready to explore one of the most basic uses for template metaprogramming techniques: adding static type checking to traditionally unchecked operations. We'll look at a practical example from science and engineering that can find applications in almost any numerical code. Along the way you'll learn some important new concepts and get a taste of metaprogramming at a high level using the MPL.

3.1 Dimensional Analysis

The first rule of doing physical calculations on paper is that the numbers being manipulated don't stand alone: most quantities have attached *dimensions,* to be ignored at our peril. As computations become more complex, keeping track of dimensions is what keeps us from inadvertently assigning a mass to what should be a length or adding acceleration to velocity—it establishes a type system for numbers.

Manual checking of types is tedious, and as a result, it's also error-prone. When human beings become bored, their attention wanders and they tend to make mistakes. Doesn't type checking seem like the sort of job a computer might be good at, though? If we could establish a framework of C++ types for dimensions and quantities, we might be able to catch errors in formulae before they cause serious problems in the real world.

Preventing quantities with different dimensions from interoperating isn't hard; we could simply represent dimensions as classes that only work with dimensions of the same type. What makes this problem interesting is that different dimensions *can* be combined, via multiplication or division, to produce arbitrarily complex new dimensions. For example, take Newton's law, which relates force to mass and acceleration:

$$F = ma$$

Since mass and acceleration have different dimensions, the dimensions of force must somehow capture their combination. In fact, the dimensions of acceleration are already just such a composite, a change in velocity over time:

$$dv/dt$$

Since velocity is just change in distance (l) over time (t), the fundamental dimensions of acceleration are:

$$(l/t)/t = l/t^2$$

And indeed, acceleration is commonly measured in "meters per second squared." It follows that the dimensions of force must be:

$$ml/t^2$$

and force is commonly measured in kg(m/s^2), or "kilogram-meters per second squared." When multiplying quantities of mass and acceleration, we multiply their dimensions as well and carry the result along, which helps us to ensure that the result is meaningful. The formal name for this bookkeeping is **dimensional analysis**, and our next task will be to implement its rules in the C++ type system. John Barton and Lee Nackman were the first to show how to do this in their seminal book, *Scientific and Engineering C++* [BN94]. We will recast their approach here in metaprogramming terms.

3.1.1 Representing Dimensions

An international standard called *Système International d'Unites* breaks every quantity down into a combination of the dimensions *mass, length* or *position, time, charge, temperature, intensity,* and *angle.* To be reasonably general, our system would have to be able to represent seven or more fundamental dimensions. It also needs the ability to represent composite dimensions that, like *force,* are built through multiplication or division of the fundamental ones.

In general, a composite dimension is the product of powers of fundamental dimensions.[1] If we were going to represent these powers for manipulation at runtime, we could use an array of seven ints, with each position in the array holding the power of a different fundamental dimension:

```
typedef int dimension[7]; // m  l  t  ...
dimension const mass      = {1, 0, 0, 0, 0, 0, 0};
dimension const length    = {0, 1, 0, 0, 0, 0, 0};
dimension const time      = {0, 0, 1, 0, 0, 0, 0};
...
```

In that representation, force would be:

```
dimension const force  = {1, 1, -2, 0, 0, 0, 0};
```

---

1. Divisors just contribute negative exponents, since $1/x = x^{-1}$.

that is, mlt^{-2}. However, if we want to get dimensions into the type system, these arrays won't do the trick: they're all the same type! Instead, we need types that *themselves* represent sequences of numbers, so that two masses have the same type and a mass is a different type from a length.

Fortunately, the MPL provides us with a collection of **type sequences**. For example, we can build a sequence of the built-in signed integral types this way:

```
#include <boost/mpl/vector.hpp>

typedef boost::mpl::vector<
    signed char, short, int, long> signed_types;
```

How can we use a type sequence to represent numbers? Just as numerical metafunctions pass and return wrapper *types* having a nested `::value`, so numerical sequences are really sequences of wrapper types (another example of polymorphism). To make this sort of thing easier, MPL supplies the `int_<N>` class template, which presents its integral argument as a nested `::value`:

```
#include <boost/mpl/int.hpp>

namespace mpl = boost::mpl; // namespace alias
static int const five = mpl::int_<5>::value;
```

> ## Namespace Aliases
>
> `namespace` *alias* `=` *namespace-name* ;
>
> declares *alias* to be a synonym for *namespace-name*. Many examples in this book will use `mpl::` to indicate `boost::mpl::`, but will omit the alias that makes it legal C++.

In fact, the library contains a whole suite of integral constant wrappers such as `long_` and `bool_`, each one wrapping a different type of integral constant within a class template.

Now we can build our fundamental dimensions:

```
typedef mpl::vector<
    mpl::int_<1>, mpl::int_<0>, mpl::int_<0>, mpl::int_<0>
  , mpl::int_<0>, mpl::int_<0>, mpl::int_<0>
> mass;

typedef mpl::vector<
    mpl::int_<0>, mpl::int_<1>, mpl::int_<0>, mpl::int_<0>
  , mpl::int_<0>, mpl::int_<0>, mpl::int_<0>
> length;
...
```

Whew! That's going to get tiring pretty quickly. Worse, it's hard to read and verify: The essential information, the powers of each fundamental dimension, is buried in repetitive syntactic "noise." Accordingly, MPL supplies **integral sequence wrappers** that allow us to write:

```
#include <boost/mpl/vector_c.hpp>

typedef mpl::vector_c<int,1,0,0,0,0,0,0> mass;
typedef mpl::vector_c<int,0,1,0,0,0,0,0> length; // or position
typedef mpl::vector_c<int,0,0,1,0,0,0,0> time;
typedef mpl::vector_c<int,0,0,0,1,0,0,0> charge;
typedef mpl::vector_c<int,0,0,0,0,1,0,0> temperature;
typedef mpl::vector_c<int,0,0,0,0,0,1,0> intensity;
typedef mpl::vector_c<int,0,0,0,0,0,0,1> angle;
```

Even though they have different types, you can think of these `mpl::vector_c` specializations as being equivalent to the more verbose versions above that use `mpl::vector`.

If we want, we can also define a few composite dimensions:

```
// base dimension:      m l  t ...
typedef mpl::vector_c<int,0,1,-1,0,0,0,0> velocity;     // l/t
typedef mpl::vector_c<int,0,1,-2,0,0,0,0> acceleration; // l/(t²)
typedef mpl::vector_c<int,1,1,-1,0,0,0,0> momentum;     // ml/t
typedef mpl::vector_c<int,1,1,-2,0,0,0,0> force;        // ml/(t²)
```

And, incidentally, the dimensions of scalars (like pi) can be described as:

```
typedef mpl::vector_c<int,0,0,0,0,0,0,0> scalar;
```

3.1.2   Representing Quantities

The types listed above are still pure metadata; to typecheck real computations we'll need to somehow bind them to our runtime data. A simple numeric value wrapper, parameterized on the number type T and on its dimensions, fits the bill:

```
template <class T, class Dimensions>
struct quantity
{
```

```
    explicit quantity(T x)
        : m_value(x)
    {}

    T value() const { return m_value; }
 private:
    T m_value;
};
```

Now we have a way to represent numbers associated with dimensions. For instance, we can say:

```
quantity<float,length> l( 1.0f );
quantity<float,mass> m( 2.0f );
```

Note that `Dimensions` doesn't appear anywhere in the definition of `quantity` outside the template parameter list; its *only* role is to ensure that l and m have different types. Because they do, we cannot make the mistake of assigning a length to a mass:

```
m = l;     // compile time type error
```

3.1.3   Implementing Addition and Subtraction

We can now easily write the rules for addition and subtraction, since the dimensions of the arguments must always match.

```
template <class T, class D>
quantity<T,D>
operator+(quantity<T,D> x, quantity<T,D> y)
{
   return quantity<T,D>(x.value() + y.value());
}

template <class T, class D>
quantity<T,D>
operator-(quantity<T,D> x, quantity<T,D> y)
{
   return quantity<T,D>(x.value() - y.value());
}
```

These operators enable us to write code like:

```
quantity<float,length> len1( 1.0f );
quantity<float,length> len2( 2.0f );

len1 = len1 + len2;    // OK
```

but prevent us from trying to add incompatible dimensions:

```
len1 = len2 + quantity<float,mass>( 3.7f ); // error
```

3.1.4 Implementing Multiplication

Multiplication is a bit more complicated than addition and subtraction. So far, the dimensions of the arguments and results have all been identical, but when multiplying, the result will usually have different dimensions from either of the arguments. For multiplication, the relation:

$$\left(x^a\right)\left(x^b\right) = x^{(a+b)}$$

implies that the exponents of the result dimensions should be the sum of corresponding exponents from the argument dimensions. Division is similar, except that the sum is replaced by a **difference**.

To combine corresponding elements from two sequences, we'll use MPL's transform algorithm. transform is a metafunction that iterates through two input sequences in parallel, passing an element from each sequence to an arbitrary binary metafunction, and placing the result in an output sequence.

```
template <class Sequence1, class Sequence2, class BinaryOperation>
struct transform;  // returns a Sequence
```

The signature above should look familiar if you're acquainted with the STL transform algorithm that accepts two *runtime* sequences as inputs:

```
template <
    class InputIterator1, class InputIterator2
  , class OutputIterator, class BinaryOperation
>
void transform(
    InputIterator1 start1, InputIterator2 finish1
  , InputIterator2 start2
  , OutputIterator result, BinaryOperation func);
```

Now we just need to pass a BinaryOperation that adds or subtracts in order to multiply or divide dimensions with mpl::transform. If you look through the MPL reference manual, you'll come across plus and minus metafunctions that do just what you'd expect:

```
#include <boost/static_assert.hpp>
#include <boost/mpl/plus.hpp>
#include <boost/mpl/int.hpp>
namespace mpl = boost::mpl;

BOOST_STATIC_ASSERT((
    mpl::plus<
        mpl::int_<2>
      , mpl::int_<3>
    >::type::value == 5
));
```

> **BOOST_STATIC_ASSERT**
>
> is a macro that causes a compilation error if its argument is false. The double paren-
> theses are required because the C++ preprocessor can't parse templates: it would
> otherwise be fooled by the comma into treating the condition as two separate macro
> arguments. Unlike its runtime analogue `assert(...)`, BOOST_STATIC_ASSERT can
> also be used at class scope, allowing us to put assertions in our metafunctions.
> See Chapter 8 for an in-depth discussion.

At this point it might seem as though we have a solution, but we're not quite there yet. A naive attempt to apply the `transform` algorithm in the implementation of `operator*` yields a compiler error:

```
#include <boost/mpl/transform.hpp>

template <class T, class D1, class D2>
quantity<
    T
  , typename mpl::transform<D1,D2,mpl::plus>::type
>
operator*(quantity<T,D1> x, quantity<T,D2> y) { ... }
```

It fails because the protocol says that metafunction arguments must be types, and `plus` is not a type, but a class template. Somehow we need to make metafunctions like `plus` fit the metadata mold.

One natural way to introduce polymorphism between metafunctions and metadata is to employ the wrapper idiom that gave us polymorphism between types and integral constants. Instead of a nested integral constant, we can use a class template nested within a **metafunction class**:

```
struct plus_f
{
    template <class T1, class T2>
    struct apply
    {
        typedef typename mpl::plus<T1,T2>::type type;
    };
};
```

> **Definition**
>
> A **metafunction class** is a class with a publicly accessible nested metafunction called apply.

Whereas a metafunction is a template but not a type, a metafunction class wraps that template within an ordinary non-templated class, which *is* a type. Since metafunctions operate on and return types, a metafunction class can be passed as an argument to, or returned from, another metafunction.

Finally, we have a BinaryOperation type that we can pass to transform without causing a compilation error:

```
template <class T, class D1, class D2>
quantity<
    T
  , typename mpl::transform<D1,D2,plus_f>::type  // new dimensions
>
operator*(quantity<T,D1> x, quantity<T,D2> y)
{
    typedef typename mpl::transform<D1,D2,plus_f>::type dim;
    return quantity<T,dim>( x.value() * y.value() );
}
```

Now, if we want to compute the force exerted by gravity on a five kilogram laptop computer, that's just the acceleration due to gravity (9.8 m/sec^2) times the mass of the laptop:

```
quantity<float,mass> m(5.0f);
quantity<float,acceleration> a(9.8f);
std::cout << "force = " << (m * a).value();
```

Our operator* multiplies the runtime values (resulting in 6.0f), and our metaprogram code uses transform to sum the meta-sequences of fundamental dimension exponents, so that the result type contains a representation of a new list of exponents, something like:

```
vector_c<int,1,1,-2,0,0,0,0>
```

However, if we try to write:

```
quantity<float,force> f = m * a;
```

we'll run into a little problem. Although the result of m * a does indeed represent a force with exponents of mass, length, and time 1, 1, and -2 respectively, the type returned by transform isn't a specialization of vector_c. Instead, transform works generically on the elements of its inputs and builds a new sequence with the appropriate elements: a type with many of the same sequence properties as vector_c<int,1,1,-2,0,0,0,0>, but with a different C++ type altogether. If you want to see the type's full name, you can try to compile the example yourself and look at the error message, but the exact details aren't important. The point is that force names a different type, so the assignment above will fail.

In order to resolve the problem, we can add an implicit conversion from the multiplication's result type to quantity<float,force>. Since we can't predict the exact types of the dimensions involved in any computation, this conversion will have to be templated, something like:

```
template <class T, class Dimensions>
struct quantity
{
    // converting constructor
    template <class OtherDimensions>
    quantity(quantity<T,OtherDimensions> const& rhs)
      : m_value(rhs.value())
    {
    }
    ...
```

Unfortunately, such a general conversion undermines our whole purpose, allowing nonsense such as:

```
// Should yield a force, not a mass!
quantity<float,mass> bogus = m * a;
```

We can correct that problem using another MPL algorithm, equal, which tests that two sequences have the same elements:

```
template <class OtherDimensions>
quantity(quantity<T,OtherDimensions> const& rhs)
  : m_value(rhs.value())
```

```
{
    BOOST_STATIC_ASSERT((
        mpl::equal<Dimensions,OtherDimensions>::type::value
    ));
}
```

Now, if the dimensions of the two quantities fail to match, the assertion will cause a compilation error.

3.1.5 Implementing Division

Division is similar to multiplication, but instead of adding exponents, we must subtract them. Rather than writing out a near duplicate of plus_f, we can use the following trick to make minus_f much simpler:

```
struct minus_f
{
    template <class T1, class T2>
    struct apply
      : mpl::minus<T1,T2> {};
};
```

Here minus_f::apply uses inheritance to expose the nested type of its base class, mpl::minus, so we don't have to write:

```
typedef typename ...::type type
```

We don't have to write typename here (in fact, it would be illegal), because the compiler knows that dependent names in apply's initializer list must be base classes.[2] This powerful simplification is known as **metafunction forwarding**; we'll apply it often as the book goes on.[3]

Syntactic tricks notwithstanding, writing trivial classes to wrap existing metafunctions is going to get boring pretty quickly. Even though the definition of minus_f was far less verbose than that of plus_f, it's still an awful lot to type. Fortunately, MPL gives us a *much* simpler way to pass metafunctions around. Instead of building a whole metafunction class, we can invoke transform this way:

---

2. In case you're wondering, the same approach could have been applied to plus_f, but since it's a little subtle, we introduced the straightforward but verbose formulation first.

3. Users of EDG-based compilers should consult Appendix C for a caveat about metafunction forwarding. You can tell whether you have an EDG compiler by checking the preprocessor symbol __EDG_VERSION__, which is defined by all EDG-based compilers.

```
typename mpl::transform<D1,D2, mpl::minus<_1,_2> >::type
```

Those funny looking arguments (_1 and _2) are known as **placeholders**, and they signify that when the `transform`'s `BinaryOperation` is invoked, its first and second arguments will be passed on to `minus` in the positions indicated by _1 and _2, respectively. The whole type `mpl::minus<_1,_2>` is known as a **placeholder expression**.

Note

MPL's placeholders are in the `mpl::placeholders` namespace and defined in `boost/mpl/placeholders.hpp`. In this book we will usually assume that you have written:

```
#include<boost/mpl/placeholders.hpp>
using namespace mpl::placeholders;
```

so that they can be accessed without qualification.

Here's our division operator written using placeholder expressions:

```
template <class T, class D1, class D2>
quantity<
    T
  , typename mpl::transform<D1,D2,mpl::minus<_1,_2> >::type
>
operator/(quantity<T,D1> x, quantity<T,D2> y)
{
    typedef typename
      mpl::transform<D1,D2,mpl::minus<_1,_2> >::type dim;

    return quantity<T,dim>( x.value() / y.value() );
}
```

This code is considerably simpler. We can simplify it even further by factoring the code that calculates the new dimensions into its own metafunction:

```
template <class D1, class D2>
struct divide_dimensions
    : mpl::transform<D1,D2,mpl::minus<_1,_2> > // forwarding again
{};

template <class T, class D1, class D2>
quantity<T, typename divide_dimensions<D1,D2>::type>
```

```
operator/(quantity<T,D1> x, quantity<T,D2> y)
{
    return quantity<T, typename divide_dimensions<D1,D2>::type>(
        x.value() / y.value());
}
```

Now we can verify our "force-on-a-laptop" computation by reversing it, as follows:

```
quantity<float,mass> m2 = f/a;
float rounding_error = std::abs((m2 - m).value());
```

If we got everything right, rounding_error should be very close to zero. These are boring calculations, but they're just the sort of thing that could ruin a whole program (or worse) if you got them wrong. If we had written a/f instead of f/a, there would have been a compilation error, preventing a mistake from propagating throughout our program.

3.2 Higher-Order Metafunctions

In the previous section we used two different forms—metafunction classes and placeholder expressions—to pass and return metafunctions just like any other metadata. Bundling metafunctions into "first class metadata" allows transform to perform an infinite variety of different operations: in our case, multiplication and division of dimensions. Though the idea of using functions to manipulate other functions may seem simple, its great power and flexibility [Hudak89] has earned it a fancy title: **higher-order functional programming**. A function that operates on another function is known as a **higher-order function**. It follows that transform is a higher-order metafunction: a metafunction that operates on another metafunction.

Now that we've seen the power of higher-order metafunctions at work, it would be good to be able to create new ones. In order to explore the basic mechanisms, let's try a simple example. Our task is to write a metafunction called twice, which—given a unary metafunction f and arbitrary metadata x—computes:

$$twice(f, x) := f(f(x)) \,.$$

This might seem like a trivial example, and in fact it is. You won't find much use for twice in real code. We hope you'll bear with us anyway: Because it doesn't do much more than accept and invoke a metafunction, twice captures all the essential elements of "higher-orderness" without any distracting details.

If f is a metafunction class, the definition of twice is straightforward:

```
template <class F, class X>
struct twice
{
    typedef typename F::template apply<X>::type once;    // f(x)
    typedef typename F::template apply<once>::type type; // f(f(x))
};
```

Or, applying metafunction forwarding:

```
template <class F, class X>
struct twice
  : F::template apply<
        typename F::template apply<X>::type
    >
{};
```

C++ Language Note

The C++ standard requires the `template` keyword when we use a **dependent name** that refers to a member template. `F::apply` may or may not name a template, *depending* on the particular F that is passed. See Appendix B for more information about `template`.

Given the need to sprinkle our code with the `template` keyword, it would be nice to reduce the syntactic burden of invoking metafunction classes. As usual, the solution is to factor the pattern into a metafunction:

```
template <class UnaryMetaFunctionClass, class Arg>
struct apply1
  : UnaryMetaFunctionClass::template apply<Arg>
{};
```

Now `twice` is just:

```
template <class F, class X>
struct twice
  : apply1<F, typename apply1<F,X>::type>
{};
```

To see `twice` at work, we can apply it to a little metafunction class built around the `add_pointer` metafunction:

```
struct add_pointer_f
{
    template <class T>
    struct apply : boost::add_pointer<T> {};
};
```

Now we can use twice with add_pointer_f to build pointers-to-pointers:

```
BOOST_STATIC_ASSERT((
    boost::is_same<
        twice<add_pointer_f, int>::type
      , int**
    >::value
));
```

3.3   Handling Placeholders

Our implementation of twice already works with metafunction classes. Ideally, we would like it to work with placeholder expressions, too, much the same as mpl::transform allows us to pass either form. For example, we would like to be able to write:

```
template <class X>
struct two_pointers
    : twice<boost::add_pointer<_1>, X>
{};
```

But when we look at the implementation of boost::add_pointer, it becomes clear that the current definition of twice can't work that way.

```
template <class T>
struct add_pointer
{
    typedef T* type;
};
```

To be invokable by twice, boost::add_pointer<_1> would have to be a metafunction class, along the lines of add_pointer_f. Instead, it's just a nullary metafunction returning the almost senseless type _1*. Any attempt to use two_pointers will fail when apply1 reaches for a nested ::apply metafunction in boost::add_pointer<_1> and finds that it doesn't exist.

We've determined that we don't get the behavior we want automatically, so what next? Since mpl::transform can do this sort of thing, there ought to be a way for us to do it too—and so there is.

3.3.1   The lambda Metafunction

We can *generate* a metafunction class from boost::add_pointer<_1>, using MPL's lambda metafunction:

```
template <class X>
struct two_pointers
  : twice<typename mpl::lambda<boost::add_pointer<_1> >::type, X>
{};

BOOST_STATIC_ASSERT((
    boost::is_same<
        two_pointers<int>::type
      , int**
    >::value
));
```

We'll refer to metafunction classes like add_pointer_f and placeholder expressions like boost::add_pointer<_1> as **lambda expressions**. The term, meaning "unnamed function object," was introduced in the 1930s by the logician Alonzo Church as part of a fundamental theory of computation he called the *lambda-calculus*.[4] MPL uses the somewhat obscure word lambda because of its well-established precedent in functional programming languages.

Although its primary purpose is to turn placeholder expressions into metafunction classes, mpl::lambda can accept any lambda expression, even if it's already a metafunction class. In that case, lambda returns its argument unchanged. MPL algorithms like transform call lambda internally, before invoking the resulting metafunction class, so that they work equally well with either kind of lambda expression. We can apply the same strategy to twice:

```
template <class F, class X>
struct twice
  : apply1<
        typename mpl::lambda<F>::type
      , typename apply1<
            typename mpl::lambda<F>::type
          , X
        >::type
    >
{};
```

---

4. See http://en.wikipedia.org/wiki/Lambda_calculus for an in-depth treatment, including a reference to Church's paper proving that the equivalence of lambda expressions is in general not decidable.

Now we can use `twice` with metafunction classes *and* placeholder expressions:

```
int* x;

twice<add_pointer_f, int>::type        p = &x;
twice<boost::add_pointer<_1>, int>::type q = &x;
```

3.3.2   The `apply` Metafunction

Invoking the result of `lambda` is such a common pattern that MPL provides an `apply` metafunction to do just that. Using `mpl::apply`, our flexible version of `twice` becomes:

```
#include <boost/mpl/apply.hpp>

template <class F, class X>
struct twice
    : mpl::apply<F, typename mpl::apply<F,X>::type>
{};
```

You can think of `mpl::apply` as being just like the `apply1` template that we wrote, with two additional features:

1. While `apply1` operates only on metafunction classes, the first argument to `mpl::apply` can be any lambda expression (including those built with placeholders).

2. While `apply1` accepts only one additional argument to which the metafunction class will be applied, `mpl::apply` can invoke its first argument on any number from zero to five additional arguments.[5] For example:

```
// binary lambda expression applied to 2 additional arguments
mpl::apply<
    mpl::plus<_1,_2>
  , mpl::int_<6>
  , mpl::int_<7>
>::type::value // == 13
```

> **Guideline**
>
> When writing a metafunction that invokes one of its arguments, use `mpl::apply` so that it works with lambda expressions.

---

5. See the Configuration Macros section of the MPL reference manual for a description of how to change the maximum number of arguments handled by `mpl::apply`.

3.4   More Lambda Capabilities

Lambda expressions provide much more than just the ability to pass a metafunction as an argument. The two capabilities described next combine to make lambda expressions an invaluable part of almost every metaprogramming task.

3.4.1   Partial Metafunction Application

Consider the lambda expression `mpl::plus<_1,_1>`. A single argument is directed to both of `plus`'s parameters, thereby adding a number to itself. Thus, a *binary* metafunction, `plus`, is used to build a *unary* lambda expression. In other words, we've created a whole new computation! We're not done yet, though: By supplying a non-placeholder as one of the arguments, we can build a unary lambda expression that adds a fixed value, say 42, to its argument:

```
mpl::plus<_1, mpl::int_<42> >
```

The process of binding argument values to a subset of a function's parameters is known in the world of functional programming as **partial function application**.

3.4.2   Metafunction Composition

Lambda expressions can also be used to assemble more interesting computations from simple metafunctions. For example, the following expression, which multiplies the sum of two numbers by their difference, is a **composition** of the three metafunctions `multiplies`, `plus`, and `minus`:

```
mpl::multiplies<mpl::plus<_1,_2>, mpl::minus<_1,_2> >
```

When evaluating a lambda expression, MPL checks to see if any of its arguments are themselves lambda expressions, and evaluates each one that it finds. The results of these inner evaluations are substituted into the outer expression before it is evaluated.

3.5   Lambda Details

Now that you have an idea of the semantics of MPL's `lambda` facility, let's formalize our understanding and look at things a little more deeply.

3.5.1   Placeholders

The definition of "placeholder" may surprise you:

Definition

A **placeholder** is a metafunction class of the form mpl::arg<X>.

3.5.1.1 Implementation

The convenient names _1, _2,... _5 are actually typedefs for specializations of mpl::arg that simply select the Nth argument for any N.[6] The implementation of placeholders looks something like this:

```
namespace boost { namespace mpl { namespace placeholders {

template <int N> struct arg; // forward declarations
struct void_;

template <>
struct arg<1>
{
    template <
      class A1, class A2 = void_, ... class Am = void_>
    struct apply
    {
        typedef A1 type; // return the first argument
    };
};
typedef arg<1> _1;

template <>
struct arg<2>
{
    template <
      class A1, class A2, class A3 = void_, ...class Am = void_
    >
    struct apply
    {
        typedef A2 type; // return the second argument
    };
};
```

---

6. MPL provides five placeholders by default. See the Configuration Macros section of the MPL reference manual for a description of how to change the number of placeholders provided.

```
typedef arg<2> _2;
```

more specializations and typedefs...

```
}}}
```

Remember that invoking a metafunction class is the same as invoking its nested `apply` meta-function. When a placeholder in a lambda expression is evaluated, it is invoked on the expression's actual arguments, returning just one of them. The results are then substituted back into the lambda expression and the evaluation process continues.

3.5.1.2   The Unnamed Placeholder

There's one special placeholder, known as the **unnamed placeholder**, that we haven't yet defined:

```
namespace boost { namespace mpl { namespace placeholders {

typedef arg<-1> _; // the unnamed placeholder

}}}
```

The details of its implementation aren't important; all you really need to know about the unnamed placeholder is that it gets special treatment. When a lambda expression is being transformed into a metafunction class by `mpl::lambda`,

> the *n*th appearance of the unnamed placeholder *in a given template specialization* is replaced with *_n*.

So, for example, every row of Table 3.1 contains two equivalent lambda expressions.

Table 3.1 Unnamed Placeholder Semantics

`mpl::plus<_,_>`	`mpl::plus<_1,_2>`

`boost::is_same<`
 	
`    _`
`  , boost::add_pointer<_>`
`>`
	`boost::is_same<`
	`    _1`
	`  , boost::add_pointer<_1>`
	`>`

`mpl::multiplies<`
`    mpl::plus<_,_>`
`  , mpl::minus<_,_>`
`>`
	`mpl::multiplies<`
	`    mpl::plus<_1,_2>`
	`  , mpl::minus<_1,_2>`
	`>`

Especially when used in simple lambda expressions, the unnamed placeholder often eliminates just enough syntactic "noise" to significantly improve readability.

3.5.2   Placeholder Expression Definition

Now that you know just what *placeholder* means, we can define **placeholder expression**:

Definition

A placeholder expression is either:

- a placeholder

or

- a template specialization with at least one argument that is a placeholder expression.

In other words, a placeholder expression always involves a placeholder.

3.5.3   Lambda and Non-Metafunction Templates

There is just one detail of placeholder expressions that we haven't discussed yet. MPL uses a special rule to make it easier to integrate ordinary templates into metaprograms: After all of the placeholders have been replaced with actual arguments, if the resulting template specialization X doesn't have a nested `::type`, the result of lambda is just X itself.

For example, `mpl::apply<std::vector<_>, T>` is always just `std::vector<T>`. If it weren't for this behavior, we would have to build trivial metafunctions to create ordinary template specializations in lambda expressions:

```
// trivial std::vector generator
template<class U>
struct make_vector { typedef std::vector<U> type; };
typedef mpl::apply<make_vector<_>, T>::type vector_of_t;
```

Instead, we can simply write:

```
typedef mpl::apply<std::vector<_>, T>::type vector_of_t;
```

3.5.4 The Importance of Being Lazy

Recall the definition of `always_int` from the previous chapter:

```
struct always_int
{
    typedef int type;
};
```

Nullary metafunctions might not seem very important at first, since something like `add_pointer<int>` could be replaced by `int*` in any lambda expression where it appears. Not all nullary metafunctions are that simple, though:

```
struct add_pointer_f
{
    template <class T>
    struct apply : boost::add_pointer<T> {};
};
typedef mpl::vector<int, char*, double&> seq;
typedef mpl::transform<seq, boost::add_pointer<_> > calc_ptr_seq;
```

Note that `calc_ptr_seq` is a nullary metafunction, since it has `transform`'s nested `::type`. A C++ template is not instantiated until we actually "look inside it," though. Just naming `calc_ptr_seq` does not cause it to be evaluated, since we haven't accessed its `::type` yet.

Metafunctions can be invoked *lazily,* rather than immediately upon supplying all of their arguments. We can use **lazy evaluation** to improve compilation time when a metafunction result is only going to be used conditionally. We can sometimes also avoid contorting program structure by *naming* an invalid computation without actually performing it. That's what we've done with `calc_ptr_seq` above, since you can't legally form `double&*`. Laziness and all of its virtues will be a recurring theme throughout this book.

3.6 Details

By now you should have a fairly complete view of the fundamental concepts and language of both template metaprogramming in general and of the Boost Metaprogramming Library. This section reviews the highlights.

Metafunction forwarding. The technique of using public derivation to supply the nested `type` of a metafunction by accessing the one provided by its base class.

Metafunction class.   The most basic way to formulate a compile-time function so that it can be treated as polymorphic metadata; that is, as a type. A metafunction class is a class with a nested metafunction called `apply`.

MPL.   Most of this book's examples will use the Boost Metaprogramming Library. Like the Boost type traits headers, MPL headers follow a simple convention:

```
#include <boost/mpl/component-name.hpp>
```

If the component's name ends in an underscore, however, the corresponding MPL header name does not include the trailing underscore. For example, `mpl::bool_` can be found in `<boost/mpl/bool.hpp>`. Where the library deviates from this convention, we'll be sure to point it out to you.

Higher-order function.   A function that operates on or returns a function. Making metafunctions polymorphic with other metadata is a key ingredient in higher-order metaprogramming.

Lambda expression.   Simply put, a lambda expression is callable metadata. Without some form of callable metadata, higher-order metafunctions would be impossible. Lambda expressions have two basic forms: *metafunction classes* and *placeholder expressions.*

Placeholder expression.   A kind of lambda expression that, through the use of placeholders, enables in-place *partial metafunction application* and *metafunction composition.* As you will see throughout this book, these features give us the truly amazing ability to build up almost any kind of complex type computation from more primitive metafunctions, right at its point of use:

```
// find the position of a type x in some_sequence such that:
//        x is convertible to 'int'
//     && x is not 'char'
//     && x is not a floating type
typedef mpl::find_if<
      some_sequence
    , mpl::and_<
          boost::is_convertible<_1,int>
        , mpl::not_<boost::is_same<_1,char> >
        , mpl::not_<boost::is_float<_1> >
      >
    >::type iter;
```

Placeholder expressions make good on the promise of algorithm reuse without forcing us to write new metafunction classes. The corresponding capability is often sorely missed in the runtime world of the STL, since it is often much easier to write a loop by hand than it is to use standard algorithms, despite their correctness and efficiency advantages.

The `lambda` metafunction.   A metafunction that transforms a lambda expression into a corresponding metafunction class. For detailed information on `lambda` and the lambda evaluation process, please see the MPL reference manual.

The `apply` metafunction.   A metafunction that invokes its first argument, which must be a lambda expression, on its remaining arguments. In general, to invoke a lambda expression, you should always pass it to `mpl::apply` along with the arguments you want to apply it to in lieu of using `lambda` and invoking the result "manually."

Lazy evaluation.   A strategy of delaying evaluation until a result is required, thereby avoiding any unnecessary computation and any associated unnecessary errors. Metafunctions are only invoked when we access their nested `::type`s, so we can supply all of their arguments without performing any computation and delay evaluation to the last possible moment.

3.7   Exercises

3-0.   Use `BOOST_STATIC_ASSERT` to add error checking to the `binary` template presented in section 1.4.1, so that `binary<N>::value` causes a compilation error if N contains digits other than 0 or 1.

3-1.   Turn `vector_c<int,1,2,3>` into a type sequence with elements (2,3,4) using `transform`.

3-2.   Turn `vector_c<int,1,2,3>` into a type sequence with elements (1,4,9) using `transform`.

3-3.   Turn T into T**** by using `twice` twice.

3-4.   Turn T into T**** using `twice` on itself.

3-5.   There's still a problem with the dimensional analysis code in section 3.1. Hint: What happens when you do:

```
f = f + m * a;
```

Repair this example using techniques shown in this chapter.

3-6.   Build a lambda expression that has functionality equivalent to `twice`. Hint: `mpl::apply` is a metafunction!

3-7*. What do you think would be the semantics of the following constructs:

```
typedef mpl::lambda<mpl::lambda<_1> >::type t1;
typedef mpl::apply<_1,mpl::plus<_1,_2> >::type t2;
typedef mpl::apply<_1,std::vector<int> >::type t3;
```

```
typedef mpl::apply<_1,std::vector<_1> >::type t4;
typedef mpl::apply<mpl::lambda<_1>,std::vector<int> >::type  t5;
typedef mpl::apply<mpl::lambda<_1>,std::vector<_1> >::type t6;
typedef mpl::apply<mpl::lambda<_1>,mpl::plus<_1,_2> >::type t7;
typedef mpl::apply<_1,mpl::lambda< mpl::plus<_1,_2> > >::type t8;
```

Show the steps used to arrive at your answers and write tests verifying your assumptions. Did the library behavior match your reasoning? If not, analyze the failed tests to discover the actual expression semantics. Explain why your assumptions were different, what behavior you find more coherent, and why.

3-8*. Our dimensional analysis framework dealt with dimensions, but it entirely ignored the issue of *units*. A length can be represented in inches, feet, or meters. A force can be represented in newtons or in kg m/sec^2. Add the ability to specify units and test your code. Try to make your interface as syntactically friendly as possible for the user.

## 4

Integral Type Wrappers and Operations

As we hinted earlier, the MPL supplies a group of wrapper templates that, like `int_`, are used to make integer values into polymorphic metadata. There's actually more to these wrappers than meets the eye, and in this chapter we'll uncover the details of their structure. We'll also explore some of the metafunctions that operate on them, and discuss how best to write metafunctions returning integral constants.

4.1 Boolean Wrappers and Operations

`bool` is not just the simplest integral type, but also one of the most useful. Most of the type traits are `bool`-valued, and as mentioned earlier, play an important role in many metaprograms. The MPL type wrapper for `bool` values is defined this way:

```
template< bool x > struct bool_
{
    static bool const value = x;        // 1
    typedef bool_<x> type;              // 2
    typedef bool value_type;            // 3
    operator bool() const { return x; } // 4
};
```

Let's walk through the commented lines above one at a time:

1. By now this line should come as no surprise to you. As we've said earlier, every integral constant wrapper contains a `::value`.

2. Every integral constant wrapper is a nullary metafunction that returns *itself*. The reasons for this design choice will become clear in short order.

3. The wrapper's `::value_type` indicates the (*cv*-unqualified) type of its `::value`.

4. Each `bool_<x>` specialization is quite naturally convertible to a `bool` of value x.

The library also supplies two convenient `typedef`s:

```
typedef bool_<false> false_;
typedef bool_<true> true_;
```

4.1.1 Type Selection

So far, we've only made decisions at compile time by embedding them in ad hoc class template specializations: the terminating conditions of recursive algorithms (like the `binary` template we wrote in Chapter 1) say "if the argument is zero, calculate the result this way, otherwise, do it the other (default) way." We also specialized `iter_swap_impl` to select one of two implementations inside `iter_swap`:

```
iter_swap_impl<use_swap>::do_it(*i1,*i2);
```

Instead of hand-crafting a template specialized for each choice we make, we can take advantage of an MPL metafunction whose purpose is to make choices: `mpl::if_<C,T,F>::type` is T if `C::value` is `true`, and F otherwise. Returning to our `iter_swap` example, we can now use classes with mnemonic names in lieu of an `iter_swap_impl` template:

```
#include <boost/mpl/if.hpp>

struct fast_swap
{
    template <class ForwardIterator1, class ForwardIterator2>
    static void do_it(ForwardIterator1 i1, ForwardIterator2 i2)
    {
        std::swap(*i1, *i2);
    }
};

struct reliable_swap
{
    template <class ForwardIterator1, class ForwardIterator2>
    static void do_it(ForwardIterator1 i1, ForwardIterator2 i2)
    {
        typename
          std::iterator_traits<ForwardIterator1>::value_type
        tmp = *i1;
```

```
            *i1 = *i2;
            *i2 = tmp;
        }
    };
```

The line of `iter_swap` that invoked `iter_swap_impl`'s `do_it` member can be rewritten as:

```
mpl::if_<
    mpl::bool_<use_swap>
  , fast_swap
  , reliable_swap
>::type::do_it(i1,i2);
```

That may not seem like much of an improvement: complexity has just been moved from the definition of `iter_swap_impl` into the body of `iter_swap`. It does clarify the code, though, by keeping the logic for choosing an implementation of `iter_swap` inside its definition.

For another example, let's look at how we might optimize the passing of function parameters in generic code. In general, an argument type's copy-constructor might be expensive, so a generic function ought to accept parameters by reference. That said, it's usually wasteful to pass anything so trivial as a scalar type by reference: on some compilers, scalars are passed by value in registers, but when passed by reference they are forced onto the stack. What's called for is a metafunction, `param_type<T>`, that returns T when it is a scalar, and T `const&` otherwise.

We might use it as follows:

```
template <class T>
class holder
{
 public:
    holder(typename param_type<T>::type x);
    ...
 private:
    T x;
};
```

The parameter to the constructor of `holder<int>` is of type `int`, while `holder<std::vector<int> >`'s constructor takes a `std::vector<int> const&`. To implement `param_type`, we might use `mpl::if_` as follows:

```
#include <boost/mpl/if.hpp>
#include <boost/type_traits/is_scalar.hpp>
```

```
template <class T>
struct param_type
  : mpl::if_<
        typename boost::is_scalar<T>::type
      , T
      , T const&
    >
{};
```

Unfortunately, that implementation would prevent us from putting reference types in a `holder`: since it's illegal to form a reference to a reference, instantiating `holder<int&>` is an error. The Boost.Type Traits give us a workaround, since we *can* instantiate `add_reference<T>` on a reference type—in that case it just returns its argument:

```
#include <boost/mpl/if.hpp>
#include <boost/type_traits/add_reference.hpp>

template <class T>
struct param_type
  : mpl::if_<
        typename boost::is_scalar<T>::type
      , T
      , typename boost::add_reference<T const>::type
    >
{};
```

4.1.2   Lazy Type Selection

This approach isn't entirely satisfying, because it causes `add_reference<T const>` to be instantiated even if T is a scalar, wasting compilation time. Delaying a computation until it's absolutely needed is called **lazy evaluation**. Some functional programming languages, such as Haskell, do every computation lazily, with no special prompting. In C++, we have to do lazy evaluation explicitly. One way to delay instantiation of `add_reference` until it's needed is to have `mpl::if_` select one of two nullary metafunctions, and then invoke the one selected:

```
#include <boost/mpl/if.hpp>
#include <boost/mpl/identity.hpp>
#include <boost/type_traits/add_reference.hpp>

template <class T>
struct param_type
```

```
  : mpl::if_<              // forwarding to selected transformation
      typename boost::is_scalar<T>::type
    , mpl::identity<T>
    , boost::add_reference<T const>
  >::type
{};
```

Note our use of `mpl::identity`, a metafunction that simply returns its argument. Now `param_type<T>` *returns the result of invoking* either `mpl::identity<T>` or `boost::add_reference<T const>`, depending on whether T is a scalar.

This idiom is so common in metaprograms that MPL supplies a metafunction called `eval_if`, defined this way:

```
template <class C, class TrueMetafunc, class FalseMetafunc>
struct eval_if
  : mpl::if_<C,TrueMetafunc,FalseMetafunc>::type
{};
```

Whereas `if_` *returns* one of two arguments based on a condition, `eval_if` *invokes* one of two nullary metafunction arguments based on a condition and returns the result. We can now simplify our definition of `param_type` slightly by forwarding directly to `eval_if`:

```
#include <boost/mpl/eval_if.hpp>
#include <boost/mpl/identity.hpp>
#include <boost/type_traits/add_reference.hpp>

template <class T>
struct param_type
  : mpl::eval_if<
        typename boost::is_scalar<T>::type
      , mpl::identity<T>
      , boost::add_reference<T const>
    >       // no ::type here
{};
```

By taking advantage of the fact that Boost's integral metafunctions all supply a nested `::value`, we can make yet another simplification to `param_type`:

```
template <class T>
struct param_type
  : mpl::eval_if<
```

```
      boost::is_scalar<T>
    , mpl::identity<T>
    , boost::add_reference<T const>
  >
{};
```

Specializations of Boost metafunctions that, like is_scalar, return integral constant wrappers, happen to be publicly *derived* from those very same wrappers. As a result, the metafunction specializations are not just valid integral constant wrappers in their own right, but they inherit *all* the useful properties outlined above for wrappers such as bool_:

```
if (boost::is_scalar<X>()) // invokes inherited operator bool()
{
    // code here runs iff X is a scalar type
}
```

4.1.3   Logical Operators

Suppose for a moment that we didn't have such a smart add_reference at our disposal.   If add_reference were just defined as shown below, we wouldn't be able to rely on it to avoid forming references to references:

```
template <class T>
struct add_reference { typedef T& type; };
```

In that case, we'd want to do something like this with param_type to avoid passing references to add_reference:

```
template <class T>
struct param_type
  : mpl::eval_if<
        mpl::bool_<
          boost::is_scalar<T>::value
          || boost::is_reference<T>::value
      >
    , mpl::identity<T>
    , add_reference<T const>
  >
{};
```

Pretty ugly, right? Most of the syntactic cleanliness of our previous version has been lost. If we wanted to build a lambda expression for `param_type` on-the-fly instead of writing a new metafunction, we'd have even worse problems:

```
typedef mpl::vector<int, long, std::string> argument_types;

// build a list of parameter types for the argument types
typedef mpl::transform<
    argument_types
  , mpl::if_<
        mpl::bool_<
           boost::is_scalar<_1>::value
           || boost::is_reference<_1>::value
        >
      , mpl::identity<_1>
      , add_reference<boost::add_const<_1> >
    >
>::type param_types;
```

This one isn't just ugly, it actually fails to work properly. Because touching a template's nested `::value` forces instantiation, the logical expression `boost::is_scalar<_1>::value || is_reference<_1>::value` is evaluated immediately. Since `_1` is neither a scalar nor a reference, the result is `false`, and our lambda expression is equivalent to `add_reference<boost::add_const<_1> >`. We can solve both of these problems by taking advantage of MPL's logical operator metafunctions. Using `mpl::or_`, we can recapture the syntactic cleanliness of our original `param_type`:

```
#include <boost/mpl/or.hpp>

template <class T>
struct param_type
  : mpl::eval_if<
        mpl::or_<boost::is_scalar<T>, boost::is_reference<T> >
      , mpl::identity<T>
      , add_reference<T const>
    >
{};
```

Because `mpl::or_<x,y>` is derived from its result `::type` (a specialization of `bool_<n>`), and is thus *itself* a valid MPL Boolean constant wrapper, we have been able to completely eliminate the explicit use of `bool_` and access to a nested `::type`. Despite the fact that we're not using operator notation, the code is actually *more* readable than before.

Similar benefits accrue when we apply the same change to our lambda expression, and it works properly, to boot:

```
typedef mpl::transform<
    argument_types
  , mpl::if_<
        mpl::or_<boost::is_scalar<_1>, boost::is_reference<_1> >
      , mpl::identity<_1>
      , add_reference<boost::add_const<_1> >
    >
>::type param_types;
```

What if we wanted to change param_type to pass all stateless class types, in addition to scalars, by value? We could simply nest another invocation of or_:

```
# include <boost/type_traits/is_stateless.hpp>

template <class T>
struct param_type
  : mpl::eval_if<
        mpl::or_<
            boost::is_stateless<T>
          , mpl::or_<
                boost::is_scalar<T>
              , boost::is_reference<T>
            >
        >
      , mpl::identity<T>
      , add_reference<T const>
    >
{};
```

While that works, we can do better. mpl::or_ accepts anywhere from two to five arguments, so we can just write:

```
# include <boost/type_traits/is_stateless.hpp>

template <class T>
struct param_type
  : mpl::eval_if<
        mpl::or_<
```

```
            boost::is_scalar<T>
          , boost::is_stateless<T>
          , boost::is_reference<T>
        >
      , mpl::identity<T>
      , add_reference<T const>
    >
{};
```

In fact, most of the MPL metafunctions that operate on integral arguments (e.g., `mpl::plus<...>`) have the same property.

The library contains a similar `and_` metafunction, and a unary `not_` metafunction for inverting Boolean conditions.[1] It's worth noting that, just like the built-in operators `&&` and `||`, `mpl::and_` and `mpl::or_` exhibit "short circuit" behavior. For example, in the example above, if T is a scalar, `boost::is_stateless<T>` and `is_reference<T>` will never be instantiated.

4.2   Integer Wrappers and Operations

We've already used MPL's `int_` wrapper in our dimensional analysis example (see section 3.1). Now we can examine it in more detail, starting with its definition:

```
template< int N >
struct int_
{
    static const int value = N;
    typedef int_<N> type;

    typedef int value_type;

    typedef mpl::int_<N+1> next;
    typedef mpl::int_<N-1> prior;
    operator int() const { return N; }
};
```

As you can see, `int_` is very similar to `bool_`; in fact, the only major difference is the presence of its `::next` and `::prior` members. We'll explain their purpose later in this chapter. The library

---

1. These names all end in underscores because `and`, `or`, and `not` are C++ keywords that function as aliases for the better known operator tokens `&&`, `||`, and `!`.

supplies similar numeric wrappers for `long` and `std::size_t`, known as `long_` and `size_t` respectively.

To represent values of any other integral type, the library provides a generic wrapper defined this way:

```
template<class T, T N>
struct integral_c
{
    static const T value = N;
    typedef integral_c<T,N> type;

    typedef T value_type;

    typedef mpl::integral_c<T,N+1> next;
    typedef mpl::integral_c<T,N-1> prior;
    operator T() const { return N; }
};
```

Integral sequence wrappers, like the `vector_c` template we used to implement dimensional analysis in Chapter 3 take an initial type parameter T, which is used to form their contained `integral_c<T, ...>` specializations.

If the existence of both `int_<...>` *and* `integral_c<int,...>` is causing you a raised eyebrow, we can hardly blame you. After all, two otherwise equivalent integer wrappers can be different types. If we try to compare two integer wrappers this way:

```
boost::is_same<mpl::integral_c<int,3>, mpl::int_<3> >::value
```

the result (`false`) may be a little bit surprising. It's perhaps a little less surprising that the following is also `false`:

```
boost::is_same<mpl::long_<3>, mpl::int_<3> >::value
```

Whatever your reaction to these two examples may be, however, it should be clear by now that there's more to value equality of integral constant wrappers than simple type matching. The MPL metafunction for testing value equality is called `equal_to`, and is defined simply:

```
template<class N1, class N2>
struct equal_to
  : mpl::bool_<(N1::value == N2::value)>
{};
```

It's important not to confuse `equal_to` with `equal`, which compares the elements of two sequences. The names of these two metafunctions were taken from those of similar components in the STL.

4.2.1 Integral Operators

MPL supplies a whole suite of metafunctions for operating on integral constant wrappers, of which you've already seen a few (e.g., `plus` and `minus`). Before we get into the details, a word about naming conventions: When the metafunction corresponds to a built-in C++ operator for which the language has a textual alternative token name, like `&&`/`and`, the MPL metafunction is named for the alternative token followed by an underscore, thus `mpl::and_`. Otherwise, the MPL metafunction takes its name from the corresponding STL function object, thus `mpl::equal_to`.

The operators fall into four groups. In the tables below, $n = 5$ by default. See the Configuration Macros section of the MPL reference manual for information about how to change n.

4.2.1.1 Boolean-Valued Operators

The metafunctions in this group all have `bool` constant results. We've already covered the logical operators, but they're included here for completeness (see Table 4.1).

Table 4.1 Logical Operators

Metafunction Specialization	`::value` and `::type::value`
`not_<X>`	`!X::value`
`and_<T1,T2,...Tn>`	`T1::value && ...  Tn ::value`
`or_<T1,T2,...Tn>`	`T1::value || ...  Tn ::value`

Table 4.2 lists value comparison operators.

Table 4.2 Value Comparison Operators

Metafunction Specialization	`::value` and `::type::value`
`equal_to<X,Y>`	`X::value == Y::value`
`not_equal_to<X,Y>`	`X::value != Y::value`
`greater<X,Y>`	`X::value > Y::value`
`greater_equal<X,Y>`	`X::value >= Y::value`
`less<X,Y>`	`X::value < Y::value`
`less_equal<X,Y>`	`X::value <= Y::value`

4.2.1.2   Integral-Valued Operators

The operators section all have integral constant results whose type is the same as the type of the expression they evaluate (see Tables 4.3 and 4.4). In other words, since the type of 3+2L is long,

```
mpl::plus<mpl::int_<3>, mpl::long_<2> >::type::value_type
```

is also long.

Table 4.3 Bitwise Operators

Metafunction Specialization	::value and ::type::value
bitand_<X,Y>	X::value & Y::value
bitor_<X,Y>	X::value | Y::value
bitxor_<X,Y>	X::value ^ Y::value

Table 4.4 Arithmetic Operators

Metafunction Specialization	::value and ::type::value
divides<T1,T2,...T*n*>	T1::value / ... T*n* ::value
minus<T1,T2,...T*n*>	T1::value - ... T*n* ::value
multiplies<T1,T2,...T*n*>	T1::value * ... T*n* ::value
plus<T1,T2,...T*n*>	T1::value + ... T*n* ::value
modulus<X,Y>	X::value % Y::value
shift_left<X,Y>	X::value << Y::value
shift_right<X,Y>	X::value >> Y::value
next<X>	X::next
prior<X>	X::prior

The next and prior metafunctions are somewhat analogous to the C++ unary operators ++ and --. Since metadata is immutable, though, next and prior can't modify their arguments. As a matter of fact, mpl::next and mpl::prior are *precisely* analogous to two runtime functions declared in namespace boost that simply return incremented and decremented versions of their arguments:

```
namespace boost
{
  template <class T>
  inline T next(T x) { return ++x; }
```

```
template <class T>
inline T prior(T x) { return --x; }
}
```

You might find it curious that `mpl::next<X>` and `mpl::prior<X>` are not simply defined to return wrappers for `X::value+1` and `X::value-1`, respectively, even though they function that way when used on integral constant wrappers. The reasons should become clear in the next chapter, when we discuss the use of `next` and `prior` for sequence iteration.

4.2.2   The _c Integral Shorthand

Occasionally we find ourselves in a situation where the need to explicitly build wrapper types becomes an inconvenience. It happened in our dimensional analysis code (Chapter 3), where the use of `mpl::vector_c<int, ...>` instead of `mpl::vector<...>` eliminated the need to write `int_` specializations for each of seven powers of fundamental units.

We actually sidestepped another such circumstance while working on the `param_type` metafunction earlier in this chapter. Before `mpl::or_` came along to save our bacon, we were stuck with this ugly definition:

```
template <class T>
struct param_type
  : mpl::eval_if<
        mpl::bool_<
          boost::is_scalar<T>::value
          || boost::is_reference<T>::value
        >
      , mpl::identity<T>
      , add_reference<T const>
    >
{};
```

With MPL's `eval_if_c`, also supplied by `<boost/mpl/eval_if.hpp>`, we might have written:

```
template <class T>
struct param_type
  : mpl::eval_if_c<
        boost::is_scalar<T>::value
        || boost::is_reference<T>::value
      , mpl::identity<T>
```

```
    , add_reference<T const>
  >
{};
```

By now you've probably begun to notice some commonality in the use of _c: it always adorns templates that take raw integral constants, instead of wrappers, as parameters. The _c suffix can be thought of as an abbreviation for "constant" or "of integral constants."

4.3 Exercises

4-0. Write tests for mpl::or_ and mpl::and_ metafunctions that use their short-circuit behavior.

4-1. Implement binary metafunctions called logical_or and logical_and that model the behavior of mpl::or_ and mpl::and_, correspondingly. Use tests from exercise 4-0 to verify your implementation.

4-2. Extend the implementation of logical_or and logical_and metafunctions from exercise 4-1 to accept up to five arguments.

4-3. Eliminate the unnecessary instantiations in the following code snippets:

1.
```
template< typename N, typename Predicate >
struct next_if
  : mpl::if_<
        typename mpl::apply<Predicate,N>::type
      , typename mpl::next<N>::type
      , N
    >
{};
```

2.
```
template< typename N1, typename N2 >
struct formula
  : mpl::if_<
        mpl::not_equal_to<N1,N2>
      , typename mpl::if_<
            mpl::greater<N1,N2>
          , typename mpl::minus<N1,N2>::type
          , N1
        >::type
      , typename mpl::plus<
            N1
```

```
                , typename mpl::multiplies<N1,
                                        mpl::int_<2> >::type
            >::type
        >::type
    {};
```

Write the tests to verify that the semantics of the transformed metafunctions remained unchanged.

4-4. Use integral operators and the type traits library facilities to implement the following composite traits:

```
is_data_member_pointer
is_pointer_to_function
is_reference_to_function_pointer
is_reference_to_non_const
```

4-5. Consider the following function template, which is designed to provide a "container-based" (as opposed to iterator-based) interface to std::find:

```
template <class Container, class Value>
typename Container::iterator
container_find(Container& c, Value const& v)
{
    return std::find(c.begin(), c.end(), v);
}
```

As coded, container_find won't work for const containers; Container will be deduced as const X for some container type X, but when we try to convert the Container::const_iterator returned by std::find into a Container::iterator, compilation will fail. Fix the problem using a small metaprogram to compute container_find's return type.

5

Sequences and Iterators

If the STL can be described as a framework based on runtime algorithms, function objects, and iterators, we could say that the MPL is founded on compile-time algorithms, metafunctions, *sequences, and iterators*.[1]

We used sequences and algorithms informally in Chapter 3 to implement our dimensional analysis logic. If you're familiar with the STL, you might have guessed that under the hood we were also using iterators. The library, however, has so far allowed us to remain happily ignorant of their role, by virtue of its sequence-based algorithm interfaces.

In this chapter you will gain a general familiarity with "compile-time STL," and then proceed to formalize sequences and iterators, study their interactions with algorithms, look at a number of specific implementations offered by the library, and learn how to implement new examples of each one.

5.1 Concepts

First, we'll define an important term that originated in the world of runtime generic programming. A **concept** is a description of the requirements placed by a generic component on one or more of its arguments. We've already covered a few concepts in this book. For example, the `apply1` metafunction that we wrote in Chapter 3 required a first argument that was a Metafunction Class.

A type or group of types that satisfies a concept's requirements is said to **model** the concept or to **be a model of** the concept. So `plus_f`, also from Chapter 3, *is a model of* Metafunction Class. A concept is said to **refine** another concept when its requirements are a superset of those of the other concept.

Concept requirements usually come from the following categories.

---

1. Though indispensable in everyday programming, STL containers are not a fundamental part of that library's conceptual framework, and they don't interact directly with the other STL abstractions. By contrast, MPL's sequences play a direct role in its algorithm interfaces.

Valid expressions.   C++ expressions that must compile successfully for the objects involved in the expression to be considered models of the concept. For example, an Iterator x is expected to support the expressions ++x and *x.

Associated types.   Types that participate in one or more of the valid expressions and that can be computed from the type(s) modeling the concept. Typically, associated types can be accessed either through typedefs nested within a class definition for the modeling type or through a traits class. For example, as described in Chapter 2, an iterator's value type is associated with the iterator through `std::iterator_traits`.

Invariants.   Runtime characteristics of a model's instances that must always be true; that is, all operations on an instance must preserve these characteristics. The invariants often take the form of pre-conditions and post-conditions. For instance, after a Forward Iterator is copied, the copy and the original must compare equal.

Complexity guarantees.   Maximum limits on how long the execution of one of the valid expressions will take, or how much of various resources its computation will use. Incrementing an Iterator, for example, is required to have constant complexity.

In this chapter we'll be introducing several new concepts and refinement relationships with associated types and complexity guarantees.

5.2   Sequences and Algorithms

Most of the algorithms in the MPL operate on sequences. For example, searching for a type in a vector looks like this:

```
typedef mpl::vector<char,short,int,long,float,double> types;

// locate the position of long in types
typedef mpl::find<types,long>::type long_pos;
```

Here, `find` accepts two parameters—a sequence to search (`types`) and the type to search for (`long`)—and returns an iterator indicating the position of the first element in the sequence that is identical to `long`. Except for the fact that `mpl::find` takes a single sequence parameter instead of two iterators, this is precisely how you would search for a value in a `std::list` or `std::vector`:

```
std::vector<int> x(10);
std::vector<int>::iterator five_pos
    = std::find(x.begin(), x.end(), 5);
```

If no matching element exists, `mpl::find` returns the sequence's *past-the-end* iterator, which is quite naturally accessed with the `mpl::end` metafunction:

```
// assert that long was found in the sequence
typedef mpl::end<types>::type finish;
BOOST_STATIC_ASSERT((!boost::is_same<long_pos, finish>::value));
```

A similar `begin` metafunction returns an iterator to the beginning of the sequence.

5.3   Iterators

As with STL iterators, the most fundamental service provided by MPL iterators is **access** to the sequence element to which they refer. To dereference a compile-time iterator, we can't simply apply the prefix * operator: runtime operator overloading is unavailable at compile time. Instead, the MPL provides us with an aptly named `deref` metafunction that takes an iterator and returns the referenced element.

```
typedef mpl::vector<char,short,int,long,float,double> types;

// locate the position of long in types
typedef mpl::find<types,long>::type long_pos;

// dereference the iterator
typedef mpl::deref<long_pos>::type x;

// check that we have the expected result
BOOST_STATIC_ASSERT((boost::is_same<x,long>::value));
```

An iterator can also provide access to adjacent positions in a sequence, or **traversal**. In Chapter 4 we described the `mpl::next` and `mpl::prior` metafunctions, which produce an incremented or decremented copy of their integral argument. These primitives apply equally well to iterators:

```
typedef mpl::next<long_pos>::type float_pos;
BOOST_STATIC_ASSERT((
    boost::is_same<
        mpl::deref<float_pos>::type
      , float
    >::value
));
```

5.4   Iterator Concepts

In this section we'll define the MPL iterator concepts. If you're familiar with STL iterators, you'll probably notice similarities between these and the STL categories of the same name. There are also a few differences, which are a direct consequence of the immutable nature of C++ metadata. For example, there are no separate categories for input iterators and output iterators in the MPL. We'll point out these similarities and differences as we encounter them, along with a few key properties of all iterators, which we'll introduce in **bold text**.

Just as the fundamental iterator operations of the STL are O(1) at runtime, all the fundamental MPL iterator operations detailed in this chapter are O(1) at compile time.[2]

5.4.1   Forward Iterators

Forward Iterator is the simplest MPL iterator category; it has only three operations: forward traversal, element access, and category detection. An MPL iterator can either be both **incrementable** and **dereferenceable**, or it can be **past-the-end** of its sequence. These two states are mutually exclusive: None of the Forward Iterator operations are allowed on a past-the-end iterator.

Since MPL iterators are immutable, we can't increment them "in place" the way we can with STL iterators. Instead, we pass them to `mpl::next`, which yields the next position in the sequence. The author of an incrementable iterator can either specialize `mpl::next` to support her iterator type, or she can simply leverage its default implementation, which reaches in to access the iterator's `::next` member:

```
namespace boost { namespace mpl {
   template <class It> struct next
   {
       typedef typename It::next type;
   };
}}
```

A dereferenceable iterator supports element access through the `mpl::deref` metafunction, whose default implementation similarly accesses the iterator's nested `::type`:

---

2. In this book we measure compile-time complexity of an operation in terms of the number of template instantiations required. There are of course other factors that will determine the time it takes to compile any program. See Appendix C for more details.

```
namespace boost { namespace mpl {
  template <class It> struct deref
  {
      typedef typename It::type type;
  };
}}
```

To check for equivalence of iterators, use the `boost::is_same` metafunction from the Boost Type Traits library. Two iterators are equivalent only if they have the same type. Since `is_same` works on any type, this applies equally well to past-the-end iterators. An iterator j is said to be **reachable** from an iterator i if they are equivalent, or if there exists some sequence:

```
typedef mpl::next<i>::type i₁;
typedef mpl::next<i₁>::type i₂;
  .
  .
  .
typedef mpl::next<iₙ₋₁>::type iₙ;
```

such that i_n is equivalent to j. We'll use the "half-open range" notation [i,j) to denote a range of sequence elements starting with `mpl::deref<i>::type` and ending with `mpl::deref<i`$_{n-1}$`>::type`.

Table 5.1 details the requirements for MPL forward iterators, where i is a model of *Forward Iterator*.

Table 5.1 Forward Iterator Requirements

Expression	Result	Precondition
`mpl::next<i>::type`	A Forward Iterator.	i is incrementable.
`mpl::deref<i>::type`	Any type.	i is dereferenceable.
`i::category`	Convertible to `mpl::forward_iterator_tag`.	

5.4.2 Bidirectional Iterators

A Bidirectional Iterator is a Forward Iterator with the additional ability to traverse a sequence in reverse. A Bidirectional Iterator is either **decrementable** or it refers to the beginning of its sequence.

Given a decrementable iterator, the `mpl::prior` metafunction yields the previous position in the sequence. The author of an decrementable iterator can either specialize `mpl::prior` to support her iterator type, or she can simply leverage its default implementation, which reaches in to access the iterator's `::prior` member:

```
namespace boost { namespace mpl {
    template <class It> struct prior
    {
        typedef typename It::prior type;
    };
}}
```

Table 5.2 details the additional requirements for MPL bidirectional iterators, where i is a model of Bidirectional Iterator.

Table 5.2 Additional Requirements for Bidirectional Iterators

Expression	Result	Assertion/Precondition
`mpl:: next<i>::type`	A Bidirectional Iterator.	`mpl::prior<` `mpl::next<i>::type` `>::type` is equivalent to i. Precondition: i is incrementable.
`mpl:: prior<i>::type`	A Bidirectional Iterator.	Precondition: i is decrementable.
`i::category`	Convertible to `mpl:: bidirectional_iterator_tag`.	

5.4.3 Random Access Iterators

A Random Access Iterator is a Bidirectional Iterator that also provides movement by an arbitrary number of positions forward or backward, and distance measurement between iterators in the same sequence, all in constant time.

Random access traversal is achieved using the `mpl::advance` metafunction, which, given a random access iterator i and an integral constant type n, returns an advanced iterator in the same sequence. Distance measurement is available through the `mpl::distance` metafunction, which, given random access iterators i and j into the same sequence, returns the number of positions between i and j. Note that these two operations have an intimate relationship:

```
mpl::advance<i, mpl::distance<i,j>::type>::type
```

is identical to j, and both operations have constant complexity.

As with the STL functions of the same names, `advance` and `distance` are in fact available for bidirectional and forward iterators as well, though only with *linear* complexity: The default implementations simply go through as many invocations of `mpl::next` or `mpl::prior` as necessary to get the job done. Consequently, the author of a random access iterator *must specialize* `advance` and `distance` for her iterator to work in constant time, or she won't have met the random access iterator requirements.

Table 5.3 details the additional requirements for MPL Random Access Iterators. The names `i` and `j` represent iterators into the same sequence, N represents an integral constant type, and *n* is `N::value`.

Table 5.3 Additional Requirements for Random Access Iterators

Expression	Result	Assertion/Precondition
`mpl::next<i>::type`	A Random Access Iterator.	Precondition: `i` is incrementable.
`mpl::prior<i>::type`	A Random Access Iterator.	Precondition: `i` is decrementable.

`mpl::advance<`
  `i, N`
`>::type`
	If *n*>0 , equivalent to *n* applications of `mpl::next` to `i`. Otherwise, equivalent to −*n* applications of `mpl::prior` to `i`.	Constant time.
		`mpl::advance<`
		   `i`
		  `, mpl::distance<`
		    `i,j`
		   `>::type`
		`>::type`
		is equivalent to `j`.

`mpl::distance<`
  `i, j`
`>::type`
	An integral constant wrapper.	Constant time.

`i::category`	Convertible to `mpl::random_access_iterator_tag`.	

5.5 Sequence Concepts

The MPL has a taxonomy of sequence concepts similar to those in the STL. Each level of concept refinement introduces a new set of capabilities and interfaces. In this section we'll walk through each of the concepts in turn.

5.5.1 Sequence Traversal Concepts

For each of the three iterator traversal categories—forward, bidirectional, and random access—there

is a corresponding sequence concept. A sequence whose iterators are forward iterators is called a
Forward Sequence, and so forth.

If the sequence traversal concepts detailed below seem a bit thin, it's because (apart from extensibility, which we'll get to in a moment), a sequence is not much more than a pair of iterators into its
elements. Most of what's needed to make a sequence work is provided by its iterators.

5.5.1.1 Forward Sequences

Any MPL sequence (for example, `mpl::list`, which we'll cover later in this chapter) is a Forward
Sequence.

In Table 5.4, S represents a Forward Sequence.

Table 5.4 Forward Sequence Requirements

Expression	Result	Assertion
`mpl::begin<S>::type`	A Forward Iterator.	
`mpl::end<S>::type`	A Forward Iterator.	Reachable from `mpl::begin<S>::type`.

Because we can access any sequence's `begin` iterator, we can trivially get its first element.
Accordingly, every nonempty MPL sequence also supports the expression

```
mpl::front<S>::type
```

which is equivalent to

```
mpl::deref<
    mpl::begin<S>::type
>::type
```

5.5.1.2 Bidirectional Sequences

In Table 5.5, S is any Bidirectional Sequence.

Table 5.5 Additional Requirements for Bidirectional Sequences

Expression	Result
`mpl::begin<S>::type`	A Bidirectional Iterator.
`mpl::end<S>::type`	A Bidirectional Iterator.

Because we can access any sequence's end iterator, we can trivially get to its last element if its iterators are bidirectional. Accordingly, every nonempty Bidirectional Sequence also supports the expression

```
mpl::back<S>::type
```

which is equivalent to

```
mpl::deref<
    mpl::prior<
        mpl::end<S>::type
    >::type
>::type
```

5.5.1.3 Random Access Sequences

`mpl::vector` is an example of a Random Access Sequence. In Table 5.6 , S is any Random Access Sequence.

Table 5.6 Additional Requirements for Random Access Sequences

Expression	Result
`mpl::begin<S>::type`	A Random Access Iterator.
`mpl::end<S>::type`	A Random Access Iterator.

Because a Random Access Sequence has random access iterators, we can trivially get to any element of the sequence in one step. Accordingly, every Random Access Sequence also supports the expression

```
mpl::at<S,N>::type
```

which is equivalent to

```
mpl::deref<
    mpl::advance<
        mpl::begin<S>::type
      , N
    >::type
>::type
```

5.5.2 Extensibility

An Extensible Sequence is one that supports `insert`, `erase`, and `clear` operations. Naturally, since metadata is immutable, none of these operations can modify the original sequence. Instead, they all return a modified *copy* of the original sequence.

Given that S is an Extensible Sequence, `pos` is some iterator into S, `finish` is an iterator reachable from `pos`, and X is any type, the expressions in Table 5.7 return a new sequence that models the same sequence concept that S does:

Table 5.7 Extensible Sequence Requirements

Expression	Elements of Result

`mpl::insert<S,pos,X>::type`	`[mpl::begin<S>::type, pos),`
	`X,`
	`[pos, mpl::end<S>::type)`

`mpl::erase<S,pos>::type`	`[mpl::begin<S>::type, pos),` `[mpl::next<pos>::type, mpl::end<S>::type)`

`mpl::erase<`
`    S, pos, finish`
`>::type`
	`[mpl::begin<S>::type, pos),`
	`[finish, mpl::end<S>::type)`

`mpl::clear<S>::type`	*None.*

Many of the MPL sequences are extensible, but with different complexity for the different operations. For example, insertion and erasure at the head of an `mpl::list` is O(1) (i.e., takes constant time and compiler resources), while making a `list` that differs only at the tail is O(N), meaning that the cost is proportional to the original list's length. Insertion and erasure at the back of an `mpl::vector` is O(1), though modifications at other positions are only guaranteed to be O(N).

MPL also supplies `push_front` and `pop_front` metafunctions, which insert and erase a single element at the head of a sequence respectively, and also `push_back` and `pop_back`, which do the same at the tail of a sequence. Each of these operations is only available for sequences that can support it with O(1) complexity.

5.5.3 Associative Sequences

An Associative Sequence is a mapping whose set of unique **key** types is mapped to one or more of its **value** types. Each of the sequence's **element** types—those accessible through its iterators—is associated with a single (key, value) pair.[3] In addition to supporting `begin<S>::type` and `end<S>::type` as required for any Forward Sequence, an Associative Sequence supports the following operations.

In Tables 5.8 and 5.9, `k` and `k2` can be any type and `pos1` and `pos2` are iterators into `S`.

Table 5.8 Associative Sequences Requirements

Expression	Result	Precondition/Assertion

`mpl::has_key<`
`  S, k`
`>::value`
	`true` if `k` is in `S`'s set of keys; `false` otherwise.	

`mpl::at<`
`  S, k`
`>::type`
	The value type associated with `k`.	Precondition: `k` is in `S`'s set of keys

`mpl::order<`
`  S, k`
`>::type`
	An unsigned integral constant wrapper.	If
		`    mpl::order<S,k>::type::value`
		`    == mpl::order<S,k2>::type::value`
		then `k` is identical to `k2`.
		Precondition: `k` is in `S`'s set of keys.

`mpl::key_type<`
`  S, t`
`>::type`
	The key type that `S` would use for an element type `t`.	If
		`    mpl::key_type<`
		`        S, mpl::deref<pos1>::type`
		`    >::type`
		is identical to
		`    mpl::key_type<`
		`        S, mpl::deref<pos2>::type`
		`    >::type`
		then `pos1` is identical to `pos2`.

`mpl::value_type<`
`  S, t`
`>::type`
	The value type that `S` would use for an element type `t`.	

Note that there are no guarantees about the values returned by the `order` metafunction other than that each key will be associated with a unique value. In particular, `order` values are not required to have any relationship to iterator traversal order. Also note that unlike an STL associative container, which always has an associated ordering relation (it defaults to `std::less<KeyType>`), an associative meta-sequence has no such ordering relation: The order that elements will be traversed during iteration is entirely up to the sequence implementation.

---

3. For some concrete examples, see section 5.8, which covers `mpl::map` and `mpl::set`.

5.5.4   Extensible Associative Sequences

Like an ordinary Extensible Sequence, an Extensible Associative Sequence supports `insert`, `erase`, and `clear` operations, each of which produces a new sequence as a result. Since the ordering of elements in an Associative Sequence is arbitrary, an inserted element won't necessarily end up in the position indicated by the iterator passed to the `insert` metafunction. In this respect, associative meta-sequences resemble STL associative containers such as `std::map` and `std::set`, but in some ways they are quite different. For example, while an STL sequence can use an iterator as a "hint" to improve the performance of insertion from O(log(N)) to O(1), an associative meta-sequence ignores the iterator argument to `insert` altogether: In fact, insertion is always O(1). While it is convenient—even crucial—for authors of generic sequence algorithms to have a uniform `insert` metafunction that always takes an iterator argument, it is equally *in*convenient to come up with an iterator every time you want to insert a new element in a `set`. Therefore, in addition to `mpl::insert<S,pos,t>`, an Extensible Associative Sequence must also support the equivalent `mpl::insert<S,t>` form.

Another difference from runtime associative containers is that erasures actually have an effect on the efficiency of iteration: A complete traversal of an associative meta-sequence has a worst-case complexity of O(N+E), where N is the number of elements in the sequence and E is the number of elements that have been erased. When an element is erased from an Associative Sequence, the library *adds* a special marker element that causes the erased element to be skipped during iteration. Note that applying `clear` to an Associative Sequence does not come with a similar penalty: The result is a brand new sequence.

The following expressions have constant complexity and return a new sequence that models all the same MPL sequence concepts as S does.

Table 5.9 Extensible Associative Sequence

Expression	Result	Note

`mpl::insert<`
`    S, pos1, t`
`>::type`
 	
`mpl::insert<`
`  S, t`
`>::type`
	S' equivalent to S except that
	
	`mpl::at<`
	`    S'`
	`  , mpl::key_type<S,t>::type`
	`>::type`
	
	is `mpl::value_type<S,t>::type`.
		May incur an erasure penalty if
		`mpl::has_key<`
		`    S,`
		`    mpl::key_type<`
		`      S, t`
		`    >::type`
		`>::value`
		is `true`.

Table 5.9 Extensible Associative Sequence (continued)

Expression	Result	Note

`mpl::erase<`
`    S, pos1`
`>::type`
	S' equivalent to S except that
	`mpl::has_key<`
	`      S'`
	`    , mpl::key_type<`
	`        S`
	`        , mpl::deref<pos1>::type`
	`      >::type`
	`>::value`
	is `false`.	

`mpl::erase_key<`
`    S, k`
`>::type`
	S' equivalent to S except that
	`mpl::has_key<S',k>::value`
	is `false`.	

`mpl::clear<`
`    S`
`>::type`
	An empty sequence with the same properties as S.	

Because erasure anywhere in an Extensible Associative Sequence is O(1), `pop_front` and `pop_back` are both available. Since insertion is also O(1), `mpl::push_front<S,t>` and `mpl::push_back<S,t>` are also supported, but are both equivalent to `mpl::insert<S,t>` because the iterator argument in `mpl::insert<S,pos,t>` is ignored.

5.6   Sequence Equality

It's important, particularly when handling computed results, not to fall into the trap of relying on sequence *type identity*. For example, you should not expect the following assertion to pass:

```
BOOST_STATIC_ASSERT((       // error
  boost::is_same<
      mpl::pop_back<mpl::vector<int, short> >::type
    , mpl::vector<int>
  >::value
));
```

For most purposes, the two types being compared above will act the same, and most of the time you'll never notice a difference. That said, the result of using `mpl::pop_back` on a specialization of `mpl::vector` will *not* be another specialization of `mpl::vector`!

As you saw in our exploration of dimensional analysis in Chapter 3, a function template that can only be called with two identical types is likely not to work as expected if those types are sequences. The same goes for a class template partial specialization that matches only when two type arguments are identical.

The correct way to check for sequence equality is always to use the `equal` algorithm, as follows:

```
BOOST_STATIC_ASSERT((          // OK
  mpl::equal<
      mpl::pop_back<mpl::vector<int, short> >::type
    , mpl::vector<int>
  >::value
));
```

5.7   Intrinsic Sequence Operations

MPL supplies a catalog of sequence metafunctions whose STL counterparts are usually implemented as member functions. We've already discussed `begin`, `end`, `front`, `back`, `push_front`, `push_back`, `pop_front`, `pop_back`, `insert`, `erase`, and `clear`; the rest are summarized in Table 5.10, where R is any sequence.

Table 5.10 Intrinsic Sequence Operations

Expression	Result	Worst-Case Complexity
`mpl::empty<S>::type`	A `bool` constant wrapper; `true` iff the sequence is empty.	Constant.

`mpl::insert_range<`
`    S, pos, R`
`>::type`
	Identical to S but with the elements of R inserted at `pos`.	Linear in the length of the result.

`mpl::size<S>::type`	An integral constant wrapper whose `::value` is the number of elements in S.	Linear in the length of S.

All of these metafunctions are known as **intrinsic sequence operations**, to distinguish them from generic sequence algorithms, because they generally need to be implemented separately for each new kind of sequence. They're not implemented as nested metafunctions (corresponding to similar container member functions in the STL) for three good reasons.

1. **Syntactic overhead.** Member templates are a pain to use in most metaprogramming contexts

because of the need to use the extra `template` keyword:

```
Sequence::template erase<pos>::type
```

as opposed to:

```
mpl::erase<Sequence,pos>::type
```

As you know, reducing the burdens of C++ template syntax is a major design concern for MPL.

2. **Efficiency.** Most sequences are templates that are instantiated in many different ways. The presence of template members, even if they're unused, may have a cost for each instantiation.

3. **Convenience.** Despite the fact that we call these operations "intrinsic," there are reasonable ways to supply default implementations for many of them. For example, the default `size` measures the distance between the sequence's `begin` and `end` iterators. If these operations were member templates, every sequence author would be required to write all of them.

5.8   Sequence Classes

In this section we'll describe the specific sequences provided by the MPL, and discuss how they fit the sequence concepts detailed above.

Before we begin, you should know that all of the MPL sequences have both an unnumbered and a numbered form. The unnumbered forms are the ones you're already familiar with, like `mpl::vector<int, long, int>`. The corresponding numbered forms include the sequence's length as part of its template name, for example, `mpl::vector3<int, long, int>`. The length of unnumbered forms is limited to 20 elements by default[4] to reduce coupling in the library and to limit compilation times. To use the numbered form of a sequence with length *N*, you must include a corresponding "numbered header" file, named for the sequence whose length is *N* rounded up to the nearest multiple of ten. For example:

```
#include <boost/mpl/vector/vector30.hpp> // 28 rounded up

// declare a sequence of 28 elements
typedef boost::mpl::vector28<
    char, int, long ... 25 more types
> s;
```

---

4. See the Configuration Macros section of the MPL reference manual for details on how to change this limit.

5.8.1 list

mpl::list is the simplest of the extensible MPL sequences, and it is structurally very similar to a runtime singly-linked list. Since it is a Forward Sequence, it supports begin and end, and, of course, access to the first element via front. It supports O(1) insertion and erasure at the head of the sequence, so it also supports push_front and pop_front.

5.8.2 vector

MPL's vector is almost an exact analogue to the STL vector: it is a Random Access Sequence, so naturally it has Random Access Iterators. Since every Random Access Iterator is a Bidirectional Iterator, and we have access to the vector's end iterator, back is supported in addition to front. Like an STL vector, MPL's vector also supports efficient push_back and pop_back operations.

In addition to the usual compile-time/runtime differences, this sequence may differ from those in the STL in one significant detail: It may have a maximum size that is limited not just by the usual compiler resources, such as memory or template instantiation depth, but also by the way the sequence was implemented. In that case, the sequence can normally be extended only as far as the maximum numbered sequence header included in the translation unit. For example:

```
#include <boost/mpl/vector/vector10.hpp>

typedef boost::mpl::vector9<
      int[1], int[2], int[3], int[4]
    , int[5], int[6], int[7], int[8], int[9]
> s9;

typedef mpl::push_back<s9, int[10]>::type s10;   // OK
typedef mpl::push_back<s10, int[11]>::type s11; // error
```

To make the code work, we'd have to replace the #include directive with:

```
#include <boost/mpl/vector/vector20.hpp>
```

This limitation is not as serious as it may sound, for two reasons:

1. The library headers provide you with numbered vector forms allowing up to 50 elements by default, and that number can be adjusted just by defining some preprocessor symbols.[5]

---

5. See the Configuration Macros section of the MPL reference manual for details on how to change this limit.

2. Since meta-code executes at compile time, exceeding the limit causes a compile-time error. Unless you're writing generic metafunction libraries to be used by other metaprogrammers, you can never ship code that will fail in the customer's hands because of this limitation, as long as your code compiles on your local machine.

We wrote that it *may* differ in this respect because on compilers that support the `typeof` language extension, the maximum size limitation vanishes. Chapter 9 describes some of the basic techniques that make that possible.

Operations on `mpl::vector` tend to compile much more quickly than those on `mpl::list`, and, due to its random-access capability, `mpl::vector` is far more flexible. Taken together, these factors should make `mpl::vector` your first choice when selecting a general-purpose Extensible Sequence. However, if your clients will be using your code for compile-time computation that may require sequences of arbitrary length, it may be better to use `mpl::list`.

Guideline

Reach for `mpl::vector` first when choosing a general-purpose type sequence.

5.8.3   deque

MPL's `deque` is almost exactly like its `vector` in all respects, except that `deque` allows efficient operations at the head of the sequence with `push_front` and `pop_front`. Unlike the corresponding STL components, the efficiency of `deque` is very close to that of `vector`—so much so, in fact, that on many C++ compilers, a `vector` really *is* a `deque` under-the-covers.

5.8.4   range_c

range_c is a "lazy" random access sequence that contains consecutive integral constants. That is, mpl::range_c<long, N, M> is roughly equivalent to:

```
mpl::vector<
    mpl::integral_c<long,N>
  , mpl::integral_c<long,N+1>
  , mpl::integral_c<long,N+2>
  ...
  , mpl::integral_c<long,M-3>
  , mpl::integral_c<long,M-2>
  , mpl::integral_c<long,M-1> // Note: M-1, not M
>
```

By saying range_c is "lazy," we mean that its elements are not explicitly represented: It merely stores the endpoints and produces new integral constants from within the range on demand. When iterating over large sequences of integers, using range_c is not only convenient, but can result in a significant savings in compilation time over the use of a non-lazy alternative like the vector shown above.

The price of this economy is that range_c comes with a limitation not shared by vector and list: It is not extensible. If the library could support insertion of arbitrary elements into range_c, the elements would need to be explicitly represented. Though not extensible, range_c supports pop_front and pop_back, because contracting a range is easy.

5.8.5 map

An MPL map is an Extensible Associative Sequence in which each element supports the interface of mpl::pair.

```
template <class T1, class T2>
struct pair
{
    typedef pair type;
    typedef T1 first;
    typedef T2 second;
};
```

An element's first and second types are treated as its key and value, respectively. To create a map, just list its elements in sequence as template parameters. The following example shows a mapping from built-in integral types to their next "larger" type:

```
typedef mpl::map<
    mpl::pair<bool, unsigned char>
  , mpl::pair<unsigned char, unsigned short>
  , mpl::pair<unsigned short, unsigned int>
  , mpl::pair<unsigned int, unsigned long>
  , mpl::pair<signed char, signed short>
  , mpl::pair<signed short, signed int>
  , mpl::pair<signed int, signed long>
>::type to_larger;
```

Like mpl::vector, the mpl::map implementation has a bounded maximum size on C++ compilers that don't support the typeof language extension, and the appropriate numbered sequence headers must be included if you're going to grow a map beyond the next multiple of ten elements.

It's not all bad news for users whose compiler doesn't go beyond the standard requirements, though: When `map` has a bounded maximum size, iterating over all of its elements is O(N) instead of O(N+E), where N is the size of the map and E is the number of erasures that have been applied to it.

5.8.6 `set`

A `set` is like a `map`, except that each element is identical to its key type and value type. The fact that the key and value types are identical means that `mpl::at<S,k>::type` is a fairly uninteresting operation—it just returns k unchanged. The main use for an MPL `set` is efficient membership testing with `mpl::has_key<S,k>::type`. A `set` is never subject to a maximum size bound, and therefore operation is always O(N+E) for complete traversal.

5.8.7 `iterator_range`

An `iterator_range` is very similar to `range_c` in intent. Instead of representing its elements explicitly, an `iterator_range` stores two iterators that denote the sequence endpoints. Because MPL algorithms operate on sequences instead of iterators, `iterator_range` can be indispensable when you want to operate on just part of a sequence: Once you've found the sequence endpoints, you can form an `iterator_range` and pass that to the algorithm, rather than building a modified version of the original sequence.

5.9   Integral Sequence Wrappers

We've already discussed the use of the `vector_c` class template as a shortcut for writing lists of integral constants. MPL also supplies `list_c`, `deque_c`, and `set_c` for representing the corresponding vectors, deques, and sets. Each of these sequences takes the form:

```
sequence-type_c<T, n₁, n₂,... nₖ>
```

The first argument to each of these sequence wrappers is the integer type T that it will store, and the following arguments are the values of T that it will store. You can think of these as being equivalent to:

```
sequence-type<
    integral_c<T,n₁>
  , integral_c<T,n₂>
  , ...
  , integral_c<T,nₖ>
>
```

That said, they are not precisely the same type, and, as we've suggested, you should not rely on type identity when comparing sequences.

Note that the MPL also provides _c-suffixed versions of the numbered sequence forms:

```
#include <boost/mpl/vector/vector10_c.hpp>
```

```
typedef boost::mpl::vector10_c<int,1,2,3,4,5,6,7,8,9,10> v10;
```

5.10 Sequence Derivation

Typically, the unnumbered form of any sequence is derived from the corresponding numbered form, or else shares with it a common base class that provides the sequence's implementation. For example, `mpl::vector` might be defined this way:

```
namespace boost { namespace mpl {

   struct void_; // "no argument" marker

   // primary template declaration
   template <class T0 = void_, class T1 = void_, etc....>
   struct vector;

   // specializations
   template<>
   struct vector<> : vector0<> {};

   template<class T0>
   struct vector<T0> : vector1<T0> {};

   template<class T0, class T1>
   struct vector<T0,T1> : vector2<T0,T1> {};

   template<class T0, class T1, class T2>
   struct vector<T0,T1,T2> : vector3<T0,T1,T2> {};

   etc.
}}
```

The integral sequence wrappers are similarly derived from equivalent underlying type sequences.

All of the built-in MPL sequences are designed so that nearly any subclass functions as an equivalent type sequence. Derivation is a powerful way to provide a new interface, or just a new name, to an existing family of sequences. For example, the Boost Python library provides the following type sequence:

```
namespace boost { namespace python {

  template <class T0=mpl::void_, ... class T4=mpl::void_>
  struct bases : mpl::vector<T0,T1,T2,T3,T4> {};

}}
```

You can use the same technique to create a plain class that is an MPL type sequence:

```
struct signed_integers
  : mpl::vector<signed char, short, int, long> {};
```

On some compilers, using `signed_integers` instead of the underlying `vector` can dramatically improve metaprogram efficiency. See Appendix C for more details.

5.11 Writing Your Own Sequence

In this section we'll show you how to write a simple sequence. You might be wondering at this point why you'd ever want to do that; after all, the built-in facilities provided by MPL are pretty complete. Usually it's a matter of efficiency. While the MPL sequences are well-optimized for general-purpose use, you may have a specialized application for which it's possible to do better. For example, it's possible to write a wrapper that presents the argument types of a function pointer as a sequence [Nas03]. If you happen to already have the function pointer type in hand for other reasons, iterating over the wrapper directly rather than assembling another sequence containing those types could save quite a few template instantiations.

For this example, we'll write a limited-capacity *Random Access Sequence* called `tiny` with up to three elements. This sequence will be very much like MPL's implementation of `vector` for compilers that are merely conforming but do not supply `typeof`.

5.11.1 Building Tiny Sequence

The first step is to choose a representation. Not much more is required of the representation than to encode the (up to three) types it can contain in the sequence type itself:

```
struct none {}; // tag type to denote no element

template <class T0 = none, class T1 = none, class T2 = none>
struct tiny
{
    typedef tiny type;
```

```
typedef T0 t0;
typedef T1 t1;
typedef T2 t2;

...
};
```

As you can see, we've jumped the gun and filled in some of the implementation: tiny's nested
::type refers back to the sequence itself, which makes tiny a sort of "self-returning metafunction."
All of the MPL sequences do something similar, and it turns out to be terribly convenient. For
example, to return sequence results from a metafunction, you can just derive the metafunction from
the sequence you want to return. Also, when one branch of an eval_if needs to return a sequence,
you don't have to wrap it in the identity metafunction described in Chapter 4. That is, given a
tiny sequence S, the following two forms are equivalent:

```
// pop the front element off S, unless it is empty
typedef mpl::eval_if<
    mpl::empty<S>
  , mpl::identity<S>
  , mpl::pop_front<S>
>::type r1;

// likewise
typedef mpl::eval_if<
    mpl::empty<S>
  , S                          // when invoked, S returns S
  , mpl::pop_front<S>
>::type r2;
```

The other three nested typedefs, t0, t1, and t2, make it easy for any metafunction to access a
tiny sequence's elements:[6]

---

6. The alternative would be a cumbersome partial specialization:

```
template <class Tiny>
struct manipulate_tiny;

template <class T0, class T1, class T2>
struct manipulate_tiny<tiny<T0,T1,T2> >
{
    // T0 is known
};
```

Embedding the element types will save us a lot of code in the long run.

```
template <class Tiny>
struct manipulate_tiny
{
    // what's T0?
    typedef typename Tiny::t0 t0;
};
```

As long as we can all agree not to use none for any other purpose than to mark the beginning of tiny's empty elements, we now have a convenient interface for holding up to three elements. It's not an MPL sequence yet, though.

Looking back at the most basic sequence requirements, we find that every sequence has to return iterators from MPL's begin and end metafunctions. Right away it's clear we'll need an iterator representation. Because Random Access Iterators can move in both directions, they must have access to all the elements of the sequence. The simplest way to handle that is to embed the entire sequence in the iterator representation. In fact, it's typical that MPL iterators embed all or part of the sequence they traverse (since list iterators only move forward, they only hold the part of the list that's accessible to them).

5.11.2 The Iterator Representation

Once our iterator has access to the sequence, we just need to represent the position somehow. An integral constant wrapper (Pos in the example below) will do:

```
#include <boost/mpl/iterator_tag.hpp>

template <class Tiny, class Pos>
struct tiny_iterator
{
    typedef mpl::random_access_iterator_tag category;
};
```

The most basic operations on any iterator are dereferencing, via mpl::deref, and forward traversal, via mpl::next. In this case, we can handle incremental traversal in either direction by building a new tiny_iterator with an incremented (or decremented) position:[7]

---

7. We could have also taken advantage of the default mpl::next and mpl::prior implementations and realized the requirements by simply supplying tiny_iterator with the corresponding nested typedefs (::next/::prior). The price for a somewhat reduced amount of typing would be slower metaprograms—such an iterator would be a typical instance of the "Blob" anti-pattern discussed in Chapter 2.

```
namespace boost { namespace mpl {

    // forward iterator requirement
    template <class Tiny, class Pos>
    struct next<tiny_iterator<Tiny,Pos> >
    {
        typedef tiny_iterator<
            Tiny
          , typename mpl::next<Pos>::type
        > type;
    };
     // bidirectional iterator requirement
    template <class Tiny, class Pos>
    struct prior<tiny_iterator<Tiny,Pos> >
    {
        typedef tiny_iterator<
            Tiny
          , typename mpl::prior<Pos>::type
        > type;
    };

}}
```

Dereferencing our `tiny_iterator` is a bit more involved: We need some way to index our `tiny` sequence with the iterator's position. If you're thinking, "Hang on, to do that you'd need to implement the `at` operation," you're right: It's time to leave our iterators alone for a while.

5.11.3 Implementing `at` for `tiny`

One reasonable way to implement `at` is to use partial specialization. First we'll write a template that selects an element of the sequence based on a numerical argument:

```
template <class Tiny, int N> struct tiny_at;

// partially specialized accessors for each index
template <class Tiny>
struct tiny_at<Tiny,0>
{
    typedef typename Tiny::t0 type;
};

template <class Tiny>
```

```
struct tiny_at<Tiny,1>
{
    typedef typename  Tiny::t1 type;
};

template <class Tiny>
struct tiny_at<Tiny,2>
{
    typedef typename Tiny::t2 type;
};
```

Note that if you try to access `tiny_at`'s nested `::type` when the second argument is a number outside the range 0...2, you'll get an error: The unspecialized (or "primary") template is not defined.

Next, we could simply partially specialize `mpl::at` for `tiny` instances:

```
namespace boost { namespace mpl {

  template <class T0, class T1, class T2, class Pos>
  struct at<tiny<T0,T1,T2>, Pos>
    : tiny_at<tiny<T0,T1,T2>,Pos::value>
  {
  };

}}
```

On the face of it, there's nothing wrong with using partial specialization, but let's see how we could get the unspecialized version of `mpl::at` to work for `tiny`. This is what the `at` supplied by MPL looks like:

```
template<class Sequence, class N>
struct at
  : at_impl<typename Sequence::tag>
      ::template apply<Sequence,N>
{
};
```

By default, `at` forwards its implementation to `at_impl<Sequence::tag>`, a metafunction class that knows how to perform the `at` function for all sequences with that `tag` type. So we could add a `::tag` to `tiny` (call it `tiny_tag`), and write an explicit (full) specialization of `mpl::at_impl`:

struct tiny_tag {};

```
template <class T0 = none, class T1 = none, class T2 = none>
```

```
struct tiny
{
    typedef tiny_tag tag;
    typedef tiny type;
    typedef T0 t0;
    typedef T1 t1;
    typedef T2 t2;
};

namespace boost { namespace mpl {
    template <>
    struct at_impl<tiny_tag>
    {
        template <class Tiny, class N>
        struct apply : tiny_at<Tiny, N::value>
        {};
    };
}}
```

This might not seem to be a big improvement over the results of partially specializing `at` for `tiny` sequences, but it is. In general, writing partial specializations that will match all the forms taken by a particular sequence family can be impractical. It's very common for equivalent sequence forms *not* to be instances of the same template, so normally at least one partial specialization for each form would be required: You can't write a partial template specialization that matches both `mpl::vector<int>` and `mpl::vector1<int>`, for example. For the same reasons, specializing `at` limits the ability of third parties to quickly build new members of the sequence family through derivation.

> **Recommendation**
>
> To implement an intrinsic sequence operation, always provide a sequence tag and a specialization of the operation's `_impl` template.

5.11.4 Finishing the `tiny_iterator` Implementation

With our implementation of `at` in hand, we're ready to implement our `tiny_iterator`'s dereference operation:

```
namespace boost { namespace mpl {

    template <class Tiny, class Pos>
```

```
struct deref< tiny_iterator<Tiny,Pos> >
  : at<Tiny,Pos>
{
};

}}
```

The only thing missing now are constant-time specializations of `mpl::advance` and `mpl::distance` metafunctions:

```
namespace boost { namespace mpl {

  // random access iterator requirements
  template <class Tiny, class Pos, class N>
  struct advance<tiny_iterator<Tiny,Pos>,N>
  {
      typedef tiny_iterator<
          Tiny
        , typename mpl::plus<Pos,N>::type
      > type;
  };

  template <class Tiny, class Pos1, class Pos2>
  struct distance<
      tiny_iterator<Tiny,Pos1>
    , tiny_iterator<Tiny,Pos2>
  >
    : mpl::minus<Pos2,Pos1>
  {};

}}
```

Note that we've left the job of checking for usage errors to you in exercise 5-0.

5.11.5   begin and end

Finally, we're ready to make `tiny` into a real sequence; all that remains is to supply `begin` and `end`. Like `mpl::at`, `mpl::begin` and `mpl::end` use traits to isolate the implementation for a particular family of sequences. Writing our `begin`, then, is straightforward:

```
namespace boost { namespace mpl {

    template <>
    struct begin_impl<tiny_tag>
    {
        template <class Tiny>
        struct apply
        {
            typedef tiny_iterator<Tiny,int_<0> > type;
        };
    };
}}
```

Writing end is a little more complicated than writing begin was, since we'll need to deduce the sequence length based on the number of none elements. One straightforward approach might be:

```
namespace boost { namespace mpl {

    template <>
    struct end_impl<tiny_tag>
    {
        template <class Tiny>
        struct apply
          : eval_if<
                is_same<none,typename Tiny::t0>
              , int_<0>
              , eval_if<
                    is_same<none,typename Tiny::t1>
                  , int_<1>
                  , eval_if<
                        is_same<none,typename Tiny::t2>
                      , int_<2>
                      , int_<3>
                    >
                >
            >
        {};
    };
}}
```

Unfortunately, that code doesn't satisfy the O(1) complexity requirements of end: It costs O(N) template instantiations for a sequence of length N, since eval_if/is_same pairs will be instantiated until a none element is found. To find the size of the sequence in constant time, we need only write a few partial specializations:

```
template <class T0, class T1, class T2>
struct tiny_size
  : mpl::int_<3> {};

template <class T0, class T1>
struct tiny_size<T0,T1,none>
  : mpl::int_<2> {};

template <class T0>
struct tiny_size<T0,none,none>
  : mpl::int_<1> {};

template <>
struct tiny_size<none,none,none>
  : mpl::int_<0> {};

namespace boost { namespace mpl {
   template <>
   struct end_impl<tiny_tag>
   {
       template <class Tiny>
       struct apply
       {
           typedef tiny_iterator<
               Tiny
             , typename tiny_size<
                   typename Tiny::t0
                 , typename Tiny::t1
                 , typename Tiny::t2
               >::type
           >
           type;
       };
   };
}}
```

Here, each successive specialization of tiny_size is "more specialized" than the previous one, and only the appropriate version will be instantiated for any given tiny sequence. The best-matching tiny_size specialization will always correspond directly to the length of the sequence.

If you're a little uncomfortable (or even peeved) at the amount of boilerplate code repetition here, we can't blame you. After all, didn't we promise that metaprogramming would help save us from all that? Well, yes we did. We have two answers for you. First, metaprogramming libraries save their *users* from repeating themselves, but once you start writing new sequences you're now working at the level of a library designer.[8] Your users will thank you for going to the trouble (even if they're just you!). Second, as we hinted earlier, there are other ways to automate code generation. You'll see how even the library designer can be spared the embarrassment of repeating herself in Appendix A.

It's so easy to do at this point, that we may as well implement a specialized `mpl::size`. It's entirely optional; MPL's default implementation of `size` just measures the distance between our `begin` and `end` iterators, but since we are going for efficiency, we can save a few more template instantiations by writing our own:

```
namespace boost { namespace mpl {
    template <>
    struct size_impl<tiny_tag>
    {
        template <class Tiny>
        struct apply
          : tiny_size<
                typename Tiny::t0
              , typename Tiny::t1
              , typename Tiny::t2
            >
        {};
    };
}}
```

You've probably caught on by now that the same tag-dispatching technique keeps cropping up over and over. In fact, it's used for all of the MPL's intrinsic sequence operations, so you can always take advantage of it to customize any of them for your own sequence types.

5.11.6 Adding Extensibility

In this section we'll write some of the operations required for `tiny` to fulfill the *Extensible Sequence* requirements. We won't show you all of them because they are so similar in spirit. Besides, we need to leave something for the exercises at the end of the chapter!

---

8. This need for repetition, at least at the metaprogramming library level, seems to be a peculiarity of C++. Most other languages that support metaprogramming don't suffer from the same limitation, probably because their metaprogramming capabilities are more than just a lucky accident.

First let's tackle clear and push_front. It's illegal to call push_front on a full tiny, because our tiny sequence has a fixed capacity. Therefore, any valid tiny<T0,T1,T2> passed as a first argument to push_front must always have length <= 2 and T2 = none, and it's okay to just drop T2 off the end of the sequence:[9]

```
namespace boost { namespace mpl {
    template <>
    struct clear_impl<tiny_tag>
    {
        template <class Tiny>
        struct apply : tiny<>
        {};
    };
    template <>
    struct push_front_impl<tiny_tag>
    {
        template <class Tiny, class T>
        struct apply
          : tiny<T, typename Tiny::t0, typename Tiny::t1>
        {};
    };
}}
```

That was easy! Note that because every tiny sequence is a metafunction returning itself, we were able to take advantage of metafunction forwarding in the body of apply.

> **Recommendation**
>
> For maximum MPL interoperability, when writing a class template that isn't already a metafunction, consider making it one by adding a nested ::type that refers to the class itself. When writing a metafunction that will always return a class type, consider deriving it from that class and having the metafunction return itself.

Writing push_back isn't going to be such a cakewalk: The transformation we apply depends on the length of the input sequence. Not to worry; we've already written one operation whose implementation depended on the length of the input sequence: end. Since we have the length computation conveniently at hand, all we need is a tiny_push_back template, specialized for each sequence length:

---

9. Actually *enforcing* our assumption that the sequence is not full when push_front is invoked is left for you as an exercise.

```
template <class Tiny, class T, int N>
struct tiny_push_back;

template <class Tiny, class T>
struct tiny_push_back<Tiny,T,0>
  : tiny<T,none,none>
{};

template <class Tiny, class T>
struct tiny_push_back<Tiny,T,1>
  : tiny<typename Tiny::t0,T,none>
{};

template <class Tiny, class T>
struct tiny_push_back<Tiny,T,2>
  : tiny<typename Tiny::t0,typename Tiny::t1,T>
{};

namespace boost { namespace mpl {
   template <>
   struct push_back_impl<tiny_tag>
   {
       template <class Tiny, class T>
       struct apply
         : tiny_push_back<
             Tiny, T, size<Tiny>::value
           >
       {};
   };
}}
```

Note that what is missing here is just as important as what is present. By not defining a tiny_push_back specialization for sequences of length 3, we made it a compile-time error to push_back into a full sequence.

5.12 Details

By now you should have a fairly clear understanding of what goes into an MPL sequence—and what comes out of it! In upcoming chapters you can expect to get more exposure to type sequences and their practical applications, but for now we'll just review a few of this chapter's core concepts.

Sequence concepts. MPL sequences fall into three traversal concept categories (forward, bidirectional, and random access) corresponding to the capabilities of their iterators. A sequence may also be front-extensible, meaning that it supports `push_front` and `pop_front`, or back-extensible, meaning that it supports `push_back` and `pop_back`. An Associative Sequence represents a mapping from type to type with O(1) lookup.

Iterator concepts. MPL iterators model one of three traversal concepts: Forward Iterator, Bidirectional Iterator, and Random Access Iterator. Each iterator concept refines the previous one, so that all bidirectional iterators are also forward iterators, and all random access iterators are also bidirectional iterators. A Forward Iterator x can be incrementable and dereferenceable, meaning that `next<x>::type` and `deref<x>::type` are well-defined, or it can be past-the-end of its sequence. A Bidirectional Iterator may be decrementable, or it may refer to the beginning of its sequence.

Sequence algorithms. The purely functional nature of C++ template metaprogramming really dictates that MPL algorithms operate on sequences rather than on iterator pairs. Otherwise, passing the result of one algorithm to another one would be unreasonably difficult. Some people feel that the same logic applies to STL algorithms, and several algorithm libraries for operating on whole *runtime* sequences have cropped up. Look for one in an upcoming Boost release.

Intrinsic sequence operations. Not all sequence operations can be written generically; some, such as `begin` and `end`, need to be written specifically to work with particular sequences. These MPL metafunctions all use a tag dispatching technique to allow for easy customization.

5.13 Exercises

5-0. Write a test program that exercises the parts of `tiny` we've implemented. Try to arrange your program so that it will only compile if the tests succeed.

5-1. Write a metafunction `double_first_half` that takes a Random Access Sequence of integral constant wrappers of length N as an argument, and returns a copy with the first N/2 elements doubled in value, such that the following is `true`:

```
mpl::equal<
    double_first_half< mpl::vector_c<int,1,2,3,4> >::type
  , mpl::vector_c<int,2,4,3,4>
>::type::value
```

5-2. Note that `push_back` won't compile if its `tiny` argument already has three elements. How can we get the same guarantees for `push_front`?

5-3. Drawing on the example of our `push_back` implementation, implement `insert` for `tiny` sequences. Refactor the implementation of `push_back` so that it shares more code with `insert`.

5-4. How could we reduce the number of template instantiations required by our implementation of `push_back`? (Hint: Look at our implementation of `end` in section 5.11.5 again.) How does that interact with the refactoring in the previous exercise?

5-5. Implement the `pop_front`, `pop_back`, and `erase` algorithms for `tiny`.

5-6. Write a sequence adapter template called `dimensions` that, when instantiated on an array type, presents the array's dimensions as a forward, non-extensible sequence:

```
typedef dimensions<char [10][5][2]> seq;
BOOST_STATIC_ASSERT( mpl::size<seq>::value == 3 );
BOOST_STATIC_ASSERT(( mpl::at_c<seq,0>::type::value == 2 ));
BOOST_STATIC_ASSERT(( mpl::at_c<seq,1>::type::value == 5 ));
BOOST_STATIC_ASSERT(( mpl::at_c<seq,2>::type::value == 10 ));
```

Consider using the type traits library facilities to simplify the implementation.

5-7. Modify the `dimensions` sequence adapter from exercise 5-6 to provide bidirectional iterators and `push_back` and `pop_back` operations.

5-8. Write a `fibonacci_series` class that represents an infinite forward sequence of Fibonacci numbers:

```
typedef mpl::lower_bound< fibonacci_series, int_<10> >::type n;
BOOST_STATIC_ASSERT( n::value == 8 );

typedef mpl::lower_bound< fibonacci_series, int_<50> >::type m;
BOOST_STATIC_ASSERT( m::value == 34 );
```

Each element of the Fibonacci series is the sum of the previous two elements. The series begins 0, 1, 1, 2, 3, 5, 8, 13. . . .

5-9. Modify the `fibonacci_series` sequence from exercise 5-8 to be limited by a maximum number of elements in the series. Make the sequence's iterators bidirectional:

```
typedef fibonacci_series<8> seq;
BOOST_STATIC_ASSERT( mpl::size<seq>::value == 8 );
BOOST_STATIC_ASSERT( mpl::back<seq>::type::value == 21 );
```

5-10*.   Write a `tree` class template for composing compile-time binary tree data structures:

```
typedef tree<                       //       double
    double                          //       /  \
  , tree<void*,int,long>            //    void* char
  , char                            //    /  \
  > tree_seq;                       // int   long
```

Implement iterators for pre-order, in-order, and post-order traversal of the tree elements:

```
BOOST_STATIC_ASSERT(( mpl::equal<
      preorder_view<tree_seq>
    , mpl::vector<double,void*,int,long,char>
    , boost::is_same<_1,_2>
    >::value ));

BOOST_STATIC_ASSERT(( mpl::equal<
      inorder_view<tree_seq>
    , mpl::vector<int,void*,long,double,char>
    , boost::is_same<_1,_2>
    >::value ));

BOOST_STATIC_ASSERT(( mpl::equal<
      postorder_view<tree_seq>
    , mpl::vector<int,long,void*,char,double>
    , boost::is_same<_1,_2>
    >::value ));
```

Important

Extend the tests from exercise 5-0 to cover the algorithms you implemented in exercises 5-3, 5-4, and 5-5.

6

Algorithms

Alexander Stepanov, the father of the STL, has often stressed the central role of algorithms in his library. The MPL is no different, and now that you understand the sequences and iterators on which they operate, we are ready to give algorithms the in-depth treatment they deserve.

We'll start by discussing the relationship between algorithms and abstraction. Then we'll cover the similarities and differences between algorithms in the STL and MPL, in particular the design choices made in the MPL to deal with the fact that metadata is immutable. Then we'll describe the most useful algorithms in the MPL's three algorithm categories, and conclude with a brief section on implementing your own sequence algorithms.

6.1   Algorithms, Idioms, Reuse, and Abstraction

Abstraction can be defined as generalization away from specific instances or implementations, and toward the "essence" of an object or process. Some abstractions, like that of an STL iterator, become so familiar that they can be called **idiomatic**. In software design, the *idea* reuse achieved through idiomatic abstractions can be just as important as code reuse. The best libraries provide both reusable code components *and* reusable idioms.

Because most of them operate at the relatively low level of sequence traversal, it's easy to miss the fact that the STL algorithms represent powerful abstractions. In fact, it's commonly argued—not entirely without cause—that for trivial tasks, the algorithms are inferior to handwritten loops. For example:[1]

```
// "abstraction"
std::transform(
    v.begin(), v.end(), v.begin()
  , std::bind2nd(std::plus<int>(),42)
);
```

---

1. In all fairness to the STL algorithms, this example was deliberately chosen to make the case for writing loops by hand.

```
// handwritten loop
typedef std::vector<int>::iterator v_iter;
for (v_iter i = v.begin(), last = v.end(); i != last; ++i)
    *i += 42;
```

So, what's wrong with the use of `transform` above?

- The user needs to handle iterators even if she wants to operate on the whole sequence.

- The mechanism for creating function objects is cumbersome and ugly, and brings in at least as many low-level details as it hides.

- Unless the person reading the code eats and breathes the STL components every day, the "abstraction" actually seems to obfuscate what's going on instead of clarifying it.

These weaknesses, however, can be overcome quite easily. For example, we can use the Boost Lambda library, which inspired MPL's compile time lambda expressions, to simplify and clarify the runtime function object:[2]

```
std::transform(v.begin(), v.end(), v.begin(), _1 + 42);
```

or even:

```
std::for_each(v.begin(), v.end(), _1 += 42);
```

Both statements do exactly the same thing as the raw loop we saw earlier, yet once you are familiar with the idioms of the Lambda library, iterators, and `for_each`, the use of algorithms is far clearer.

We could raise the abstraction level a bit further by rewriting STL algorithms to operate on whole sequences (like the MPL algorithms do), but let's stop here for now. From the simplification above, you can already see that many of the problems with our example weren't the fault of the algorithm at all. The real culprit was the STL function object framework used to generate the algorithm's function argument. Setting aside those problems, we can see that these "trivial" algorithms abstract away several deceptively simple low-level details:

- Creation of temporary iterators.

- Correct declaration of the iterator type, even in generic code.

---

2. In these examples, `_1` refers to a placeholder *object* from the Boost Lambda library (in namespace `boost::lambda`). MPL's placeholder *types* were inspired by the Lambda library's placeholder objects.

- Avoiding known inefficiencies[3]

- Taking advantage of known optimizations (e.g., loop unrolling)

- And correct generic loop termination: `for_each` uses `pos != finish` instead of `pos < finish`, which would lock it into random access iterators

These all seem easy enough to get right when you consider a single loop, but when that pattern is repeated throughout a large project the chance of errors grows rapidly. The optimizations mentioned above only tend to increase that risk, as they generally introduce even more low-level detail.

More importantly, the use of `for_each` achieves *separation of concerns:* the common pattern of traversing and modifying all the elements of a sequence is neatly captured in the name of the algorithm, leaving us only to specify the details of the modification. In the compile time world, this division of labor can be especially important, because as you can see from the `binary` template we covered in Chapter 1, coding even the simplest repeated processes is not so simple. It's a great advantage to be able to use the library's pre-written algorithms, adding only the details that pertain to the problem you're actually trying to solve.

When you consider the complexity hidden behind algorithms such as `std::lower_bound`, which implements a customized binary search, or `std::stable_sort`, which gracefully degrades performance under low memory conditions, it's much easier to see the value of reusing the STL algorithms. Even if we haven't convinced you to call `std::for_each` whenever you have to operate on all elements of a sequence, we hope you'll agree that even simple sequence algorithms provide a useful level of abstraction.

6.2   Algorithms in the MPL

Like the STL algorithms, the MPL algorithms capture useful sequence operations and can be used as primitive building blocks for more complex abstractions. In the MPL algorithm set, you'll find just about everything you get from the standard `<algorithm>` header, similarly named.

That said, there are a few notable differences between the STL and MPL algorithms. You already know that metadata is immutable and therefore MPL algorithms must return new sequences rather than changing them in place, and that MPL algorithms operate directly on sequences rather than on iterator ranges. Aside from the fact that the choice to operate on sequences gives us a higher-level interface, it is also strongly related to the functional nature of template metaprogramming. When

---

3. When efficiency counts, it's best to avoid post-incrementing most iterators (`iter++`), since the `operator++` implementation must make a copy of the iterator *before* it is incremented, in order to return its original value. Standard library implementators know about this pitfall and go out of their way to use pre-increment (`++iter`) instead wherever possible.

result sequences must be returned, it becomes natural to pass the result of one operation directly to another operation. For example:

```
// Given a nonempty sequence Seq, returns the largest type in an
// identical sequence where all instances of float have been
// replaced by double.
template <class Seq>
struct biggest_float_as_double
  : mpl::deref<
        typename mpl::max_element<
            typename mpl::replace<
                Seq
              , float
              , double
            >::type
          , mpl::less<mpl::sizeof_<_1>, mpl::sizeof_<_2> >
        >::type
    >
{};
```

If `max_element` and `replace` operated on iterators instead of sequences, though, `biggest_float_as_double` would probably look something like this:

```
template <class Seq>
struct biggest_float_as_double
{
    typedef typename mpl::replace<
        , typename mpl::begin<Seq>::type
        , typename mpl::end<Seq>::type
        , float
        , double
    >::type replaced;

    typedef typename mpl::max_element<
        , typename mpl::begin<replaced>::type
        , typename mpl::end<replaced>::type
        , mpl::less<mpl::sizeof_<_1>, mpl::sizeof_<_2> >
    >::type max_pos;

    typedef typename mpl::deref<max_pos>::type type;
};
```

The upshot of operating primarily on whole sequences is an increase in interoperability, because the results of one algorithm can be passed smoothly to the next.

6.3   Inserters

There's another important difference between MPL and STL algorithms that is also a consequence of the functional nature of template metaprogramming. The family of "sequence-building" STL algorithms such as `copy`, `transform`, and `replace_copy_if` all accept an output iterator into which a result sequence is written. The whole point of output iterators is to create a stateful change—for example, to modify an existing sequence or extend a file—but there is no state in functional programming. How would you write into an MPL iterator? Where would the result go? None of our examples have used anything that looks remotely like an output iterator—instead, they have simply constructed a new sequence of the same type as some input sequence.

Each of the STL's mutating algorithms can write output into a sequence whose type differs from that of any input sequence or, when passed an appropriate output iterator, it can do something completely unrelated to sequences, like printing to the console. The MPL aims to make the same kind of thing possible at compile time, allowing us to arbitrarily customize the way algorithm results are handled, by using inserters.[4]

An **inserter** is nothing more than a type with two type members:

- `::state`, a representation of information being carried through the algorithm, and

- `::operation`, a binary operation used to build a new `::state` from an output sequence element and the existing `::state`.

For example, an inserter that builds a new vector might look like:

```
mpl::inserter<mpl::vector<>, mpl::push_back<_,_> >
```

where `mpl::inserter` is defined to be:

```
template <class State, class Operation>
struct inserter
{
    typedef State state;
    typedef Operation operation;
};
```

---

4.   The name "inserter" is inspired by the STL's family of output-iterator-creating function adaptors that includes `std::front_inserter` and `std::back_inserter`.

In fact, inserters built on push_back and push_front are so useful that they've been given familiar names: back_inserter and front_inserter. Here's another, more evocative way to spell the vector-building inserter:

```
mpl::back_inserter<mpl::vector<> >
```

When passed to an MPL algorithm such as copy, it functions similarly to std::back_inserter in the following STL code:

```
std::vector<any> v; // start with empty vector
std::copy(start, finish, std::back_inserter(v));
```

Now let's see how an inserter actually works by using mpl::copy to copy the elements of a list into a vector. Naturally, mpl::copy takes an input sequence in place of std::copy's input iterator pair, and an inserter in place of std::copy's output iterator, so the invocation looks like this:

```
typedef mpl::copy<
    mpl::list<A, B, C>
  , mpl::back_inserter<mpl::vector<> >
>::type result_vec;
```

At each step of the algorithm, the inserter's binary operation is invoked with the result from the previous step (or, in the first step, the inserter's initial type) as its first argument, and the element that would normally be written into the output iterator as its second argument. The algorithm returns the result of the final step, so the above is equivalent to:

```
typedef

  mpl::push_back<          // >---------------+
                           //                 |
      mpl::push_back<      // >-------------+ |
                           //               | |
          mpl::push_back<  // >-----------+ | |
              mpl::vector<> //            | | |
            , A            //             | | |
          >::type          // first step <-+ | |
        , B                //                 | |
      >::type              // second step <--+ |
    , C                    //                 |
  >::type                  // third step <-----+

result_vec;
```

Because it's very common to want to build the same kind of sequence you're operating on, MPL supplies default inserters for all of its sequence-building algorithms. That's why we were able to use `transform` so effectively without specifying an inserter.

Note that an inserter need not do anything that looks like insertion. The following example uses an inserter to sum the initial elements of each element in a sequence of sequences:

```
typedef mpl::vector<
    mpl::vector_c<int, 1, 2, 3>
  , mpl::vector_c<int, 4, 5, 6>
  , mpl::vector_c<int, 7, 8, 9>
> S;

typedef mpl::transform<
    S                      // input sequence
  , mpl::front<_>          // transformation selects front element

  , mpl::inserter<
        mpl::int_<0>       // result starts with 0
      , mpl::plus<_,_>     // and adds each output element
    >
>::type sum; // 0 + 1 + 4 + 7 == 12
```

Without the inserter, `transform` would build a vector consisting of the initial elements of each sequence in S; with the inserter, those initial elements are fed into `mpl::plus<_,_>`, starting with the initial value of `mpl::int_<0>`.

6.4   Fundamental Sequence Algorithms

The pattern used by `back_inserter` of "folding" sequence elements into a result, is at the heart of the way sequences are processed in a functional environment. Users of Haskell and ML will immediately recognize it as the pattern used by the `fold` function (and hardcore STL users will recognize it as the pattern of `std::accumulate`). In pseudocode:

```
fold(Seq, Prev, BinaryOp) :=
    if Seq is empty then:
        Prev
    else:          // combine the first element with Prev
        fold(     // and process the rest recursively
            tail(Seq)
          , BinaryOp(Prev, head(Seq))
          , BinaryOp
        )
```

From the caller's viewpoint, `Prev` should probably be called `InitialType`. We chose the name `Prev` because it makes understanding the algorithm's implementation easier. At each step of processing other than the first, `Prev` is the result from the previous step of processing.

You can build many other more complicated sequence traversal algorithms on top of `fold`. For example, we can reverse any front-extensible sequence with:

```
template <class Seq>
struct reverse
  : mpl::fold<
      Seq
    , typename mpl::clear<Seq>::type // initial type
    , mpl::push_front<_,_>           // binary operation
    >
{};
```

It's worth noticing the curious property of `fold` that, when we use it with `push_front`, the result always comes out in reverse order. Since `list`s can only be built with `push_front` and it's mighty inefficient to have to use `reverse` just to put things back in the right order every time we generate a `list` result, MPL also provides a `reverse_fold` metafunction that processes elements in reverse order. To do that efficiently with a sequence that can only be traversed in the forward direction may seem like quite a trick at first, but it's actually pretty simple. Instead of operating on the sequence's first element and folding the rest, we first fold the rest and *then* operate on the first element:

```
reverse_fold(Seq, Prev, BinaryOp) :=
   if Seq is empty then:
      Prev
    else:            // process the rest of the sequence
      BinaryOp(      // and combine with the first element
          reverse_fold(tail(seq), Prev, BinaryOp)
        , head(seq)
      )
```

Instead of processing each sequence element "on the way in" to the traversal, we're processing it "on the way out."

If we can process elements either "going in" or "coming back out," why not both? MPL's `reverse_fold` is actually a little more general than what we've shown you. A fourth optional argument can be used to supply an "inward," or forward, operation. So the algorithm actually looks more like this:

```
reverse_fold(Seq, Prev, OutOp, InOp = _1) :=
    if Seq is empty then:
        Prev
      else:
      OutOp(
            reverse_fold(
                tail(Seq)
              , InOp(Prev,head(Seq)) // just Prev by default
              , OutOp
              , InOp)
          , head(Seq)
        )
```

This generalization allows us to take full advantage of the inherently bidirectional pattern of a recursive sequence traversal. Note that InOp is, by default, just a function that returns its first argument. When we don't supply InOp, it's as though Prev were passed directly to the recursive call.

Before we finish with low-level iteration algorithms and move on to more exciting fare, there's just one more generalization in MPL's fold algorithm family we need to cover: Instead of iterating over *elements* of the sequence, we can iterate over *positions,* that is, iterator values. That's useful, for example, if we want to process consecutive subranges of the input sequence. Since we can always retrieve the element referenced by an iterator, it's slightly more general to fold sequence iterators with iter_fold than to fold sequence elements with plain fold. In pseudocode, iter_fold is defined as follows:

```
iter_fold(Seq, Prev, BinaryOp) :=
    if Seq is empty then:
        Prev
      else:              // combine the first position with Prev
        iter_fold(     // and process the rest recursively
            tail(Seq)
          , BinaryOp(Prev, begin(Seq))
          , BinaryOp
        )
```

The main difference between fold and iter_fold is that the second argument to BinaryOp is an iterator instead of an element. Naturally, the full generalization, reverse_iter_fold, is provided too:

```
reverse_iter_fold(Seq, Prev, OutOp, InOp = _1) :=
    if Seq is empty then:
        Prev
      else:
      OutOp(
          reverse_iter_fold(
              tail(Seq)
            , InOp(Prev, begin(Seq))
            , OutOp
            , InOp)
          , begin(Seq)
      )
```

6.5   Querying Algorithms

Table 6.1 describes the MPL's sequence querying algorithms. Most of these should be immediately familiar to STL users, with the possible exception of `contains`, which is so simple and useful that it probably should have been one of the STL algorithms to begin with. Similarly to the corresponding STL algorithms, `compare` predicates default to `mpl::less<_,_>` but, if supplied, must induce a *strict weak ordering* on their arguments.

Table 6.1 Sequence Querying Algorithms

Metafunction	Result `::type`	Complexity
`mpl::find<seq, T>`	An iterator to the first occurrence of T in `seq`, or `mpl::end<seq>::type` if not found.	Linear.
`mpl::find_if<seq, T, pred>`	An iterator to the first element of `seq` that satisfies predicate `pred`, or `mpl::end<seq>::type` if not found.	Linear.
`mpl::contains<seq, T>`	True iff `seq` contains T.	Linear.
`mpl::count<seq, T>`	The number of occurrences of T in `seq`.	Linear.
`mpl::count_if<seq, pred>`	The number of elements in `seq` that satisfy predicate `pred`.	Linear.

Table 6.1 Sequence Querying Algorithms (continued)

Metafunction	Result `::type`	Complexity
`mpl::equal<seq1, seq2>`	True iff `seq1` and `seq2` contain the same elements in the same order.	Linear.

`mpl::lower_bound<`
`    seq, T`
`  , compare`
`>`
	The earliest order-preserving position at which `T` could be inserted in a sequence `seq` sorted according to comparison `compare`.	Logarithmic in invocations to `compare`. Logarithmic traversal of *Random Access Sequences;* linear traversal otherwise.

`mpl::upper_bound<`
`    seq, T`
`  , compare`
`>`
	The latest order-preserving position at which `T` could be inserted in a sequence `seq` sorted according to comparison `compare`.	Logarithmic in invocations to `compare`. Logarithmic traversal of *Random Access Sequences;* linear traversal otherwise.

`mpl::max_element<`
`    seq`
`  , compare`
`>`
	The first position i in `seq` such that for all positions j:
	`mpl::apply<`
	`        compare`
	`      , mpl::deref<i>::type`
	`      , mpl::deref<j>::type`
	`>::type::value == false`
		Linear.

`mpl::min_element<`
`    seq`
`  , compare`
`>`
	The first position i in `seq` such that for all positions j:
	`mpl::apply<`
	`        compare`
	`      , mpl::deref<j>::type`
	`      , mpl::deref<i>::type`
	`>::type::value == false`
		Linear.

6.6   Sequence Building Algorithms

All of MPL's sequence building algorithms follow the same pattern. It's a little bit elaborate, but as a result the algorithms are extremely easy to use. The pattern is as follows, for any sequence building algorithm xxxx.

- There is a corresponding algorithm, `reverse_xxxx`, which accepts the same arguments but operates on input sequence elements in reverse order. We call `xxxx` and `reverse_xxxx` **counterpart algorithms**.

- The algorithm's last argument is an optional inserter.

- If the inserter is not specified:

  - If the first sequence argument `Seq` is back-extensible, the result is *as if*

    ```
    mpl::back_inserter<mpl::clear<Seq>::type>
    ```

    had been passed as the inserter.

  - Otherwise, the result is *as if* the counterpart algorithm had been invoked with

    ```
    mpl::front_inserter<mpl::clear<Seq>::type>
    ```

    as the inserter.

Let's see how this plays out in practice. In the following examples, `v123` indicates a type with "vector properties" equivalent to `mpl::vector_c<int, 1,2,3>`. Similarly, `l876` indicates a type equivalent to `mpl::list_c<int, 8,7,6>`.

```
// starting sequences
typedef mpl::vector_c<int, 1, 2, 3> v123;
typedef mpl::list_c<int, 1, 2, 3>   l123;

// transformation
typedef mpl::plus<_1,mpl::int_<5> > add5;

// using the default inserters
typedef mpl::transform<v123, add5>::type          v678;
typedef mpl::transform<l123, add5>::type          l678;
typedef mpl::reverse_transform<v123, add5>::type  v876;
typedef mpl::reverse_transform<l123, add5>::type  l876;
```

Thus, the simple no-inserter forms produce the expected result for both front-extensible and back-extensible sequences. In order to use the versions with inserters, though, we have to be aware of both the algorithm's traversal direction and the properties of the sequence we're building:

```
// this inserter is equivalent to the default
typedef mpl::transform<
    v123, add5, mpl::back_inserter<mpl::vector<> >
>::type                                           v678;
```

```
// also equivalent to the default
typedef mpl::reverse_transform<
    l123, add5, mpl::front_inserter<mpl::list<> >
>::type                                                    l678;

// properties of input sequence don't affect the result
typedef mpl::reverse_transform<
    v123, add5, mpl::front_inserter<mpl::list<> >
>::type                                                    l678;
```

The inserter used in building a new sequence should always be determined by the front- or back-extensibility of the *result* sequence. The library's default inserter selection follows the same rule; it just happens that the properties of the result sequence when there is no user-supplied inserter are the same as those of the input sequence.

Table 6.2 summarizes the sequence building algorithms. Note that neither the reverse_ forms nor those with the optional inserter arguments are listed, but it should be possible to deduce their existence and behavior from the description above. They are also covered in detail in the MPL reference manual. We should note that copy and reverse are exceptions to the naming rule: They are reversed versions of one another, and there is neither a reverse_copy nor a reverse_reverse algorithm in the library.

The sequence building algorithms all have linear complexity, and all return a sequence of the same type as their first input sequence by default, but using an appropriate inserter you can produce any kind of result you like.

Table 6.2 Sequence Building Algorithms

Metafunction	**Result::type**
mpl::copy<seq>	The elements of seq.
mpl::copy_if<seq, pred>	The elements of seq that satisfy predicate pred.
mpl::remove<seq, T>	A sequence equivalent to seq, but without any elements identical to T.
mpl::remove_if<seq, pred>	Equivalent to seq, but without any elements that satisfy predicate pred.
mpl::replace<seq, old, new>	Equivalent to seq, but with all occurrences of old replaced by new.
mpl::replace_if<seq, pred, new>	Equivalent to seq, but with all elements satisfying pred replaced by new.
mpl::reverse<seq>	The elements of seq in reverse order.

Table 6.2 Sequence Building Algorithms (continued)

Metafunction	Result::type

`mpl::transform<seq, unaryOp>`
`mpl::transform<seq1, seq2,`
`                binaryOp>`
	The results of invoking `unaryOp` with consecutive elements of `seq`, or of invoking `binaryOp` with consecutive pairs of elements from `seq1` and `seq2`.

`mpl::unique<seq>` `mpl::unique<seq, equiv>`	The sequence composed of the initial elements of every subrange of `seq` whose elements are all the same. If the equivalence relation `equiv` is supplied, it is used to determine sameness.

Functional Algorithms Under Aliases

Many of these sequence building algorithms, whose names are taken from similar STL algorithms, actually originated in the functional programming world. For example, the two-argument version of `transform` is known to functional programmers as "map," the three-argument `transform` is sometimes called "zip_with," and `copy_if` is also known as "filter."

Because we've left the `reverse_` algorithms out of Table 6.2 it's only fair that we point out that the form of `unique` that accepts an equivalence relation is, well, *unique* among all of the sequence building algorithms. The `reverse_` forms of most algorithms produce the same elements as the normal forms do (in reverse order), but the elements of sequences produced by `unique` and `reverse_unique` for the same arguments may differ. For example:

```
typedef mpl::equal_to<
    mpl::shift_right<_1, mpl::int_<1> >
  , mpl::shift_right<_2, mpl::int_<1> >
> same_except_last_bit;                  // predicate

typedef mpl::vector_c<int, 0,1,2,3,4,5> v;

typedef unique<
    v, same_except_last_bit
>::type                   v024;          // 0, 2, 4

typedef reverse_unique<
    v, same_except_last_bit
>::type                   v531;          // 5, 3, 1
```

6.7   Writing Your Own Algorithms

Our first piece of advice for anyone wishing to implement a metafunction that does low-level sequence traversal is, "Leave the traversal to us!" It's usually much more effective to simply reuse the MPL algorithms as primitives for building higher-level ones. You could say we took that approach in Chapter 3, when we implemented `divide_dimensions` in terms of `transform`. You'll save more than just coding effort: MPL's primitive iteration algorithms have been specially written to avoid deep template instantiations, which can drastically slow down compilation or even cause it to fail.[5] Many of the MPL algorithms are ultimately implemented in terms of `iter_fold` for the same reasons.

Because the MPL provides such an extensive repertoire of linear traversal algorithms, if you find you *must* write a metafunction that does its own sequence traversal, it will probably be because you need some other traversal pattern. In that case your implementation will have to use the same basic recursive formulation that we introduced in Chapter 1 with the `binary` template, using a specialization to terminate the recursion. We recommend that you operate on iterators rather than on successive incremental modifications of the same sequence for two reasons. First, it's going to be efficient for a wider variety of sequences. Not all sequences support O(1) `pop_front` operations, and some that do may have a rather high constant factor, but all iterators support O(1) incrementation via `next`. Second, as we saw with `iter_fold`, operating on iterators is slightly more general than operating on sequence elements. That extra generality costs very little at implementation time, but pays great dividends in algorithm reusability.

6.8   Details

Abstraction.   An idea that emphasizes high-level concepts and de-emphasizes implementation details. Classes in runtime C++ are one kind of abstraction commonly used to package state with associated processes. Functions are one of the most fundamental kinds of abstraction and are obviously important in any functional programming context. The MPL algorithms are abstractions of repetitive processes and are implemented as metafunctions. The abstraction value of algorithms in MPL is often higher than that of corresponding STL algorithms simply because the alternative to using them is so much worse at compile time. While we can traverse an STL sequence with a `for` loop and a couple of iterators, a hand-rolled compile-time sequence traversal always requires at least one new class template and an explicit specialization.

Fold.   A primitive functional abstraction that applies a binary function repeatedly to the elements of a sequence and an additional value, using the result of the function at each step as the additional value for the next step. The STL captures the same abstraction under the name `accumulate`.

---

5. See Appendix C for more information.

MPL generalizes `fold` in two ways: by operating on iterators instead of elements (`iter_fold`) and by supplying bidirectional traversal (`reverse_[iter_]fold`).

Querying algorithms. MPL supports a variety of algorithms that return iterators or simple values; these generally correspond exactly to STL algorithms of the same names.

Sequence building algorithms. The STL algorithms that require *Output Iterators* arguments correspond to pairs of forward and backward MPL "sequence building" algorithms that, by default, construct new sequences of the same kind as their first input sequence. They also accept an optional *inserter* argument that gives greater control over the algorithm's result.

Inserters. In the STL tradition, a function whose name ends with `inserter` creates an output iterator for adding elements to a sequence. MPL uses the term to denote a binary metafunction packaged with an additional value, which is used as an output processor for the result elements of an algorithm. The default inserters used by the algorithms are `front_inserter<S>` and `back_inserter<S>`; they fold the results into S using `push_front` or `push_back`. Using an inserter with an algorithm is equivalent to applying `fold` to the algorithm's default (no-inserter) result, the inserter's function, and its initial state. It follows that there's no reason an inserter (or a sequence building algorithm) needs to build new sequences; it can produce an arbitrary result depending on its function component.

6.9   Exercises

6-0.   Use `mpl::copy` with a hand-built inserter to write a `smallest` metafunction that finds the smallest of a sequence of types. That is:

```
BOOST_STATIC_ASSERT((
    boost::is_same<
        smallest< mpl::vector<int[2], char, double&> >::type
      , char
    >::value
));
```

Now that you've done it, is it a good way to solve that problem? Why or why not?

6-1.   Rewrite the `binary` template from section 1.4.1 using one of the MPL sequence iteration algorithms, and write a test program that will only compile if your `binary` template is working. Compare the amount of code you wrote with the version using handwritten recursion presented in Chapter 1. What characteristics of the problem caused that result?

6-2. Because `std::for_each` is the most basic algorithm in the standard library, you may be wondering why we didn't say anything about its compile time counterpart. The fact is that unlike, for example, `transform`, the algorithm does not have a pure compile time counterpart. Can you offer an explanation for that fact?

6-3. Write an inserter class template called `binary_tree_inserter` that employs the `tree` template from exercise 5-10 to incrementally build a binary search tree:

```
typedef mpl::copy<
    mpl::vector_c<int,17,25,10,2,11>
  , binary_tree_inserter< tree<> >
  >::type bst;

//        int_<17>
//        /      \
//     int_<10>  int_<25>
//      /    \
// int_<2> int_<11>
BOOST_STATIC_ASSERT(( mpl::equal<
    inorder_view<bst>
  , mpl::vector_c<int,2,10,11,17,25>
  >::value ));
```

6-4. Write an algorithm metafunction called `binary_tree_search` that performs binary search on trees built using `binary_tree_inserter` from exercise 6-3:

```
typedef binary_tree_search<bst,int_<11> >::type pos1;
typedef binary_tree_search<bst,int_<20> >::type pos2;
typedef mpl::end<bst>::type                      end_pos;

BOOST_STATIC_ASSERT((!boost::is_same< pos1,end_pos >::value));
BOOST_STATIC_ASSERT((boost::is_same< pos2,end_pos >::value));
```

6-5*. List all algorithms in the standard library and compare their set to the set of algorithms provided by MPL. Analyze the differences. What algorithms are named differently? What algorithms have different semantics? What algorithms are missing? Why do you think they are missing?

7

Views and Iterator Adaptors

Algorithms like `transform` provide one way to operate on sequences. This chapter covers the use of **sequence views**, a powerful sequence processing idiom that is often superior to the use of algorithms.

First, an informal definition:

> ### Sequence View
> A **sequence view**—or **view** for short—is a lazy adaptor that delivers an altered presentation of one or more underlying sequences.

Views are *lazy:* Their elements are only computed on demand. We saw examples of lazy evaluation when we covered nullary metafunctions in Chapter 3 and `eval_if` in Chapter 4. As with other lazy constructs, views can help us avoid premature errors and inefficiencies from computations whose results will never be used. Also sequence views sometimes fit a particular problem better than other approaches, yielding simpler, more expressive, and more maintainable code.

In this chapter you will find out how views work and we will discuss how and when to use them. Then we'll explore the view classes that come with the MPL and you will learn how to write your own.

7.1 A Few Examples

In the following sections we'll explore a few problems that are particularly well-suited to the use of views, which should give you a better feeling for what views are all about. We hope to show you that the idea of views is worth its conceptual overhead, and that these cases are either more efficient or more natural to code using views.

7.1.1 Comparing Values Computed from Sequence Elements

Let's start with a simple problem that will give you a taste of how views work:

Write a metafunction `padded_size` that, given an integer *MinSize* and a sequence *Seq* of types ordered by increasing size, returns the size of the first element *e* of *Seq* for which `sizeof(e)` >= *MinSize*.

7.1.1.1   A First Solution

Now let's try to solve the problem with the tools we've covered so far. The fact that we're searching in a *sorted* sequence is a clue we'll want to use one of the binary searching algorithms `upper_bound` or `lower_bound` at the core of our solution. The fact that we're looking for a property of the *first* element satisfying the property narrows the choice to `lower_bound`, and allows us to sketch an outline of the solution:

```
template<class Seq, class MinSize>
struct padded_size
  : mpl::sizeof_<                      // the size of
        typename mpl::deref<           // the element at
            typename mpl::lower_bound< // the first position
                Seq
              , MinSize
              , comparison predicate   // satisfying...
            >::type
        >::type
    >
{};
```

In English, this means "return the size of the result of the element at the first position satisfying *some condition*," where *some condition* is determined by the *comparison predicate* passed to `lower_bound`.

The condition we want to satisfy is `sizeof(e)` >= *MinSize*. If you look up `lower_bound` in the MPL reference manual you'll see that its simple description doesn't really apply to this situation:

> Returns the first position in the sorted `Sequence` [i.e. *Seq*] where T [i.e., *MinSize*] could be inserted without violating the ordering.

After all, `Seq` is ordered on element size, and we don't care about the size of the integral constant wrapper `MinSize`; we're not planning to insert it. The problem with this simple description of `lower_bound` is that it's geared towards *homogeneous* comparison predicates, where T is a potential sequence element. Now, if you read a bit further in the `lower_bound` reference you'll find this entry:

```
typedef lower_bound< Sequence,T,Pred >::type i;
```

Return type: A model of Forward Iterator

Semantics: i is the furthermost iterator in Sequence such that, for every
iterator j in

```
[begin<Sequence>::type, i),
apply<Pred, deref<j>::type, T >::type::value
```

is true.

In English, this means that the result of lower_bound will be the last position in Sequence such that the predicate, applied to *any* element at a prior position and T, yields true. This more precise description seems as though it may work for us: We want the last position such that, for all elements *e* at prior positions, sizeof(*e*) < MinSize::value. Therefore, the predicate will be:

```
mpl::less<mpl::sizeof_<_1>, _2>
```

Inserting the predicate into our complete metafunction, we are left with:

```
template<class Seq, class MinSize>
struct padded_size
  : mpl::sizeof_<
        typename mpl::deref<
            typename mpl::lower_bound<
                Seq
              , MinSize
              , mpl::less<mpl::sizeof_<_1>, _2>
            >::type
        >::type
    >
{};
```

7.1.1.2   Analysis

Now let's take a step back and look at what we just did. If you're like us, your code-quality spider sense has started tingling.

First of all, writing such a simple metafunction probably shouldn't require us to spend so much time with the MPL reference manual. In general, if you had a tough time writing a piece of code, you can expect maintainers to have an even harder time trying to read it. After all, the code's author at least has the advantage of knowing her own intention. In this case, the way that lower_bound deals with heterogeneous comparisons and the order of arguments to its predicate demanded significant study, and it probably won't be easy to remember; it seems unfair to ask those who come after us to pore through the manual so they can understand what we've written. After all, those who come after may be *us*!

Secondly, even if we set aside the need to consult the reference manual, there's something odd about the fact that we're computing the size of sequence elements within the `lower_bound` invocation, and then we're again asking for the size of the element at the position `lower_bound` returns to us. Having to repeat oneself is irksome, to say the least.

7.1.1.3   A Simplification

Fortunately, that repetition actually provides a clue as to how we might improve things. We're searching in a sequence of elements ordered by *size,* comparing the *size* of each one with a given value and returning the *size* of the element we found. Ultimately, we're not at all interested in the sequence elements themselves: we only care about their sizes. Furthermore, if we could do the search over a sequence of sizes, we could use a *homogeneous* comparison predicate:

```
template<class Seq, class MinSize>
struct padded_size
  : mpl::deref<
        typename mpl::lower_bound<
            typename mpl::transform<
                Seq, mpl::sizeof_<_>
             >::type
          , MinSize
          , mpl::less<_,_>
        >::type
     >
{};
```

In fact, `mpl::less<_,_>` is already `lower_bound`'s default predicate, so we can simplify the implementation even further:

```
template<class Seq, class MinSize>
struct padded_size
  : mpl::deref<
        typename mpl::lower_bound<
            typename mpl::transform<
                Seq, mpl::sizeof_<_>
          >::type
          , MinSize
        >::type
   >
{};
```

Naturally—since this chapter is building a case for views—there's a problem with this simplified implementation too: it's inefficient. While our first implementation invoked `mpl::sizeof_` only on the O(log N) elements visited by `lower_bound` during its binary search, this one uses `transform` to greedily compute the size of *every* type in the sequence.

7.1.1.4 Fast and Simple

Fortunately, we can have the best of both worlds by turning the greedy size computation into a lazy one with `transform_view`:

```
template<class Seq, class MinSize>
struct first_size_larger_than
  : mpl::deref<
        typename mpl::lower_bound<
            mpl::transform_view<Seq, mpl::sizeof_<_> >
          , MinSize
        >::type
    >
{};
```

`transform_view<S,P>` is a sequence whose elements are identical to the elements of `transform<S,P>`, but with two important differences:

1. Its elements are computed only "on demand"; in other words, it's a lazy sequence.

2. Through the `::base` member of any of its iterators, we can get an iterator to the corresponding position in S.[1]

If the approach we've taken seems a little unfamiliar, it's probably because people don't usually code this way in runtime C++. However, once exposed to the virtues of laziness, you quickly discover that there is a whole category of algorithmic problems similar to this one, and that solving them using views is only natural, even at runtime.[2]

7.1.2 Combining Multiple Sequences

Only one compile-time sequence building algorithm, `transform`, has direct support for operating on pairs of elements from two input sequences. If not for its usefulness, this nonuniformity in the

---

1. We'll explain `base` in section 7.3.
2. See the History section at the end of this chapter for some references to runtime views libraries.

library design could almost be called an aesthetic wart: It's merely a concession to convenience and consistency with the STL. For other kinds of operations on multiple sequences, or to `transform` three or more input sequences, we need a different strategy.

You *could* code any new multi-sequence algorithm variant "by hand," but as you can probably guess, we'd rather encourage you to reuse some MPL tools for that purpose. There's actually a component that lets you use your trusty single-sequence tools to solve any parallel N-sequence problem. MPL's `zip_view` transforms a sequence of N input sequences into a sequence of N-element sequences composed of elements selected from the input sequences. So, if S is $[s_1, s_2, s_3 \ldots]$, T is $[t_1, t_2, t_3 \ldots]$, and U is $[u_1, u_2, u_3 \ldots]$, then the elements of `zip_view<vector<S,T,U>` > are $[[s_1, t_1, u_1 \ldots], [s_2, t_2, u_2 \ldots], [s_3, t_3, u_3 \ldots] \ldots]$.

For example, the elementwise sum of three vectors might be written:

```
mpl::transform_view<
    mpl::zip_view<mpl::vector<V1,V2,V3> >
  , mpl::plus<
        mpl::at<_, mpl::int_<0> >
      , mpl::at<_, mpl::int_<1> >
      , mpl::at<_, mpl::int_<2> >
    >
>
```

That isn't too bad, but we have to admit that unpacking vector elements with `mpl::at` is both cumbersome and ugly. We can clean the code up using MPL's `unpack_args` wrapper, which transforms an N-argument lambda expression like `mpl::plus<_,_,_>` into a unary lambda expression. When applied to a sequence of N elements,

```
mpl::unpack_args<lambda-expression>
```

extracts each of the sequence's N elements and passes them as consecutive arguments to *lambda-expression*.

Whew! That description is a bit twisty, but fortunately a little code is usually worth 1,000 words. This equivalent rewrite of our elementwise sum uses `unpack_args` to achieve a significant improvement in readability:

```
mpl::transform_view<
    mpl::zip_view<mpl::vector<V1,V2,V3> >
  , mpl::unpack_args<mpl::plus<_,_,_> >
>
```

7.1.3   Avoiding Unnecessary Computation

Even if views don't appeal to you conceptually, you should still use them to solve problems that can benefit from their lazy nature. Real-world examples are numerous, so we'll just supply a few here:

```
// does seq contain int, int&, int const&, int volatile&,
// or int const volatile&?
typedef mpl::contains<
    mpl::transform_view<
        seq
      , boost::remove_cv< boost::remove_reference<_> > >
    >
  , int
>::type found;

// find the position of the least integer whose factorial is >= n
typedef mpl::lower_bound<
    mpl::transform_view< mpl::range_c<int,0,13>, factorial<_1> >
  , n
>::type::base number_iter;

// return a sorted vector of all the elements from seq1 and seq2
typedef mpl::sort<
    mpl::copy<
        mpl::joint_view<seq1,seq2>
      , mpl::back_inserter< mpl::vector<> >
    >::type
>::type result;
```

The last example above uses `joint_view`, a sequence consisting of the elements of its arguments "laid end-to-end." In each of these cases, the use of lazy techniques (views) saves a significant number of template instantiations over the corresponding eager approach.

7.1.4   Selective Element Processing

With `filter_view`, a lazy version of the `filter` algorithm, we can process a subset of a sequence's elements without building an intermediate sequence. When a `filter_view`'s iterators are incremented, an underlying iterator into the sequence "being viewed" is advanced until the filter function is satisfied:

```
// a sequence of the pointees of all pointer elements in Seq
mpl::transform_view<
    mpl::filter_view< Seq, boost::is_pointer<_1> >
  , boost::remove_pointer<_1>
>
```

7.2   View Concept

By now you probably have a pretty good feeling for what views are all about, but let's try to firm the idea up a bit. To begin with, this subsection should probably be titled "View concept" with a lowercase *c*, since normally when we speak of "Concepts" in C++, we're referring to formal interface requirements as described in Chapter 5. Views are a little more casual than that. From an interface perspective, a view is nothing more than a sequence, and is only a view because of two *implementation* details. First, as we've repeated until you're surely tired of reading it, views are *lazy:* their elements are computed only on demand. Not all lazy sequences are views, though. For example, range_c<...> is a familiar example of a lazy sequence, but somehow that doesn't seem much like a view onto anything. The second detail required for "view-ness" is that the elements must be generated from one or more input sequences.

An **emergent property** is one that only arises because of some more fundamental characteristics. All views share two emergent properties. First—and this really applies to all lazy sequences since their elements are computed—views are not extensible. If you need extensibility, you need to use the copy algorithm to create an extensible sequence from the view. Second, since iterators arbitrate all element accesses, most of the logic involved in implementing a sequence view is contained in its iterators.

7.3   Iterator Adaptors

The iterators of a sequence view are examples of *iterator adaptors*, an important concept (lowercase *c*) in its own right. Just as a view is a sequence built upon one or more underlying sequences, an **iterator adaptor** is an iterator that adapts the behavior of one or more underlying iterators.

Iterator adaptors are so useful in runtime C++ that there is an entire Boost library devoted to them. Even the STL contains several iterator adaptors, most notably std::reverse_iterator that traverses the same sequence of elements as its underlying iterator, but in the opposite order. The iterators of mpl::filter_view are another example of an iterator **traversal adaptor**. An iterator **access adaptor** accesses different element values from its underlying iterator, like the iterators of mpl::transform_view do.

Because you can access a `std::reverse_iterator`'s underlying iterator by calling its `base()` member function, MPL adaptors provide access to *their* underlying iterators via a nested `::base` type. In all other respects, an iterator adaptor is just like any other iterator. It can have any of the three iterator categories—possibly different from its underlying iterator(s)—and all of the usual iterator requirements apply.

7.4 Writing Your Own View

Since most of a sequence view's smarts are in its iterators, it stands to reason that most of the work of implementing a view involves implementing an iterator adaptor. Let's whip up an iterator for `zip_view` to see how it's done.

Since `zip_view` operates on a sequence of input sequences, it's natural that its iterator should operate on a sequence of iterators into those input sequences. Let's give our `zip_iterator` an iterator sequence parameter:

```
template <class IteratorSeq>
struct zip_iterator;
```

The MPL's `zip_iterator` models the least refined concept of any of its component iterators, but for the sake of simplicity our `zip_iterator` will always be a forward iterator. The only requirements we need to satisfy for a forward iterator are dereferencing with `mpl::deref` and incrementing with `mpl::next`. To dereference a zip iterator we need to dereference each of its component iterators and pack the results into a sequence. Taking advantage of the default definition of `mpl::deref`, which just invokes its argument as a metafunction, the body of `zip_iterator` is defined thus:

```
template <class IteratorSeq>
struct zip_iterator
{
    typedef mpl::forward_iterator_tag category;

    typedef typename mpl::transform<
        IteratorSeq
      , mpl::deref<_1>
    >::type type;
};
```

Similarly, to increment a zip iterator we need to increment each of its component iterators:

```
namespace boost { namespace mpl
{
  // specialize next<...> for zip_iterator
  template <class IteratorSeq>
  struct next<::zip_iterator<IteratorSeq> >
  {
      typedef ::zip_iterator<
          typename transform<
              IteratorSeq
            , next<_1>
          >::type
      > type;
  };
}}
```

The one remaining element we might want to add to the body of `zip_iterator`, as a convenience, is a `::base` member that accesses the iterators being adapted. In an iterator adaptor for a single iterator, `::base` would just be that one iterator; in this case, though, it will be a sequence of underlying iterators:

```
template <class IteratorSeq>
struct zip_iterator
{
    typedef IteratorSeq base;
    ...
};
```

Now there's almost nothing left to do for `zip_view`; it's just a sequence that uses `zip_iterator`. In fact, we can build `zip_view` out of `iterator_range`:

```
template <class Sequences>
struct zip_view
  : mpl::iterator_range<
        zip_iterator<
            typename mpl::transform_view<
                Sequences, mpl::begin<_1>
            >::type
        >
      , zip_iterator<
            typename mpl::transform_view<
                Sequences, mpl::end<_1>
```

```
            >::type
        >
    >
{};
```

7.5   History

There is a long history of lazy evaluation and lazy sequences in programming, especially in the functional programming community. The first known C++ example of the "view" concept appeared in 1995, in a (runtime) library by Jon Seymour, called, aptly, Views [Sey96]. Interestingly, the approach of the views library was inspired more by database technology than by work in functional programming. A more complete treatment of the view concept appeared in the View Template Library (VTL), by Martin Wieser and Gary Powell, in 1999 [WP99, WP00]. By 2001, implementing and adapting C++ iterators were recognized as important tasks in their own right, and the Boost Iterator Adaptor Library was developed [AS01a].

7.6   Exercises

7-0. Write a test program that exercises our `zip_view` implementation. Try to arrange your program so that it will only compile if the tests succeed.

7-1. Our implementation of `zip_iterator` uses `transform` to generate its nested `::type`, but the one in MPL uses `transform_view` instead. What advantage does the MPL approach have?

7-2. Modify `zip_iterator` so that its `::iterator_category` reflects the least-refined concept modeled by any of its underlying iterators. Extend the iterator implementation to satisfy all potential requirements of the computed category.

7-3. Use `mpl::joint_view` to implement a `rotate_view` sequence view, presenting a shifted and wrapped view onto the original sequence:

```
typedef mpl::vector_c<int,5,6,7,8,9,0,1,2,3,4> v;
typedef rotate_view<
    v
  , mpl::advance_c<mpl::begin<v>::type,5>::type
> view;
```

```
BOOST_STATIC_ASSERT(( mpl::equal<
    view
  , mpl::range_c<int,0,10>
>::value ));
```

7-4. Design and implement an iterator adaptor that adapts any Random Access Iterator by presenting the elements it traverses in an order determined by a sequence of nonnegative integer indices. Make your `permutation_iterator` a forward iterator.

7-5. Change the permutation iterator from exercise 7-4 so its traversal category is determined by the category of the sequence of indices.

7-6. Implement a `permutation_view` using your permutation iterator adaptor, so that:

```
permutation_view<
    mpl::list_c<int,2,1,3,0,2>      // indices
  , mpl::vector_c<int,11,22,33,44>  // elements
>
```

yields sequence [33,22,44,11,33]

7-7. Design and implement a reverse iterator adaptor with semantics analogous to those of `std::reverse_iterator`. Make its category the same as the category of the underlying iterator. Use the resulting iterator to implement a `reverse_view` template.

7-8. Implement a `crossproduct_view` template that adapts two original sequences by presenting all possible pairs of their elements in a right cross product order.

8

Diagnostics

Because C++ metaprograms are executed during compilation, debugging presents special challenges. There's no debugger that allows us to step through metaprogram execution, set breakpoints, examine data, and so on—that sort of debugging would require interactive inspection of the compiler's internal state. All we can really do is wait for the process to fail and then decipher the error messages it dumps on the screen. C++ template diagnostics are a common source of frustration because they often have no obvious relationship to the cause of the error and present a great deal more information than is useful. In this chapter we'll discuss how to understand the sort of errors metaprogrammers typically encounter, and even how to bend these diagnostics to our own nefarious purposes.

The C++ standard leaves the specifics of error reporting entirely up to the compiler implementor, so we'll be discussing the behaviors of several different compilers, often in critical terms. Because your compiler's error messages are all the help you're going to get, your choice of tools can have a huge impact on your ability to debug metaprograms. If you're building libraries, your *clients'* choice of tools will affect their perception of your code—and the time you spend answering questions— when mistakes are made. Therefore, we suggest you pay close attention even when we're discussing a compiler you don't normally use: You may discover that you'd like to have it in your kit, or that you'll want to do something special to support clients who may use it. Likewise, if it seems as though we're attacking your favorite tool, we hope you won't be offended!

8.1   Debugging the Error Novel

The title of this section is actually taken from another book [VJ02], but it's so wonderfully apt that we had to use it ourselves. In fact, template error reports so often resemble *War and Peace* in approachability that many programmers ignore them and resort to random code tweaks in the hope of making the right change. In this section we'll give you the tools to skim these diagnostic tomes and find your way right to the problem.

> **Note**
>
> We'll be looking at examples of error messages, many of which would be too wide to fit on the page if presented without alteration. In order to make it possible to see these messages, we've broken each long line at the right margin, and where neccessary added a blank line afterwards to separate it from the line following.

8.1.1 Instantiation Backtraces

Let's start with a simple (erroneous) example. The following code defines a simplistic compile-time "linked list" type structure, and a metafunction designed to compute the total size of all the elements in a list:

```
struct nil {};                        // the end of every list

template <class H, class T = nil>    // a list node, e.g:
struct node                          // node<X,node<Y,node<Z> > >
{
    typedef H head; typedef T tail;
};

template <class S>
struct total_size
{
    typedef typename total_size<     // total size of S::tail
        typename S::tail
    >::type tail_size;               // line 17

    typedef boost::mpl::int_<        // add size of S::head
        sizeof(S::head)
        + tail_size::value           // line 22
    > type;
};
```

The bug above is that we've omitted the specialization needed to terminate the recursion of total_size. If we try to use it as follows:

```
typedef total_size<
    node<long, node<int, node<char> > >
>::type x;                            // line 27
```

we get an error message something like this one generated by version 3.2 of the GNU C++ compiler (GCC):

```
foo.cpp: In instantiation of 'total_size<nil>':
foo.cpp:17:   instantiated from 'total_size<node<char, nil> >'
foo.cpp:17:   instantiated from 'total_size<node<int,
node<char, nil > > >'
foo.cpp:17:   instantiated from 'total_size<node<long int,
node<int, node<char, nil> > > >'
```

```
foo.cpp:27:   instantiated from here
foo.cpp:17: no type named 'tail' in 'struct nil'
continued...
```

The first step in getting comfortable with long template error messages is to recognize that the compiler is actually doing you a favor by dumping all that information. What you're looking at is called an **instantiation backtrace**, and it corresponds almost exactly to a runtime call stack backtrace. The first line of the error message shows the metafunction call where the error occurred, and each succeeding line that follows shows the metafunction call that invoked the call in the line that precedes it. Finally, the compiler shows us the low-level cause of the error: we're treating the `nil` sentinel as though it were a `node<...>` by trying to access its `::tail` member.

In this example it's easy to understand the error simply by reading that last line, but as in runtime programming, a mistake in an outer call can often cause problems many levels further down. Having the entire instantiation backtrace at our disposal helps us analyze and pinpoint the source of the problem.

Of course, the result isn't perfect. Compilers typically try to "recover" after an error like this one and report more problems, but to do so they must make some assumptions about what you really meant. Unless the error is as simple as a missing semicolon, those assumptions tend to be wrong, and the remaining errors are less useful:

```
...continued from above
foo.cpp:22: no type named 'tail' in 'struct nil'
foo.cpp:22: 'head' is not a member of type 'nil'
foo.cpp: In instantiation of 'total_size<node<char, nil> >':
foo.cpp:17:   instantiated from 'total_size<node<int, node<char,
nil> > >'

foo.cpp:17:   instantiated from 'total_size<node<long int, node<
int, node<char, nil> > > >'

foo.cpp:27:   instantiated from here
foo.cpp:17: no type named 'type' in 'struct total_size<nil>'
foo.cpp:22: no type named 'type' in 'struct total_size<nil>'
...many lines omitted here...
foo.cpp:27: syntax error before ';'token
```

In general, it's best to simply ignore any errors after the first one that results from compiling any source file.

8.1.2   Error Formatting Quirks

While every compiler is different, there are some common themes in message formatting that you may learn to recognize. In this section we'll look at some of the advanced error-reporting features of modern compilers.

8.1.2.1   A More Realistic Error

Most variations in diagnostic formatting have been driven by the massive types that programmers suddenly had to confront in their error messages when they began using the STL. To get an overview, we'll examine the diagnostics produced by three different compilers for this ill-formed program:

```
# include <map>
# include <list>
# include <iterator>
# include <string>
# include <algorithm>

using namespace std;
void copy_list_map(list<string> & l, map<string, string>& m)
{
    std::copy(l.begin(), l.end(), std::back_inserter(m));
}
```

Although the code is disarmingly simple, some compilers respond with terribly daunting error messages. If you're like us, you may find yourself fighting to stay awake when faced with the sort of unhelpful feedback that we're about to show you. If so, we urge you to grab another cup of coffee and stick it out: The point of this section is to become familiar enough with common diagnostic behaviors that you can quickly see through the mess and find the salient information in any error message. After we've gone through a few examples, we're sure you'll find the going easier.

With that, let's throw the code at Microsoft Visual C++ (VC++) 6 and see what happens.

```
C:\PROGRA~1\MICROS~4\VC98\INCLUDE\xutility(19) : error C2679:
binary '=' : no operator defined which takes a right-hand operand
of type 'class std::basic_string<char,struct std::char_traits<
char>,class std::allocator<char> >' (or there is no acceptable
conversion)

        foo.cpp(9) : see reference to function template
        instantiation 'class std::back_insert_iterator<class std::
        map<class std::basic_string<char,struct std::char_traits<
```

```
char>,class std::allocator<char> >,class std::basic_string<
char,struct std::char_traits<char>,class std::allocator<char
> >,struct std::less<class std::basic_string<char,struct std
::char_traits<char>,class std::allocator<char> > >,class std
::allocator<class std::basic_string<char,struct std::
char_traits<char>,class std::allocator<char> > > > > __cdecl
std::copy(class std::list<class std::basic_string<char,
struct std::char_traits<char>,class std::allocator<char> >,
class std::allocator<class std::basic_string<char,struct std
::char_traits<char>,class std::allocator<char> > > >::
iterator,class std::list<class std::basic_string<char,struct
std::char_traits<char>,class std::allocator<char> >,class
std::allocator<class std::basic_string<char,struct std::
char_traits<char>,class std::allocator<char> > > >::iterator
,class std::back_insert_iterator<class std::map<class std::
basic_string<char,struct std::char_traits<char>,class std::
allocator<char> >,class std::basic_string<char,struct std::
char_traits<char>,class std::allocator<char> >,struct std::
less<class std::basic_string<char,struct std::char_traits<
char>,class std::allocator<char> > >,class std::allocator<
class std::basic_string<char,struct std::char_traits<char>,
class std::allocator<char> > > > >)' being compiled
```
message continues...

Whew! Something obviously has to be done about that. We've only shown the first two (really long) lines of the error, but that alone is almost unreadable. To get a handle on it, we could copy the message into an editor and lay it out with indentation and line breaks, but it would still be fairly unmanageable: Even with no real formatting it nearly fills a whole page!

8.1.2.2   typedef Substitution

If you look closely, you can see that the long type

```
class std::basic_string<char, struct std::char_traits<char>,
                        class std::allocator<char> >
```

is repeated twelve times in just those first two lines. As it turns out, std::string happens to be a typedef (alias) for that type, so we could quickly simplify the message using an editor's search-and-replace feature:

```
C:\PROGRA~1\MICROS~4\VC98\INCLUDE\xutility(19) : error C2679:
binary '=' : no operator defined which takes a right-hand operand
of type 'std::string' (or there is no acceptable conversion)

    foo.cpp(9) : see reference to function template instantiation
    'class std::back_insert_iterator<class std::map<std::string,
    std::string,struct std::less<std::string>,class
    std::allocator<std::string> > > __cdecl std::copy(class
    std::list<std::string,class std::allocator<std::string>
    >::iterator,class std::list<std::string,class std::allocator<
    std::string> >::iterator,class std::back_insert_iterator<
    class std::map<std::string,std::string,struct std::
    less<std::string>,class std::allocator<std::string> > >)'
    being compiled
```

That's a major improvement. Once we've made that change, the project of manually inserting line breaks and indentation so we can analyze the message starts to seem more tractable. Strings are such a common type that a compiler writer could get a lot of mileage out of making just this one substitution, but of course `std::string` is not the only `typedef` in the world. Recent versions of GCC generalize this transformation by remembering all namespace-scope `typedef`s for us so that they can be used to simplify diagnostics. For example, GCC 3.2.2 says this about our test program:

```
...continued messages
/usr/include/c++/3.2/bits/stl_algobase.h:228: no match for '
    std::back_insert_iterator<std::map<std::string, std::string,
    std::less<std::string>, std::allocator<std::pair<const
    std::string, std::string> > > >& = std::basic_string<char,
    std::char_traits<char>, std::allocator<char> >&' operator
messages continue...
```

It's interesting to note that GCC didn't make the substitution on the right hand side of the assignment operator. As we shall soon see, however, being conservative in `typedef` substitution might not be such a bad idea.

8.1.2.3 "With" Clauses

Take a look back at our revised VC++ 6 error message as it appears *after* the `std::string` substitution. You can almost see, if you squint at it just right, that there's an invocation of `std::copy` in the second line. To make that fact more apparent, many compilers separate actual template arguments from the name of the template specialization. For example, the final line of the GCC instantiation backtrace preceding the error cited above is:

```
/usr/include/c++/3.2/bits/stl_algobase.h:349: instantiated from
'_OutputIter std::copy(_InputIter, _InputIter, _OutputIter)
[with _InputIter = std::_List_iterator<std::string, std::string&,
std::string*>, _OutputIter = std::back_insert_iterator<std::map<
std::string, std::string, std::less<std::string>, std::allocator<
std::pair<const std::string, std::string> > > >]'
messages continue...
```

Reserved Identifiers

The C++ standard reserves identifiers that begin with an underscore and a capital letter (like _InputIter) and identifiers containing double-underscores anywhere (e.g., __function__) for use by the language implementation. Because we're presenting diagnostics involving the C++ standard library, you'll see quite a few reserved identifiers in this chapter. Don't be misled into thinking it's a convention to emulate, though: The library is using these names to stay out of our way, but if *we* use them our program's behavior is undefined.

The "with" clause allows us to easily see that std::copy is involved. Also, seeing the formal template parameter names gives us a useful reminder of the concept requirements that the copy algorithm places on its parameters. Finally, because the same type is used for two different formal parameters, but is spelled out only once in the "with" clause, the overall size of the error message is reduced. Many of the compilers built on the Edison Design Group (EDG) front-end have been doing something similar for years.

Microsoft similarly improved the VC++ compiler's messages in version 7, and also added some helpful line breaks:

```
foo.cpp(10) : see reference to function template instantiation
'_OutIt std::copy(_InIt,std::list<_Ty,_Ax>::iterator,
std::back_insert_iterator<_Container>)' being compiled

with
[
    _OutIt=std::back_insert_iterator<std::map<std::string,std
    ::string,std::less<std::string>,std::allocator<std::pair<
    const std::string,std::string>>>>,

    _InIt=std::list<std::string,std::allocator<std::string>>::
    iterator,

    _Ty=std::string,
```

```
_Ax=std::allocator<std::string>,
_Container=std::map<std::string,std::string,std::less<std
::string>,std::allocator<std::pair<const std::string,std::
string>>>
```
```
]
```

Unfortunately, we also begin to see some unhelpful behaviors in VC++ 7.0. Instead of listing _InIt and _OutIt twice in the function signature, the second and third parameter types are written out in full and repeated in the "with" clause. There's a bit of a ripple effect here, because as a result _Ty and _Ax, which would never have shown up had _InIt and _OutIt been used consistently in the signature, also appear in a "with" clause.

8.1.2.4   Eliminating Default Template Arguments

In version 7.1, Microsoft corrected that quirk, giving us back the ability to see that the first two arguments to std::copy have the same type. Now, though, they show the full name of the std::copy specialization, so we still have to confront more information than is likely to be useful:

```
foo.cpp(10) : see reference to function template instantiation '
_OutIt std::copy<std::list<_Ty>::iterator,std::
back_insert_iterator<_Container> >(_InIt,_InIt,_OutIt)' being
compiled
with
[
    _OutIt=std::back_insert_iterator<std::map<std::string,std::
    string>>,

    _Ty=std::string,
    _Container=std::map<std::string,std::string>,
    _InIt=std::list<std::string>::iterator
]
messages continue...
```

Had the highlighted material above been replaced with std::copy<_InIt,_OutIt>, _Ty could also have been dropped from the "with" clause.

The good news is that an important simplification has been made: std::list's default allocator argument and std::map's default allocator and comparison arguments have been left out. As of this writing, VC++ 7.1 is the only compiler we know of that elides default template arguments.

8.1.2.5   Deep `typedef` Substitution

Many modern compilers try to remember if and how each type was computed through *any* `typedef` (not just those at namespace scope), so the type can be represented that way in diagnostics. We call this strategy **deep `typedef` substitution**, because `typedef`s from deep within the instantiation stack show up in diagnostics. For instance, the following example:

```
# include <map>
# include <vector>
# include <algorithm>
int  main()
{
    std::map<int,int> a;
    std::vector<int> v(20);
    std::copy(a.begin(), a.end(), v.begin());
    return 0;
}
```

produces this output with Intel C++ 8.0:

```
C:\Program Files\Microsoft Visual Studio .NET 2003\VC7\INCLUDE\
xutility(1022): error: no suitable conversion function from "std::
allocator<std::pair<const int, int>>::value_type" to "std::
allocator <std::_Tree<std::_Tmap_traits<int, int, std::less<int>,
std::allocator<std::pair<const int, int>>, false>>::key_type=
{std::_Tmap_traits<int, int, std::less<int>, std::allocator<std::
pair<const int, int>>, false>::key_type={int}}>::value_type=
{std::_Allocator_base<std::_Tree<std::_Tmap_traits<int, int,

        std::less<int>, std::allocator<std::pair<const int, int>>,
        false>>::key_type={std::_Tmap_traits<int, int, std::less<
        int>, std::allocator<std::pair<const int, int>>, false>::
        key_type={int}}>::value_type={std::_Tree<std::_Tmap_traits
        <int, int, std::less<int>, std::allocator<std::pair<const
        int, int>>, false>>::key_type={std::_Tmap_traits<int, int,
        std::less<int>, std::allocator<std::pair<const int, int>>,
        false>::key_type={int}}}}" exists

    *_Dest = *_First;
              ^

...
```

What do we need to know, here? Well, the problem is that you can't assign from a `pair<int, int>` (the `map`'s element) into an `int` (the `vector`'s element). That information is in fact buried in the message above, but it's presented badly. A literal translation of the message into something more like English might be:

No conversion exists from the `value_type` of an

`allocator<pair<int,int> >`

to the `value_type` of an

`_allocator<`

`_Tree<...>::key_type...` (which is some
`_Tmap_traits<...>::key_type`, which is `int`)
`>.`

Oh, that second `value_type` is the `value_type` of an

`_Allocator_base<`

`_Tree<...>::key_type...` (which is some
`_Tmap_traits<...>::key_type`, which is `int`)
`>,`

which is also the `key_type` of a `_Tree<...>`, which is `int`.

Ugh. It would have been a *lot* more helpful to just tell us that you can't assign from `pair<int, int>` into `int`. Instead, we're presented with a lot of information about how those types were derived inside the standard library implementation.

Here's a report of the same error from VC++ 7.1:

```
C:\Program Files \Microsoft Visual Studio .NET 2003\Vc7 \include\
xutility(1022) : error C2440: '=' : cannot convert from 'std::
allocator<_Ty>::value_type' to 'std::allocator<_Ty>::value_type'

        with
        [
            _Ty=std::pair<const int,int>
        ]
        and
        [
            _Ty=std::_Tree<std::_Tmap_traits<int,int,std::less<
            int>,std::allocator<std::pair<const int,int>>,
```

```
                    false>>::key_type

            ]
    ...
```

This message is a lot shorter, but that may not be much consolation: It appears at first to claim that `allocator<_Ty>::value_type` can't be converted to itself! In fact, the two mentions of _Ty refer to types defined in consecutive bracketed clauses (introduced by "with" and "and"). Even once we've sorted that out, this diagnostic has the same problem as the previous one: The types involved are expressed in terms of `typedef`s in `std::allocator`. It's a good thing that it's easy to remember that `std::allocator`'s `value_type` is the same as its template argument, or we'd have no clue what types were involved here.

Since `allocator<_Ty>::value_type` is essentially a metafunction invocation, this sort of deep `typedef` substitution really does a number on our ability to debug metaprograms. Take this simple example:

```
# include <boost/mpl/transform.hpp>
# include <boost/mpl/vector/vector10.hpp>

namespace mpl = boost::mpl;
using namespace mpl::placeholders;
template <class T>
struct returning_ptr
{
    typedef T* type();
};

typedef mpl::transform<
      mpl::vector5<int&,char,long[5],bool,double>
    , returning_ptr<_1>
 >::type functions;
```

The intention was to build a sequence of function types returning pointers to the types in an input sequence, but the author forgot to account for the fact that forming a pointer to a reference type (`int&`) is illegal in C++. Intel C++ 7.1 reports:

```
foo.cpp(19): error: pointer to reference is not allowed
      typedef T* type();
              ^
          detected during:
            instantiation of class "returning_ptr<T> [with T=boost::
            mpl::bind1<boost::mpl::quote1<returning_ptr>, boost::mpl
```

```
::lambda_impl<boost::mpl::_1, boost::mpl::false_>::type>
::apply<boost::mpl::vector_iterator<boost::mpl::vector5<
int &, char, long [5], bool={bool}, double>::type, boost
::mpl::integral_c<long, 0L>>::type, boost::mpl::void_,
boost::mpl::void_, boost::mpl::void_, boost::mpl::void_>
::tl]" at line 23 of "c:/boost/boost/mpl/aux_/has_type.
hpp"
```

The *general* cause of the error is perfectly clear, but the offending type is far from it. We'd really like to know what T is, but it's expressed in terms of a nested `typedef`: `mpl::bind1<...>::tl`. Unless we're prepared to crawl through the definitions of `mpl::bind1` and the other MPL templates mentioned in that line, we're stuck. Microsoft VC++ 7.1 is similarly unhelpful:[1]

```
foo.cpp(9) : error C2528: 'type' : pointer to reference is illegal
      c:\boost\boost\mpl\aux_\has_type.hpp(23) : see reference
      to class template instantiation 'returning_ptr<T>' being
      compiled

      with
      [
        T=boost::mpl::bind1<boost::mpl::quote1<returning_ptr>,
        boost::mpl::lambda_impl<boost::mpl::_1>::type>::apply<
        boost::mpl::vector_iterator<boost::mpl::vector5<int &,
        char,long [5],bool,double>::type,boost::mpl::integral_c<
        long,0>>::type >::tl

      ]
```

GCC 3.2, which only does "shallow" `typedef` substitution, reports:

```
foo.cpp: In instantiation of 'returning_ptr<int&>':
...many lines omitted...
foo.cpp:19: forming pointer to reference type 'int&'
```

This message is much more sensible. We'll explain the omitted lines in a moment.

---

1. Fortunately, Microsoft's compiler engineers have been listening to our complaints, and an evaluation version of their next compiler only injects `typedef`s defined at namespace scope into its diagnostics. With any luck, this change will survive all the way to the product they eventually release.

8.2   Using Tools for Diagnostic Analysis

Though their efforts sometimes backfire, compiler vendors are clearly going out of their way to address the problem of unreadable template error messages. That said, even the best error message formats can still leave a lot to be desired when a bug bites you from deep within a nested template instantiation. Fortunately, software tools can be an immense help, if you follow three suggestions.

8.2.1   Get a Second Opinion

Our first recommendation is to keep a few different compilers on hand, just for debugging purposes. If one compiler emits an inscutable error message, another one will likely do better. When something goes wrong, a compiler may guess at what you meant in order to report the mistake, and it often pays to have several different guesses. Also, many compilers have intrinsic deficiencies when it comes to error reporting. For example, though it is an otherwise excellent compiler—and one of the very fastest in our timing tests—Metrowerks CodeWarrior Pro 9 often fails to output filenames and line numbers for each "frame" of its instantiation backtrace, which can make the offending source code hard to find. If you need to trace the source of the error, you may want to try a different toolset.

> **Tip**
> If you don't have the budget to invest in more tools, we suggest trying to find a recent version of GCC that runs on your platform. All versions of GCC are available for free; Windows users should get the MinGW (http://www.mingw.org) or Cygwin (http://www.cygwin.com) variants. If you can't bear to install another compiler on your machine, Comeau Computing will let you try an online version of their compiler at http://www.comeaucomputing.com/tryitout. Because Comeau C++ is based on the highly conformant EDG front-end, it provides an excellent way to get a quick read on whether your code is likely to comply with the C++ standard.

8.2.2   Use Navigational Aids

For traversing instantiation stack backtraces, it's crucial to have an environment that helps you to see the source line associated with an error message. If you're one of those people who usually compiles from a command shell, you may want to issue those commands from within some kind of integrated development environment (IDE), just to avoid having to manually open files in an editor and look up line numbers. Many IDEs allow a variety of toolsets to be plugged in, but for debugging metaprograms it's important that the IDE can conveniently step between messages in the various compilers' diagnostic formats. Emacs, for example, uses an extensible set of regular expressions to extract filenames and line numbers from error messages, so it can be tuned to work with any number of compilers.

8.2.3   Clean Up the Landscape

Finally, we suggest the use of a post-processing filter such as TextFilt (http://textfilt.sourceforge.net)
or STLFilt (http://www.bdsoft.com/tools/stlfilt.html). Both of these filters were originally designed
to help programmers make sense of the types in their STL error messages. Their most basic features
include the automatic elision of default arguments from specializations of known templates, and
`typedef` substitution for `std::string` and `std::wstring`. For example, TextFilt transforms the
following mess:

```
example.cc:21: conversion from 'double' to non-scalar type
'map<vector<basic_string<char, string_char_traits<char>,
__default_alloc_template<true, 0> >,
allocator<basic_string<char, string_char_traits<char>,
__default_alloc_template<true, 0> > > >, set<basic_string<char,
string_char_traits<char>, _ _default_alloc_template<true, 0> >,
less<basic_string<char, string_char_traits<char>,
__default_alloc_template<true, 0> > >,
allocator<basic_string<char, string_char_traits<char>,
__default_alloc_template<true, 0> > > >,
less<vector<basic_string<char, string_char_traits<char>,
__default_alloc_template<true, 0> >,
allocator<basic_string<char, string_char_traits<char>,
__default_alloc_template<true, 0> > > > >,
allocator<set<basic_string<char, string_char_traits<char>,
__default_alloc_template<true, 0> >, less<basic_string<char,
string_char_traits<char>, _ _default_alloc_template<true, 0> > >,
allocator<basic_string<char, string_char_traits<char>,
__default_alloc_template<true, 0> > > > > >' requested
```

into the much more readable:

```
example.cc:21: conversion from 'double' to non-scalar type
'map<vector<string>,set<string>>' requested
```

TextFilt is interesting because it is easily customizable; you can add special handling for your
own types by writing "rulesets," which are simple sets of regular expression-based transformations.
STLFilt is not so easily customized (unless you enjoy hacking Perl), but it includes several command
line options with which you can tune how much information you see. We find these two indispensable
for template metaprogramming.

1. **GCC error message reordering.** Though GCC is by far our preferred compiler for metaprogram debugging, it's by no means perfect. Its biggest problem is that it prints the actual cause

of an error *following* the entire instantiation backtrace. As a result, you often have to step through the whole backtrace before the problem becomes apparent, and the actual error is widely separated from the nearest instantiation frame. That's why the GCC error messages in this chapter are often shown with *"many lines omitted..."*. STLFilt has two options for GCC message reordering:

- `-hdr:LD1:`, which brings the actual error message to the top of the instantiation backtrace.

- `-hdr:LD2:`, which is just like `-hdr:LD1` but adds a copy of the final line of the backtrace (the non-template code that initiated the instantiation) just after the error message.

2. **Expression wrapping and indenting.** No matter how much is done to filter irrelevant information from an error message, there's no getting around the fact that some C++ types and expressions are intrinsically complex. For example, if there were no default template arguments and `typedef`s to work with, getting a grip on the previous example would have required us to parse its nesting structure. STLFilt includes a `-meta` option that formats messages according to the conventions of this book. Even with default template argument elision and `typedef` substitution disabled, STLFilt can still help us see what's going on in the message:

```
example.cc:21: conversion from 'double' to non-scalar type
  'map<
      vector<
          basic_string<
              char, string_char_traits<char>
            , __default_alloc_template<true, 0>
          >, allocator<
              basic_string<
                  char, string_char_traits<char>
                , __default_alloc_template<true, 0>
              >
          >
      >, set<
          basic_string<
              char, string_char_traits<char>
            , __default_alloc_template<true, 0>
          >, less<
              basic_string<
                  char, string_char_traits<char>
                , __default_alloc_template<true, 0>
              >
          >, allocator<
```

```
            basic_string<
                char, string_char_traits<char>
                , __default_alloc_template<true, 0>
            >
          >
        >, less<
            ...12 lines omitted...
        >, allocator<
            ...16 lines omitted...
        >
    >' requested
```

Although the message is still huge, it has become much more readable: By scanning its first few columns we can quickly surmise that the long type is a map from vector<string> to set<string>.

Any tool can obscure a diagnostic by applying too much filtering, and STLFilt is no exception, so we encourage you to review the command line options at http://www.bdsoft.com/tools/stlfilt-opts.html and choose carefully. Fortunately, since these are external tools, you can always fall back on direct inspection of raw diagnostics.

8.3   Intentional Diagnostic Generation

Why would anyone want to generate a diagnostic on purpose? After spending most of this chapter picking through a morass of template error messages, it's tempting to wish them away. Compiler diagnostics have their place, though, even once our templates are in the hands of users who may be less well equipped to decipher them. Ultimately, it all comes down to one simple idea:

Guideline

Report every error at your first opportunity.

Even the ugliest compile-time error is better than silent misbehavior, a crash, or an assertion at runtime. Moreover, if there's going to be a compiler diagnostic anyway, it's always better to issue the message as soon as possible. The reason template error messages often provide no clue to the nature and location of an actual programming problem is that they occur far too late, when instantiation has reached deep into the implementation details of a library. Because the compiler itself has no knowledge of the library's domain, it is unable to detect usage errors at the library interface boundary and report them in terms of the library's abstractions. For example, we might try to compile:

```
#include <algorithm>
#include <list>

int main()
{
    std::list<int> x;
    std::sort(x.begin(), x.end());
}
```

Ideally, we'd like the compiler to report the problem at the point of the actual programming error, and to tell us something about the abstractions involved—iterators in this case:

```
main.cpp(7) : std::sort requires random access iterators, but
std::list<int>::iterator is only a bidirectional iterator
```

VC++ 7.1, however, reports:

```
C:\Program Files \Microsoft Visual Studio .NET 2003\Vc7 \include\
algorithm(1795) : error C2784:
'reverse_iterator<_RanIt>::difference_type std::operator -(const
std::reverse_iterator<_RanIt> &,const
std::reverse_iterator<_RanIt>  &)' : could not deduce template
argument for 'const std::reverse_iterator<_RanIt> &' from
'std::list<_Ty>::iterator'
        with
        [
            _Ty=int
        ]
continued...
```

Notice that the error is reported inside some operator- implementation in the standard library's <algorithm> header, instead of in main() where the mistake actually is. The cause of the problem is obscured by the appearance of std::reverse_iterator, which has no obvious relationship to the code we wrote. Even the use of operator-, which *hints* at the need for random access iterators, isn't directly related to what the programmer was trying to do. If the mismatch between std::list<int>::iterator and std::sort's requirement of random access had been detected earlier (ideally at the point std::sort was invoked), it would have been possible for the compiler to report the problem directly.

It's important to understand that blame for the poor error message above does not lie with the compiler. In fact, it's due to a limitation of the C++ language: While the signatures of ordinary functions clearly state the type requirements on their arguments, the same can't be said of generic functions.[2] The library authors, on the other hand, could have done a few things to limit the damage. In this section we're going to cover a few techniques we can use in our own libraries to generate diagnostics earlier and with more control over the message contents.

8.3.1   Static Assertions

You've already seen one way to generate an error when your code is being detectably misused

```
BOOST_STATIC_ASSERT(integral-constant-expression);
```

If the expression is false (or zero), a compiler error is issued. Assertions are best used as a kind of "sanity check" to make sure that the assumptions under which code was written actually hold. Let's use a classic factorial metafunction as an example:

```
#include <boost/mpl/int.hpp>
#include <boost/mpl/multiplies.hpp>
#include <boost/mpl/equal.hpp>
#include <boost/mpl/eval_if.hpp>
#include <boost/mpl/prior.hpp>
#include <boost/static_assert.hpp>

namespace mpl = boost::mpl;

template <class N>
struct factorial
  : mpl::eval_if<
        mpl::equal_to<N,mpl::int_<0> >   // check N == 0
      , mpl::int_<1>                     // 0! == 1
      , mpl::multiplies<                 // N! == N * (N-1)!
            N
          , factorial<typename mpl::prior<N>::type>
        >
    >
{
    BOOST_STATIC_ASSERT(N::value >= 0); // for nonnegative N
};
```

---

2. Several members of the C++ committee are currently working hard to overcome that limitation by making it possible to express concepts in C++ as first-class citizens of the type system. In the meantime, library solutions [SL00] will have to suffice.

Computing $N!$ only makes sense when N is nonnegative, and `factorial` was written under the assumption that its argument meets that constraint. The assertion is used to check that assumption, and if we violate it:

```
int const fact = factorial<mpl::int_<-6> >::value;
```

we'll get this diagnostic from Intel C++ 8.1:

```
foo.cpp(22): error: incomplete type is not allowed
      BOOST_STATIC_ASSERT(N::value >= 0);
      ^
         detected during instantiation of class "factorial<N>
      [with N=mpl_::int_<-6>]" at line 25
```

Note that when the condition is violated, we get an error message that refers to the line of source containing the assertion.

The implementation of `BOOST_STATIC_ASSERT` is selected by the library based on the quirks of whatever compiler you're using to ensure that the macro can be used reliably at class, function, or namespace scope, and that the diagnostic will always refer to the line where the assertion was triggered. When the assertion fails on Intel C++, it generates a diagnostic by misusing an incomplete type—thus the message "`incomplete type is not allowed`"—though you can expect to see different kinds of errors generated on other compilers.

8.3.2   The MPL Static Assertions

The contents of the diagnostic above could hardly be more informative: not only is the source line displayed, but we can see the condition in question and the argument to `factorial`. In general, though, you can't rely on such helpful results from `BOOST_STATIC_ASSERT`. In this case we got them more by lucky accident than by design.

1.   If the value being tested in the assertion (-6) weren't present in the type of the enclosing template, it wouldn't have been displayed.

2.   This compiler only displays one source line at the point of an error; had the macro invocation crossed multiple lines, the condition being tested would be at least partially hidden.

3.   Many compilers don't show any source lines in an error message. GCC 3.3.1, for example, reports:

```
foo.cpp: In instantiation of 'factorial<mpl_::int_<-6> >':
foo.cpp:25:   instantiated from here
foo.cpp:22: error: invalid application of 'sizeof' to an
incomplete type
```

Here, the failed condition is missing.

The MPL supplies a suite of static assertion macros that are actually *designed* to generate useful error messages. In this section we'll explore each of them by using it in our factorial metafunction.

8.3.2.1   The Basics

The most straightforward of these assertions is used as follows:

```
BOOST_MPL_ASSERT((bool-valued-nullary-metafunction))
```

Note that double parentheses are required even if no commas appear in the condition.

Here are the changes we might make to apply this macro in our `factorial` example:

```
...
#include <boost/mpl/greater_equal.hpp>
#include <boost/mpl/assert.hpp>

template <class N>
struct factorial
  ...
{
    BOOST_MPL_ASSERT((mpl::greater_equal<N,mpl::int_<0> >));
};
```

The advantage of BOOST_MPL_ASSERT is that it puts the name of its argument metafunction in the diagnostic. GCC now reports:

```
foo.cpp: In instantiation of 'factorial<mpl_::int_<-6> >':
foo.cpp:26:    instantiated from here
foo.cpp:23: error: conversion from '
   mpl_::failed**********boost::mpl::greater_equal<mpl_::int_<-6>,
   mpl_::int_<0> >::***********' to non-scalar type '
   mpl_::assert<false>' requested
foo.cpp:23: error: enumerator value for '
   mpl_assertion_in_line_23' not integer constant
```

Note that the violated condition is now displayed prominently, bracketed by sequences of asterisks, a feature you can count on *across all supported compilers*.

8.3.2.2   A More Likely Assertion

In truth, the diagnostic above still contains a great many characters we don't care about, but that's due more to the verbosity of using templates to express the failed condition -6 >= 0 than to anything else. BOOST_MPL_ASSERT is actually better suited to checking other sorts of conditions. For example, we might try to enforce N's conformance to the integral constant wrapper protocol as follows:

```
BOOST_MPL_ASSERT((boost::is_integral<typename N::value_type>));
```

To trigger this assertion, we could write:

```
// attempt to make a "floating point constant wrapper"
struct five : mpl::int_<5> { typedef double value_type; };
int const fact = factorial<five>::value;
```

yielding the following diagnostic, with a much better signal-to-noise ratio than our nonnegative test:

```
...
foo.cpp:24: error: conversion from
'mpl_::failed************boost::is_integral<double>::************'
to non-scalar type 'mpl_::assert<false>' requested
...
```

8.3.2.3   Negative Assertions

Negating a condition tested with BOOST_STATIC_ASSERT is as simple as preceding it with !, but to do the same thing with BOOST_MPL_ASSERT we'd need to wrap the predicate in mpl::not_<...>. To simplify negative assertions, MPL provides BOOST_MPL_ASSERT_NOT, which does the wrapping for us. The following rephrases our earlier assertion that N is nonnegative:

```
BOOST_MPL_ASSERT_NOT((mpl::less<N,mpl::int_<0> >));
```

As you can see, the resulting error message includes the mpl::not_<...> wrapper:

```
foo.cpp:24: error: conversion from 'mpl_::failed
************boost::mpl::not_<boost::mpl::less<mpl_::int_<-5>,
mpl_::int_<0> > >::************' to non-scalar type
'mpl_::assert<false>' requested
```

8.3.2.4   Asserting Numerical Relationships

We suggested that BOOST_MPL_ASSERT was not very well suited for checking numerical conditions because not only the diagnostics, but the assertions themselves tend to incur a great deal of syntactic overhead. Writing mpl::greater_equal<x,y> in order to say $x >= y$ is admittedly a bit roundabout. For this sort of numerical comparison, MPL provides a specialized macro:

```
BOOST_MPL_ASSERT_RELATION(
   integral-constant, comparison-operator, integral-constant);
```

To apply it in our factorial metafunction, we simply write:

```
BOOST_MPL_ASSERT_RELATION(N::value, >=, 0);
```

In this case, the content of generated error messages varies slightly across compilers. GCC reports:

```
...
foo.cpp:30: error: conversion from
'mpl_::failed************mpl_::assert_relation<greater_equal, -5,
0>::************' to non-scalar type 'mpl_::assert<false>'
requested
...
```

while Intel says:

```
foo.cpp(30): error: no instance of function template
"mpl_::assertion_failed" matches the argument list

  argument types are: (mpl_::failed
  ************mpl_::assert_relation< mpl_::operator>=, -5L, 0L
  >::************)

      BOOST_MPL_ASSERT_RELATION(N::value, >=, 0);
      ^
          detected during instantiation of class "factorial<N>
      [with N=mpl_::int_<-5>]" at line 33
```

These differences notwithstanding, the violated relation and the two integral constants concerned are clearly visible in both diagnostics.

8.3.2.5   Customized Assertion Messages

The assertion macros we've seen so far are great for a library's internal sanity checks, but they don't always generate messages in the most appropriate form for library users. The `factorial` metafunction probably doesn't illustrate that fact very well, because the predicate that triggers the error ($N < 0$) is such a straightforward function of the input. The prerequisite for computing $N!$ is that N be nonnegative, and any user is likely to recognize a complaint that `N >= 0` failed as a direct expression of that constraint.

Not all static assertions have that property, though: often an assertion reflects low-level details of the library implementation, rather than the abstractions that the user is dealing with. One example is found in the dimensional analysis code from Chapter 3, rewritten here with `BOOST_MPL_ASSERT`:

```
template <class OtherDimensions>
quantity(quantity<T,OtherDimensions> const& rhs)
  : m_value(rhs.value())
{
    BOOST_MPL_ASSERT((mpl::equal<Dimensions,OtherDimensions>));
}
```

What we'll see in the diagnostic, if this assertion fails, is that there's an inequality between two sequences containing integral constant wrappers. That, combined with the source line, *begins* to hint at the actual problem, but it's not very to-the-point. The first thing a user needs to know when this assertion fails is that there's a dimensional mismatch. Next, it would probably be helpful to know the identity of the first fundamental dimension that failed to match and the values of the exponents concerned. None of that information is immediately apparent from the diagnostic that's actually generated, though.

With a little more control over the diagnostic, we could generate messages that are more appropriate for users. We'll leave the specific problem of generating errors for dimensional analysis as an exercise, and return to the `factorial` problem to explore a few techniques.

Customizing the Predicate

To display a customized message, we can take advantage of the fact that `BOOST_MPL_ASSERT` places the name of its predicate into the diagnostic output. Just by writing an appropriately named predicate, we can make the compiler say anything we like—as long as it can be expressed as the name of a class. For example:

```
// specializations are nullary metafunctions that compute n>0
template <int n>
struct FACTORIAL_of_NEGATIVE_NUMBER
  : mpl::greater_equal<mpl::int_<n>, mpl::int_<0> >
{};
```

```
template <class N>
struct factorial
  : mpl::eval_if<
        mpl::equal_to<N,mpl::int_<0> >
      , mpl::int_<1>
      , mpl::multiplies<
            N
          , factorial<typename mpl::prior<N>::type>
        >
    >
{
    BOOST_MPL_ASSERT((FACTORIAL_of_NEGATIVE_NUMBER<N::value>));
};
```

Now GCC reports:

```
foo.cpp:30: error: conversion from 'mpl_::failed
************FACTORIAL_of_NEGATIVE_NUMBER<-5>::************' to
non-scalar type 'mpl_::assert<false>' requested
```

One minor problem with this approach is that it requires interrupting the flow of our code to write a predicate at namespace scope, just for the purpose of displaying an error message. This strategy has a more serious downside, though: The code now appears to be asserting that N::value is negative, when in fact it does just the opposite. That's not only likely to confuse the code's maintainers, but also its users. Don't forget that some compilers (Intel C++ in this case) will display the line containing the assertion:

```
foo.cpp(30): error: no instance of function template
"mpl_::assertion_failed" matches the argument list

    argument types are: (mpl_::failed
    ************FACTORIAL_of_NEGATIVE_NUMBER<-5>::************)

    BOOST_MPL_ASSERT((FACTORIAL_of_NEGATIVE_NUMBER<N::value>));
    ^
```

If we choose the message text more carefully, we can eliminate this potential source of confusion:

```
template <int n>
struct FACTORIAL_requires_NONNEGATIVE_argument
  : mpl::greater_equal<mpl::int_<n>, mpl::int_<0> >
{};
...
    BOOST_MPL_ASSERT((
        FACTORIAL_requires_NONNEGATIVE_argument<N::value>));
```

Those kinds of linguistic contortions, however, can get a bit unwieldy and may not always be possible.

Inline Message Generation

MPL provides a macro for generating custom messages that doesn't depend on a separately written predicate class, and therefore doesn't demand quite as much attention to exact phrasing. The usage is as follows:

```
BOOST_MPL_ASSERT_MSG(condition, message, types);
```

where *condition* is an integral constant expression, *message* is a legal C++ identifier, and *types* is a legal function parameter list. For example, to apply BOOST_MPL_ASSERT_MSG to factorial, we could write:

```
BOOST_MPL_ASSERT_MSG(
    N::value >= 0, FACTORIAL_of_NEGATIVE_NUMBER, (N));
```

yielding this message from GCC:

```
foo.cpp:31: error: conversion from 'mpl_::failed
****************(factorial<mpl_::int_<-5>
>::FACTORIAL_of_NEGATIVE_NUMBER::****************)
(mpl_::int_<-5>)' to non-scalar type 'mpl_::assert<false>'
requested.
```

We've highlighted the *message* and the *types* arguments where they appear in the diagnostic above. In this case, *types* isn't very interesting, since it just repeats mpl_::int_<-5>, which appears elsewhere in the message. We could therefore replace (N) in the assertion with the empty function parameter list, (), to get:

```
foo.cpp:31: error: conversion from 'mpl_::failed
****************(factorial<mpl_::int_<-5>
```

```
>::FACTORIAL_of_NEGATIVE_NUMBER::****************)
()' to non-scalar type 'mpl_::assert<false>'
requested.
```

In general, even using BOOST_MPL_ASSERT_MSG requires some care, because the *types* argument is used as a function parameter list, and some types we might like to display have special meaning in that context. For example, a `void` parameter will be omitted from most diagnostics, since `int f(void)` is the same as `int f()`. Furthermore, `void` can only be used once: `int f(void, void)` is illegal syntax. Also, array and function types are interpreted as pointer and function pointer types respectively:

```
int f(int x[2], char* (long))
```

is the same as

```
int f(int *x, char* (*)(long))
```

In case you don't know enough about the *types* ahead of time to be sure that they'll be displayed correctly, you can use the following form, with up to four *types:*

```
BOOST_MPL_ASSERT_MSG(condition, message, (types<types >));
```

For example, we could add the following assertion to `factorial`, based on the fact that all integral constant wrappers are classes:

```
BOOST_MPL_ASSERT_MSG(
    boost::is_class<N>::value
  , NOT_an_INTEGRAL_CONSTANT_WRAPPER
  , (types<N>));
```

If we then attempt to instantiate `factorial<void>`, VC++ 7.1 reports:

```
foo.cpp(34) : error C2664: 'mpl_::assertion_failed' : cannot
        convert parameter 1 from 'mpl_::failed
        ****************(__thiscall
        factorial<N>::NOT_an_INTEGRAL_CONSTANT_WRAPPER::*
        ****************               )(mpl_::assert_::types<T1>)
        ' to 'mpl_::assert<false>::type'
        with
        [
            N=void,
            T1=void
        ]
```

Since `types` can accept up to four arguments, the diagnostic is a little better here than on compilers that don't elide default template arguments. For example, the diagnostic from Intel C++ 8.0 is:

```
foo.cpp(31): error: no instance of function template
"mpl_::assertion_failed" matches the argument list

    argument types are: (mpl_::failed ****************
    (factorial<void>::NOT_an_INTEGRAL_CONSTANT_WRAPPER::
    ****************)(mpl_::assert_::types<void, mpl_::na,
    mpl_::na, mpl_::na>))

     BOOST_MPL_ASSERT_MSG(
     ^
          detected during instantiation of class "factorial<N>
          [with N=void]" at line 37
```

It's also worth noticing that, while the customized predicate we wrote for use with BOOST_MPL_ASSERT was written at namespace scope, the message generated by BOOST_MPL_ASSERT_MSG appears as a qualified member of the scope where the assertion was issued (`factorial<void>` in this case). As a result, compilers that do deep `typedef` substitution have one more opportunity to insert unreadable type expansions in the diagnostic. For example, if we instantiate:

```
mpl::transform<mpl::vector<void>, factorial<mpl::_> >
```

Intel C++ 8.0 generates the following:

```
foo.cpp(34): error: no instance of function template
"mpl_::assertion_failed" matches the argument list

    argument types are: (mpl_::failed
    ****************(factorial<boost::mpl::bind1<
    boost::mpl::quote1<factorial, boost::mpl::void_>,
    boost::mpl::lambda<mpl_::_,
    boost::mpl::void_>::result_>::apply<
    boost::mpl::bind1<factorial<mpl_::_>,
    mpl_::_2>::apply<boost::mpl::aux::fold_impl<1,
    boost::mpl::begin<boost::mpl::vector<void, mpl_::na,
    mpl_::na, mpl_::na, mpl_::na, mpl_::na, mpl_::na, mpl_::na,
    mpl_::na, mpl_::na, mpl_::na, mpl_::na, mpl_::na, mpl_::na,
    mpl_::na, mpl_::na, mpl_::na,
    ...four similar long lines omitted...

     mpl_::na>::t1>::NOT_an_INTEGRAL_CONSTANT_WRAPPER::
```

```
***************)(mpl_::assert_::types<boost::mpl::bind1<
line continued...

...five similar lines omitted...
BOOST_MPL_ASSERT_MSG(
^
```

The omission of nine long lines above actually contributes a great deal to the message's readability, so you can probably imagine what it's like to read the whole thing.

Selecting a Strategy

Both approaches to customized error generation we've covered here have strengths and weaknesses: BOOST_MPL_ASSERT_MSG is convenient, minimal, and highly expressive of its intent, but it can require some care if asked to display void, array, and function types, and it can have readability problems, especially in the presence of deep typedef substitution. Using custom predicates with BOOST_MPL_ASSERT offers a little more control over message formatting, though it takes more work, complicates code somewhat, and can be confusing unless the predicate name is carefully chosen. Clearly there's no perfect strategy for all needs, so consider the trade-offs carefully before selecting one.

8.3.3   Type Printing

When a template metaprogram misbehaves, it can begin to seem like an impenetrable black box, especially if the problem doesn't manifest itself in a compilation error, or if the error shows up long after the actual problem has occurred. Sometimes it's useful to intentionally generate a diagnostic just, well, for diagnostic purposes. For most situations, this simple tool suffices:

```
template <class T> struct incomplete;
```

If at any point we need to know what some type T is, all we have to do is to cause incomplete<T> to be instantiated, for example:

```
template <class T>
struct my_metafunction
{
    incomplete<T> x; // temporary diagnostic
    typedef ... type;
};
```

Most C++ compilers, indeed, *all* the compilers we've seen, will generate an error message that shows us what T is.[3] This technique is subject to the usual caveats: Compilers that do deep `typedef` substitution may show us an arbitrarily complicated name for T, depending on how T was computed.

One time-honored technique for debugging C/C++ programs is to "stick `printf`s in the code" and examine the resulting execution log. The `incomplete<T>` technique is more analogous to a runtime assertion, though: It shows us the program state in question and causes a hard error. Remember when we said that most C++ compilers don't recover well from errors? Even if your compiler forges ahead after instantiating `incomplete<T>`, the results are about as reliable as what you'd expect from a program that had reported runtime data corruption.

To generate a compile-time execution log, we'd need a way to generate a non-error diagnostic message—a warning. Because there's no single construct that will cause all compilers to generate a warning (indeed, most compilers let you disable warnings altogether), MPL has a `print` metafunction that is just like `identity` except that it is tuned to generate a warning on a variety of popular compilers with their "usual settings." For example, the following program:

```
template <class T, class U>
struct plus_dbg
{
    typedef typename
      mpl::print< typename mpl::plus<T,U>::type >::type
    type;
};

typedef mpl::fold<
    mpl::range_c<int,1,6>
  , mpl::int_<0>
  , plus_dbg<_1,_2>
>::type sum;
```

produces the following diagnostics (among others) with GCC:[4]

---

3. Note that we did not write `typedef incomplete<T> x;` because that would not cause `incomplete<T>` to be instantiated, as described in Chapter 2.

4. One peculiar quirk of GCC is that the use of metafunction forwarding interferes slightly with diagnostics. Had we instead written:

```
template <class T, class U>
struct plus_dbg
  : mpl::print< typename mpl::plus<T,U>::type >
{};
```

The diagnostics beginning with "In `instantiation of`..." would have had a filename label somewhere in MPL's implementation headers instead of in `foo.cpp`. While this problem is not enough to prevent us from recommending metafunction forwarding with GCC, it *is* worth being aware of.

```
foo.cpp: In instantiation of
'boost::mpl::print<boost::mpl::integral_c<int, 1> >':
...
foo.cpp:72: warning: comparison between signed and unsigned
integer expressions

foo.cpp: In instantiation of
'boost::mpl::print<boost::mpl::integral_c<int, 3> >':
...
foo.cpp:72: warning: comparison between signed and unsigned
integer expressions

foo.cpp: In instantiation of
'boost::mpl::print<boost::mpl::integral_c<int, 6> >':
...
foo.cpp:72: warning: comparison between signed and unsigned
integer expressions

foo.cpp: In instantiation of
'boost::mpl::print<boost::mpl::integral_c<int, 10> >':
...
foo.cpp:72: warning: comparison between signed and unsigned
integer expressions

foo.cpp: In instantiation of
'boost::mpl::print<boost::mpl::integral_c<int, 15> >':
...
foo.cpp:72: warning: comparison between signed and unsigned
integer expressions
```

Naturally, these messages are mixed into the compiler's instantiation backtraces. This is another area where diagnostic filtering tools can help: STLFilt has an option (/showback:N) that eliminates the backtrace material shown as the ellipsis (...) above, so that we're left with a simplified trace of compile time execution. Of course, if you have access to UNIX tools, piping the errors into "grep print" might do the job just as easily.

8.4   History

There is a long history of intentional compile time error generation in C++. As mentioned in Chapter 1, the very first C++ template metaprogram was a novelty written by Erwin Unruh that printed a series of prime numbers in template error messages [Unruh94]!

We first heard of the idea of encoding readable error messages in the names of types and functions from Dietmar Kuehl in 1998. By 2000, `BOOST_STATIC_ASSERT` [Mad00] had appeared and there were at least two efforts applying Kuehl's technique to improve error messages generated by STL implementations: "Static Interfaces" by Brian McNamara and Yannis Smaragdakis [MS00a] and the "Boost Concept Checking Library" by Jeremy Siek [SL00].

8.5 Details

Instantiation backtraces. Those long error messages you get when templates fail to compile are actually the compile time equivalent of the runtime call stack: They often contain valuable information that can help lead you to the source of a problem, if you can manage not to be overwhelmed by them. Compiler vendors have taken a number of steps, including the use of "with" clauses and eliminating default template parameters, to make them more readable.

`typedef` substitution. Many compilers, including Microsoft Visual C++ 7 and 7.1 and most EDG-based compilers, *attempt* to improve error messages by presenting types the way they were originally named in code. For example, they may show a `typedef` name instead of presenting the underlying type referred to by that `typedef`. We feel that substitution of class-template scoped `typedef`s actually hurts metaprogram debugging more than it helps, since metafunction results are always accessed through nested `typedef`s. We suggest you keep at least one compiler handy that doesn't do deep `typedef` substitution. GCC is one such a compiler, and it's free.

Additional tools. Because instantiation backtraces report errors at many lines of a program, we suggest you get an IDE of some kind that automatically displays the program text associated with line numbers in error messages, so you can quickly inspect the code at each level of an instantiation stack backtrace. We also suggest you try using a post-processing filter such as STLFilt to improve the readability of your template error messages.

Static assertions. `BOOST_STATIC_ASSERT`, `BOOST_MPL_ASSERT_RELATION`, and straightforward uses of `BOOST_MPL_ASSERT` are great tools for adding sanity checks to your metaprograms. They're also useful for writing metaprogram tests that are expected to compile only if the code is correct. For enforcing constraints on the way your metaprograms are *used,* we suggest something that produces more readable error messages.

Customized errors. We only know of one reasonably portable way to generate a specific message when a template is instantiated: embed it in the name of a type or function that will show up in a real compiler diagnostic. We covered two approaches: `BOOST_MPL_ASSERT` with hand written predicate metafunctions and `BOOST_MPL_ASSERT_MSG`. Each has its strengths and weaknesses. Though workable, neither is really a clean solution. In the future, we hope direct language support for custom diagnostics will be available.

Type printing. The "customized error message" technique can be extended to warnings if you need to examine a type without disturbing metaprogram execution. The `mpl::print<T>` class template can be used to generate such a warning on a wide variety of compilers, depending on your choice of compilation options.

8.6   Exercises

8-0.   Write and test a metaprogram that prints a series of prime numbers using `mpl::print`. Compare your program to Erwin Unruh's original code at http://www.erwin-unruh.de/primorig.html.

8-1.   Rewrite the assertions in the dimensional analysis code from Chapter 3 to optimize the diagnostics for library users. Analyze the resulting messages as generated by a few different compilers.

8-2.   MPL contains special macros for asserting *numeric relations*. because, when applicable, they present a much more convenient interface and higher-quality error messages than plain Boolean assertions do. What other category of test might deserve/benefit from a similar approach? Design an interface for handling these cases, and describe the kind of output you'd like to see it generate.

8-3.   Implement the interface you designed in exercise 8-2 using one of the two customized message generation techniques discussed in this chapter.

8-4.   Fix the hand written error reporting in `returning_ptr` in section 8.3.3 so that the salient information appears in the first line of the diagnostic on GCC.

## 9

Crossing the Compile-Time/Runtime Boundary

Remember runtime execution? We realize it's been a while, having spent so long in the stratospheric world of compile-time programming, but we're going to ask you to join us back on solid ground now. Ultimately, any interesting program has to do *something* at runtime. This chapter is about crossing the boundary between compile time and runtime C++—the "ozone layer," if you will—so that our metaprograms can make a difference in the lives of real users. There are probably an infinite number of ways to make that journey in C++, but some have proven themselves to be more useful than others; we'll cover a few of the most commonly used techniques next.

9.1 `for_each`

The simplest STL algorithm ought to have an MPL analogue, and so it does. Just to review, `std::for_each` traverses a (runtime) sequence and invokes some (runtime) function object on each element. Similarly, `mpl::for_each` traverses a *compile-time* sequence and invokes some runtime function object on it. Although `std::for_each` operates only at runtime, `mpl::for_each` is a hybrid, straddling the compile-time and runtime worlds.

Why Runtime Function Objects?

If you're wondering why `mpl::for_each` takes a *runtime* function object instead of a metafunction, think of it this way: Normally, the function object used with `std::for_each` returns `void`, but even if it *does* have a result, that result is discarded. In other words, that function object, if it does anything at all, has to modify the program state somehow. Since functional programming is inherently stateless and template metaprograms are functional, there wouldn't be much point in invoking a metafunction on each element of the sequence unless we were going to do something with the result.

9.1.1   Type Printing

Have you been wondering how to get a look at the contents of your type sequences? Provided we're using a compiler that produces meaningful strings from `std::type_info::name`, we can print each element of a type sequence as follows:

```
struct print_type
{
    template <class T>
    void operator()(T) const
    {
        std::cout << typeid(T).name() << std::endl;
    }
};

typedef mpl::vector<int, long, char*> s;
int main ()
{
    mpl::for_each<s>(print_type());
}
```

There are a few things we'd like you to notice about this code. First of all, `print_type`'s function-call operator is templatized, because it has to handle whatever types happen to appear in our sequence. Except when you want to process sequences whose elements are all convertible to one type, your `mpl::for_each` function objects will need a templated (or at the very least, overloaded) function call operator.

Next, note that `for_each` passes us each sequence element as a value-initialized *object* of the corresponding element type.[1]   This form is particularly convenient if you are iterating over a sequence of integral constant wrappers, which, if you remember, are implicitly convertible to their corresponding runtime constants. On the other hand, it requires some special care when iterating over an ordinary type sequence: If the element turns out to be a reference type, a class type with no

---

1. The concept of **value-initialization** was added to the C++ standard in its first "technical corrigendum" (TC1).
To **value-initialize** an object of type T means:
- If T is a class type (clause 9) with a user-declared constructor (12.1), then the default constructor for T is called.
- If T is a non-union class type without a user-declared constructor, then every nonstatic data member and base-class component of T is value-initialized.
- If T is an array type, then each element is value-initialized.
- Otherwise, the object is zero-initialized.

default constructor, or simply void, the algorithm will fail to compile since none of those types can be value-initialized.

We can avoid this pitfall by transforming the sequence through a little wrapper template to smooth out its rough edges:

```
template <class T>
struct wrap {};

// contains references
typedef mpl::vector<int&, long&, char*&> s;

mpl::for_each<
    mpl::transform<s, wrap<_1> >::type
>(print_type());
```

We'll also need to adjust our function object's signature, to account for the change in the types of arguments that will be passed:

```
struct print_type
{
    template <class T>
    void operator()(wrap<T>) const    // deduce T
    {
        std::cout << typeid(T).name() << std::endl;
    }
};
```

Because this is such a common idiom, MPL provides a second form of for_each that takes a transformation metafunction as an additional template argument. By using this second form, we can avoid building a whole new sequence of wrap specializations:

```
mpl::for_each<s, wrap<_1> >(print_type());
```

For each element T of s, the print_type object will be invoked with a wrap<T> argument.

9.1.2 Type Visitation

For a more general solution to the problem of smoothing out types at the function boundary, we can apply the Visitor pattern [GHJV95]:

```
struct visit_type    // generalized visitation function object
{
    template <class Visitor>
    void operator()(Visitor) const
    {
        Visitor::visit();
    }
};
template <class T>    // specific visitor for type printing
struct print_visitor
{
    static void visit()
    {
        std::cout << typeid(T).name() << std::endl;
    }
};

int main()
{
    mpl::for_each<s, print_visitor<_1> >(visit_type());
}
```

Here, the visit_type function object expects its argument type to have a static visit member function, and we can build new visitor objects for any purpose. This is a subtle change from our earlier examples with for_each, but note: print_visitor::visit is never passed a T object. Instead, for_each passes an instance of print_visitor<T>, for each T in our sequence, to visit_type. The information about the type of T is transmitted in print_visitor's template parameter.

9.2   Implementation Selection

In this section we'll discuss a few different ways to choose different runtime behaviors or interfaces based on the result of some compile time computation.

9.2.1   if Statements

The most straightforward way to control the implementation of a runtime function template is to test a static condition in an if statement, as follows:

```
template <class T>
void f(T x)
{
    if (boost::is_class<T>::value)
    {
        ...implementation 1...
    }
    else
    {
        ...implementation 2...
    }
}
```

Since the condition can be completely determined at compile time, many compilers will optimize away the is_class test, and will only generate code for the branch of the if that is selected.

This approach is clear and simple, with little or no conceptual overhead—when it works. Unfortunately, the technique isn't universally applicable. For example, consider what happens when the function above is implemented this way:

```
template <class T>
void f(T x)
{
    if (boost::is_class<T>::value)
    {
        std::cout << x::value;   // handle integral wrappers
    }
    else
    {
        std::cout << x;          // handle non-wrappers
    }
}
```

The intention here was for f to be able to print the value of an integral type (e.g., int) or of an integral constant wrapper (e.g., long_<5>). If we invoke f(42), though, we'll get a compilation error. The problem is that the entire function body needs to typecheck, including *both* branches of the if statement, and we can't access the nonexistent ::value member of an int.

9.2.2 Class Template Specialization

We can address the previous problem by moving each branch of our if statement into a distinct function: a static member function of a class template. By specializing the class template, we can decide which function implementation gets used:

```
template <bool> // handle integral constant wrappers
struct f_impl
{
    template <class T>
    static void print() { std::cout << T::value; }
};

template <>       // specialization for non-wrappers
struct f_impl<false>
{
    template <class T>
    static void print(T x) { std::cout << x; }
};

template <class T>
void f(T x)
{
    f_impl<boost::is_class<T>::value>::print(x);
};
```

This approach is similar to the one we used to implement `iter_swap` in Chapter 2, and the version using `mpl::if_`, introduced in Chapter 4, is a variation on the same theme. We'll see the same basic idea evolve further when we cover structure selection later in this chapter.

9.2.3 Tag Dispatching

We already got a taste of the tag dispatching concept from our work on the `tiny` sequence in Chapter 5, but the fundamental idea was actually borrowed from generic programming in the runtime domain. Runtime tag dispatching uses function overloading to generate executable code based on properties of a type.

A good example can be found in the `advance` algorithm of most C++ standard library implementations. Though conceptually simple—`advance` moves an iterator `i` by `n` positions—actually writing the algorithm is fairly complex. Depending on the traversal capabilities of the iterator, entirely distinct implementation strategies are required. For example, if `i` supports random access, then `advance` can be implemented with `i += n` and is very efficient: constant time. Other iterators must be advanced in steps, making the operation linear in `n`. If `i` is bidirectional, then it makes sense for `n` to be negative, so we must decide at runtime whether to increment or decrement the iterator. Any function that decrements an iterator, however, would fail to compile when passed an iterator supporting only forward traversal. So, `advance` requires at least three different implementations.

To select among them, we must use the concept information contained in the following category **tag types**:

```
namespace std
{
  struct input_iterator_tag { };
  struct forward_iterator_tag
    : input_iterator_tag { };

  struct bidirectional_iterator_tag
    : forward_iterator_tag { };

  struct random_access_iterator_tag
    : bidirectional_iterator_tag { };
}
```

A tag is simply an empty class whose only purpose is to convey some information at compile time, in this case the iterator concept modeled by a given iterator type. Every iterator type I has an associated category tag, which can be accessed as

```
std::iterator_traits<I>::iterator_category
```

Note that in this case the tags belong to an inheritance hierarchy that mirrors the *refinement* hierarchy of the concepts they represent. For example, every bidirectional iterator is also a forward iterator, so `bidirectional_iterator_tag` is derived from `forward_iterator_tag`.

Once again, we'll separate the three implementations into distinct function bodies, but this time we'll use overloading to select the right one by passing an *instance* of the iterator's empty tag type as an argument.

```
namespace std
{
  template <class InputIterator, class Distance>
  void __advance_impl(
      InputIterator& i
    , Distance n
    , input_iterator_tag)
  {
      while (n--) ++i;
  }

  template <class BidirectionalIterator, class Distance>
  void __advance_impl(
      BidirectionalIterator& i
    , Distance n
    , bidirectional_iterator_tag)
```

```
{
    if (n >= 0)
      while (n--) ++i;
    else
      while (n++) --i;
}
template <class RandomAccessIterator, class Distance>
void __advance_impl(
    RandomAccessIterator& i
  , Distance n
  , random_access_iterator_tag)
{
    i += n;
}

template <class InputIterator, class Distance>
void advance(InputIterator& i, Distance n)
{
    typedef typename
      iterator_traits<InputIterator>::iterator_category
    category;

    __advance_impl(i, n, category());
}
}
```

The outer advance function calls the __advance_impl overload that best matches the tag; the other overloads, which may use operations not implemented by a given iterator, are never instantiated. Here the inheritance hierarchy used for iterator tags works to our advantage: There is no __advance_impl specifically written for iterators whose category is forward_iterator_ tag, but since forward_iterator_tag is derived from input_iterator_tag, the compiler selects the input_iterator_tag version for input iterators *and* forward iterators. That would not have been possible had we used specialization on tag types to select implementations.

Note that mpl::true_ and mpl::false_ make fine dispatching tags. In the example below, desperate_cast<T>(x) is equivalent to static_cast<T>(x) unless x happens to be (a pointer to) an object of polymorphic class type, in which case desperate_cast<T>(x) is equivalent to dynamic_cast<T>(x).

```
// implementation for polymorphic types
template <class T, class U>
T desperate_cast_impl2(U& x,  mpl::true_)
```

```
{
    return dynamic_cast<T>(x); // legal iff U is polymorphic
}

// implementation for non-polymorphic types
template <class T, class U>
T desperate_cast_impl2(U& x,  mpl::false_)
{
    return static_cast<T>(x);
}

// dispatcher
template <class T, class U>
T desperate_cast_impl(U& x)
{
    return desperate_cast_impl2<T>(
        x
      , boost::is_polymorphic<
            typename boost::remove_pointer<U>::type
        >()
    );
}

// public interface
template <class T, class U>
T desperate_cast(U const& x) { return desperate_cast_impl<T>(x); }

template <class T, class U>
T desperate_cast(U& x) { return desperate_cast_impl<T>(x); }
```

Because of the way the integral-valued type traits are derived from their result types, we only need to create an object of the whole metafunction specialization boost::is_polymorphic<...>() to produce a tag that will match mpl::true_ or mpl::false_.

9.3   Object Generators

By this point in the book, you've probably grown somewhat comfortable with long nested template argument lists, but we're sure you haven't forgotten how unwieldy they can be. An **object generator** is a generic function used to deduce type information that might otherwise have to be written out the long way.

To see how that works, consider the following template, which *composes* two callable objects, f and g. The result is a new function object that, when invoked on an argument x, computes f(g(x)), yielding value of type R:

```
template <class R, class F, class G>
class compose_fg
{
 public:
    compose_fg(F const& f, G const& g)
      : f(f), g(g)
    {}

    template <class T>
    R operator()(T const& x) const
    {
        return f(g(x));
    }

 private:
    F f;
    G g;
};
```

The following example uses **compose_fg** to compute $-\sin^2(x)$ for each element of a sequence.

```
#include <functional>
#include <algorithm>
#include <cmath>

float input[5] = {0.0, 0.1, 0.2, 0.3, 0.4};
float output[5];

float sin_squared(double x)  { return std::sin(std::sin(x)); }

float* ignored = std::transform(
    input, input+5, output,
  , compose_fg<float,std::negate<float>,float(*)(float)>(
        std::negate<float>(), &sin_squared
    )
);
```

Whew, that compose_fg specialization certainly is an eyeful! It works, but it would prob-ably have been easier to handcraft a neg_sin_squared function for this purpose than to use `compose_fg`. At least the result would have been more readable that way. Fortunately, we can avoid writing out most of the template parameters for `compose_fg` if we have an auxiliary *object generator* function:

```
template <class R, class F, class G>
compose_fg<R,F,G> compose(F const& f, G const& g)
{
    return compose_fg<R,F,G>(f,g);
}
```

The entire purpose of `compose` is to serve as a vehicle for the function template argument deduction mechanism. Now the `transform` call can be written:

```
float* ignored = std::transform(
    input, input+5, seq2
  , compose<float>(std::negate<float>(), &sin_squared)
);
```

Because the compiler can deduce the type of the required `compose_fg` specialization from the types of the arguments to `compose`, there's no need to write the type out explicitly. Your C++ standard library's `bind1st` and `bind2nd` function templates are similar generators, yielding objects of type `binder1st` and `binder2nd`, respectively.[2]

When used to their full potential, object generators can allow users to generate some truly terrifying—but powerful—template types with a minimum of syntactic fuss. We'll learn more about how that works when we discuss type erasure later in this chapter.

9.4 Structure Selection

You already know how to use metafunctions to affect the types of individual class members:

```
template <class T>
struct X
{
    static int const m1 = metafunction1<T>::type::value;
    typedef typename metafunction2<T>::type m2;
```

---

2. The Boost Bind library—the basis for an entry in the first C++ standard technical report (TR1)—provides a much better way to do the same thing.

```
    int m4(typename metafunction3<T>::type p);
    ...
};
```

In this example, metaprograms are computing the value of m1, the type m2, and the parameter type of m4. Suppose, however, that we wanted to control whether m2 is present at all in a given specialization of X? The approach used above allows us to manage the details of a given class member, but fundamental *structural* changes to the class demand a more powerful technique.

Structure selection involves pushing the variable part of the class structure into public base classes or base class templates and using a metaprogram to choose among them. To see how it works, let's fix a problem in compose_fg, which is currently defined to be:

```
template <class R, class F, class G>
class compose_fg
{
 public:
    compose_fg(F const& f, G const& g)
      : f(f), g(g)
    {}

    template <class T>
    R operator()(T const& x) const
    {
        return f(g(x));
    }
 private:
    F f;
    G g;
};
```

You may be wondering what sort of problem there could possibly be: compose_fg is almost so simple that we can see its correctness at a glance. Furthermore, it works! The problem isn't one of correctness, but of efficiency. In our earlier example, we generated an object of type:

```
compose_fg<float,std::negate<float>,float(*)(float)>
```

so F is std::negate<float>. In most implementations, std::negate's only member is its function-call operator:

```
T operator()(const T& x) const { return -x; }
```

In other words, it is an empty class. The C++ standard, though, says that every one of `compose_fg`'s data members *must* occupy at least one byte. In a typical class layout scheme,[3] its first byte will be devoted to `f`, even though specializations of `negate` have no data members. There will follow a few bytes of padding (say three), as required to reach the appropriate memory alignment for a function pointer, and the memory for `g` (say four bytes) would follow thereafter, yielding an object of eight bytes. If we could do away with the storage for `f` altogether, the size would drop to four bytes. If `G` also turned out to be an empty class, the total size of the `compose_fg` object could, theoretically, be as small as one byte. We can't do better than that; the rules say even an empty class must have nonzero size.

One way to eliminate storage for empty classes might be to detect them (using the `boost::is_empty` type trait described in Chapter 2), and simply omit the corresponding data members. There are a few problems with that approach, however.

1. It's not transparent: Even empty classes can have nontrivial constructors and destructors, and if we don't store copies of `f` and `g`, the difference in `compose_fg`'s behavior could be surprising.

2. To implement `operator()` we still need F and G objects; if they weren't stored we'd need to construct them somehow, and they might not have default constructors.

Fortunately, there's a better solution. Compilers may implement an **Empty Base Optimization** (EBO), which allows an empty base class to be placed at the same address as any other subobject, as long as no two distinct subobjects *of the same type* share an address. For example,

```
compose_fg<float,std::negate<float>,float(*)(float)>
```

might have had ideal size if `compose_fg` had been written this way:

```
template <class R, class F, class G>
class compose_fg : F   // if empty, F may overlap with g
{
 public:
    typedef R result_type;

    compose_fg(F const& f, G const& g)
      : F(f), g(g)     // initialize base with f
    {}
```

---

3. The standard places almost no restriction on the way most classes are laid out, except that each distinct base or member subobject of a given type must have a distinct address, and members can't overlap one another. The only other exception occurs when the class is "plain old data" (POD), whose technical definition is given in section 2.5.4. In that case, class layout follows a more predictable set of rules.

```
    template <class T>
    R operator()(T const& x) const
    {
        F const& f = *this;    // retrieve F subobject
        return f(g(x));
    }
private:
    G g;
};
```

Naturally, we can't use that structure for all `compose_fg` specializations: If F were a function pointer, we'd get a compilation error because function pointers aren't legal base classes. Furthermore, we don't *want* to use that structure in all cases: When G is empty but F is not, we want to derive `compose_fg<R,F,G>` from G instead. The need for *structural* variation points to structure selection as the technique of choice.

The first step in applying structure selection is to delegate control over the variable part of the class structure. In this case, the way F and G are stored varies, so we can write:

```
// base class template to be defined later
template <class F, bool F_empty, class G,  bool G_empty>
class storage;
template <class R, class F, class G>
class compose_fg
  : storage<
    F,boost::is_empty<F>::value
  , G,boost::is_empty<G>::value
>{
    typedef
      storage<
    F,boost::is_empty<F>::value
  , G,boost::is_empty<G>::value
    > base;

public:
    compose_fg(F const& f, G const& g)
      : base(f, g)
    {}

    template <class T>
    R operator()(T const& x) const
    {
```

```
        F const& f = this->get_f();
        G const& g = this->get_g();
        return f(g(x));
    }
};
```

Now we only need to write storage so that it has the right structure for each of four combinations of F_empty and G_empty, and exposes access to the stored F and G via get_f and get_g members:[4]

```
template <class F, class G>
class storage<F,false,G,false> // neither F nor G is empty
{
 protected:
    storage(F const& f, G const& g)
      : f(f), g(g)
    {}
    F const& get_f() { return f; }
    G const& get_g() { return g; }
 private:
    F f;
    G g;
};

template <class F, class G>
class storage<F,false,G,true> // G is empty
  : private G
{
 protected:
    storage(F const& f, G const& g)
      : G(g), f(f)
    {}
    F const& get_f() { return f; }
    G const& get_g() { return *this; }
 private:
    F f;
};
```

---

4. If you noticed some corner cases where this code doesn't quite work, don't worry; you get to work out the fixes as part of this chapter's exercises.

```
template <class F, class G>
class storage<F,true,G,false> // F is empty
  : private F
{
 protected:
    storage(F const& f, G const& g)
      : F(f), g(g)
    {}
    F const& get_f() { return *this; }
    G const& get_g() { return g; }
 private:
    G g;
};

template <class F, class G>
class storage<F,true,G,true> // F and G are both empty
  : private F, private G
{
 protected:
    storage(F const& f, G const& g)
      : F(f), G(g)
    {}
    F const& get_f() { return *this; }
    G const& get_g() { return *this; }
};
```

Since the EBO is optional, there are no guarantees that any of this will make a difference. That said, by selecting among different bases, we've at least given the compiler the *opportunity* to optimize away the storage for empty subobjects, and most of them will take advantage of it (see the exercises for more information). You might also want to look at the Boost `compressed_pair` template [CDHM01], which implements a generalization of the EBO pattern we've used here.

9.5   Class Composition

If we can use structure selection once to control the structure of a class, we can use it over and over to create class structures in fine-grained steps. For example, to generate a struct whose members have types given by a type sequence, we could apply the `fold` algorithm:

```
// fine-grained struct element; stores a T and inherits More
template <class T, class More>
struct store : More
{
    T value;
};

typedef mpl::vector<short[2], long, char*,  int> member_types;

struct empty {};

mpl::fold<
    member_types, empty, store<_2,_1>
>::type generated;
```

Yielding an object `generated`, of type

```
store<int
  , store<char*
      , store<long
            , store<short[2], empty> > > >
```

Each specialization of `store` shown above represents a layer of inheritance containing a member of one of the types in `member_types`.

Actually *using* classes composed in this way can be tricky unless they are carefully structured. Although `generated` does indeed contain members of each of the types in `member_types`, they're hard to get at. The most obvious problem is that they're all called `value`: We can't access any other than the first one directly, because the rest are hidden by layers of inheritance. Unfortunately, there's nothing we can do about the repetition; it is a fact of life when applying class composition, because although we can easily generate member *types,* there's no way to generate member *names* using templates.[5]

Moreover, it's difficult to access the `value` member of a given type even by casting to an appropriate base class. To see why, consider what's involved in accessing the `long` value stored in `generated`. Because each `store` specialization is derived from its second argument, we'd have to write:

```
long& x = static_cast<
            store<long, store<short[2], empty> >&
          >(generated).value;
```

5. Member name generation is possible using preprocessor metaprogramming. See Appendix A for more information.

In other words, accessing any member of `store` requires knowing all the types following its type in the original sequence. We could let the compiler's function argument deduction mechanism do the work of figuring out the base class chain for us:

```
template <class T, class U>
store<T,U> const& get(store<T,U> const& e)
{
    return e;
}

char* s = get<char*>(generated).value;
```

In the example above, `get`'s first template argument is constrained to be `char*`, and the effective function parameter becomes `store<char*,U> const&`, which matches the base class of `generated` containing a `char*` member.

A slightly different pattern allows us to solve this problem a bit more neatly. As usual, the Fundamental Theorem of Software Engineering[6] applies. We'll just add a layer of indirection:

```
// fine-grained struct element; wraps a T
template <class T>
struct wrap
{
    T value;
};

// one more level of indirection
template <class U, class V>
struct inherit : U, V
{};

typedef mpl::vector<short[2], long, char*, int> member_types;

struct empty {};

mpl::fold<
    member_types, empty, inherit<wrap<_2>,_1>
>::type generated;
```

Now the type of `generated` is:

---

6. See Chapter 2 for the origin of this term.

```
inherit<wrap<int>
  , inherit<wrap<char*>
      , inherit<wrap<long>
          , inherit<wrap<short[2]>
              , empty
            >
        >
    >
>
```

Since `inherit<U,V>` is derived from both U and V, the type above is (indirectly) derived from wrap<T> for each T in the sequence. We can now access a `value` member of type `long` with:

```
long& x = static_cast<wrap<long> &>(generated).value;
```

Class generation along these lines is a common metaprogramming activity, so MPL provides ready-made tools for that purpose. In particular, we can replace `empty` and `inherit` with `mpl::empty_base` and `mpl::inherit`. The library also contains an appropriately named `inherit_linearly` metafunction that calls `fold` for us with a default initial type of `mpl::empty_base`:

```
template <class Types, class Node, class Root = empty_base>
struct inherit_linearly
  : fold<Types,Root,Node>
{
};
```

With these tools in hand, we can rewrite our last example more conveniently as:

```
#include <boost/mpl/inherit.hpp>
#include <boost/mpl/inherit_linearly.hpp>
#include <boost/mpl/vector.hpp>

// fine-grained struct element
template <class T>
struct wrap
{
    T value;
};

typedef mpl::vector<short[2], long, char*, int> member_types;
```

```
mpl::inherit_linearly<
    member_types, mpl::inherit<wrap<_2>,_1>
>::type generated;
```

Practical applications of these class composition patterns have been extensively explored by
Andrei Alexandrescu [Ale01]. For example, he uses class composition to generate visitor classes for
a generic multiple dispatch framework.

9.6   (Member) Function Pointers as Template Arguments

Integral constants are not the only kind of non-type template parameters. In fact, almost any kind of
value that can be determined at compile time is allowed, including:

- Pointers and references to specific functions

- Pointers and references to statically stored data

- Pointers to member functions

- And pointers to data members

We can achieve dramatic efficiency gains by using these kinds of template parameters. When
our earlier `compose_fg` class template is used on two function pointers, it is always at least as large
as the pointers themselves: It needs to store the values. When a function pointer is passed as a
parameter, however, no storage is needed at all.

To illustrate this technique, let's build a new composing function object template:

```
template <class R, class F, F f, class G, G g>
struct compose_fg2
{
    typedef R result_type;

    template <class T>
    R operator()(T const& x) const
    {
        return f(g(x));
    }
};
```

Note, in particular, that `compose_fg2` has no data members. We can use it to compute $\sin^2(\log_2(x))$
for each element of a sequence:

```
#include <functional>
#include <algorithm>
#include <cmath>

float input[5] = {0.0, 0.1, 0.2, 0.3, 0.4};
float output[5];

inline float log2(float x) { return std::log(x)/std::log(2.0f); }

typedef float (*floatfun)(float);

float* ignored = std::transform(
    input, input+5, output
  , compose_fg2<float, floatfun,sin_squared, floatfun,log2>()
);
```

Don't be fooled by the fact that there are function pointers involved here: on most compilers, you won't pay for an indirect function call. Because it knows the precise identity of the functions indicated by f and g, the compiler should optimize away the empty compose_fg2 object passed to std::transform and generate direct calls to log2 and sin_squared in the body of the instantiated transform algorithm.

For all its efficiency benefits, compose_fg2 comes with some notable limitations.

- Because *values* of class type are not legal template parameters, compose_fg2 can't be used to compose arbitrary function objects (but see exercise 9-4).

- There's no way to build an object generator function for compose_fg2. An object generator would have to accept the functions to be composed as function arguments and use those values as arguments to the compose_fg2 template:

```
template <class R, class F, class G>
compose_fg2<R,F,f,G,g> compose(F f, G g)
{
    return compose_fg2<R,F,f,G,g>();   // error
}
```

Unfortunately, any value passed to a function enters the runtime world irretrievably. At that point, there's no way to use it as an argument to a class template without causing a compiler error.[7]

---

[7]. Language extensions that would bypass this limitation are currently under discussion in the C++ standardization community, so watch for progress in the next few years.

9.7   Type Erasure

While most of this book's examples have stressed the value of static type information, it's sometimes more appropriate to throw that information away. To see what we mean, consider the following two expressions:

1.   `compose<float>(std::negate<float>(), &sin_squared)`

   with type

   `compose_fg<float,std::negate<float>,float(*)(float)>`

2.   `std::bind2nd(std::multiplies<float>(), 3.14159)`

   with type

   `std::binder2nd<std::multiplies<float> >`

Even though the results of these expressions have different types, they have one essential thing in common: We can invoke either one with an argument of type `float` and get a `float` result back. The common interface that allows either expression to be substituted for the other in a generic function call is a classic example of static polymorphism:

```
std::transform(
    input, input+5, output
  , compose<float>(std::negate<float>(), &sin_squared)
);

std::transform(
    input, input+5, output
  , std::bind2nd(std::multiplies<float>(), 3.14159)
);
```

Function templates aren't always the best way to handle polymorphism, though.

- Systems whose structure changes at runtime—graphical user interfaces, for example—often require runtime dispatching.

- Function templates can't be compiled into object code and shipped in libraries.

- Each instantiation of a function template typically results in new machine code. That can be a good thing when the function is in your program's critical path or is very small, because the code may be inlined and localized. If the call is not a significant bottleneck, though, your program may get bigger and sometimes even slower.

9.7.1   An Example

Imagine that we've prototyped an algorithm for an astounding screensaver and that to keep users interested we're looking for ways to let them customize its behavior. The algorithm to generate the screens is pretty complicated, but it's easily tweaked: By replacing a simple numerical function that's called once per frame in the algorithm's core, we can make it generate distinctively different patterns. It would be wasteful to templatize the whole screensaver just to allow this parameterization, so instead we decide to use a pointer to a transformation function:

```cpp
typedef float (*floatfunc)(float);

class screensaver
{
 public:
    explicit screensaver(floatfunc get_seed)
      : get_seed(get_seed)
    {}

    pixel_map next_screen()   // main algorithm
    {
        float center_pixel_brightness = ...;
        float seed = this->get_seed(center_pixel_brightness);
        complex computation using seed...
    }
 private:
    floatfunc get_seed;
    other members...
};
```

We spend a few days coming up with a menu of interesting customization functions, and we set up a user interface to choose among them. Just as we're getting ready to ship it, though, we discover a new family of customizations that allows us to generate many new astounding patterns. These new customizations require us to maintain a state vector of 128 integer parameters that is modified on each call to next_screen().

9.7.2   Generalizing

We could integrate our discovery by adding a std::vector<int> member to screensaver, and changing next_screen to pass that as an additional argument to the customize function:

```cpp
class screensaver
{
    pixel_map next_screen()
    {
        float center_pixel_brightness = ...;
        float seed = this->get_seed(center_pixel_brightness,
                                    state);
        ...
    }
 private:
    std::vector<int> state;
    float (*get_seed)(float, std::vector<int>& s);
    ...
};
```

If we did that, we'd be forced to rewrite our existing transformations to accept a state vector they don't need. Furthermore, it's beginning to look as though we'll keep discovering interesting new ways to customize the algorithm, so this hardcoded choice of customization interface looks rather unattractive. After all, our next customization might need a different type of state data altogether. If we replace the customization function pointer with a customization *class,* we can bundle the state with the class instance and eliminate the screensaver's dependency on a particular type of state:

```cpp
class screensaver
{
 public:
    struct customization
    {
        virtual ~customization() {}
        virtual float operator()(float) const = 0;
    };

    explicit screensaver(std::auto_ptr<customization> c)
      : get_seed(c)
    {}
    pixel_map next_screen()
    {
        float center_pixel_brightness = ...;
        float seed = (*this->get_seed)(center_pixel_brightness);
        ...
    }
```

```
    private:
        std::auto_ptr<customization> get_seed;
        ...
};
```

9.7.3 "Manual" Type Erasure

Now we can write a class that holds the extra state as a member, and implement our customization in its `operator()`:

```
struct hypnotic : screensaver::customization
{
    float operator()(float) const
    {
        ...use this->state...
    }
    std::vector<int> state;
};
```

To fit the customizations that don't need a state vector into this new framework, we need to wrap them in classes derived from `screensaver::customization`:

```
struct funwrapper : screensaver::customization
{
    funwrapper(floatfunc pf)
      : pf(pf) {}

    float operator()(float x) const
    {
        return this->pf(x);
    }

    floatfunc pf; // stored function pointer
};
```

Now we begin to see the first clues of type erasure at work. The runtime-polymorphic base class `screensaver::customization` is used to "erase" the details of two derived classes—from the point-of-view of `screensaver`, `hypnotic` and `funwrapper` are invisible, as are the stored state vector and function pointer type.

If you're about to object that what we've shown you is just "good old object-oriented programming," you're right. The story isn't finished yet, though: There are plenty of other types whose instances can be called with a `float` argument, yielding another `float`. If we want to customize `screensaver` with a preexisting function that accepts a `double` argument, we'll need to make another wrapper. The same goes for any callable class, even if its function call operator matches the `float (float)` signature exactly.

9.7.4 Automatic Type Erasure

Wouldn't it be far better to automate wrapper building? By templatizing the derived customization and `screensaver`'s constructor, we can do just that:

```
class screensaver
{
 private:
    struct customization
    {
        virtual ~customization() {}
        virtual float operator()(float) const = 0;
    };

    template <class F>                    // a wrapper for an F
    struct wrapper : customization
    {
        explicit wrapper(F f)
          : f(f) {}                       // store an F

        float operator()(float x) const
        {
            return this->f(x);            // delegate to stored F
        }

     private:
        F f;
    };

 public:
    template <class F>
    explicit screensaver(F const& f)
      : get_seed(new wrapper<F>(f))
    {}
    ...
```

```
    private:
        std::auto_ptr<customization> get_seed;
        ...
};
```

We can now pass any function pointer or function object to `screensaver`'s constructor, as long as what we pass can be invoked with a `float` argument and the result can be converted back into a `float`. The constructor "erases" the static type information contained in its argument while preserving access to its essential functionality—the ability to call it with a `float` and get a `float` result back—through `customization`'s virtual function call operator. To make type erasure really compelling, though, we'll have to carry this one step further by separating it from `screensaver` altogether.

9.7.5   Preserving the Interface

In its fullest expression, **type erasure** is the process of turning a wide variety of types with a common interface into one type with *that same interface.* So far, we've been turning a variety of function pointer and object types into an `auto_ptr<customization>`, which we're then storing as a member of our `screensaver`. That `auto_ptr` isn't callable, though: only its "pointee" is. However, we're not far from having a generalized `float`-to-`float` function. In fact, we could almost get there by adding a function-call operator to `screensaver` itself. Instead, let's refactor the whole function-wrapping apparatus into a separate `float_function` class so we can use it in any project. Then we'll be able to boil our `screensaver` class down to:

```
class screensaver
{
 public:
    explicit screensaver(float_function f)
      : get_seed(f)
    {}

    pixel_map next_screen()
    {
        float center_pixel_brightness = ...;
        float seed = this->get_seed(center_pixel_brightness);
        ...
    }

 private:
    float_function get_seed;
    ...
};
```

The refactoring is going to reveal another part of the common interface of all function objects that, so far, we've taken for granted: copyability. In order to make it possible to copy `float_function` objects and store them in the `screensaver`, we've gone through the same "virtualization" process with the wrapped type's copy constructor that we used on its function call operator—which explains the presence of the `clone` function in the next implementation.

```
class float_function
{

private:
    struct impl
    {
        virtual ~impl() {}
        virtual impl* clone() const = 0;
        virtual float operator()(float) const = 0;
    };

    template <class F>
    struct wrapper : impl
    {
        explicit wrapper(F const& f)
          : f(f) {}

        impl* clone() const
        {
            return new wrapper<F>(this->f); // delegate
        }

        float operator()(float x) const
        {
            return f(x);                          // delegate
        }

    private:
        F f;
    };

public:
    // implicit conversion from F
    template <class F>
    float_function(F const& f)
      : pimpl(new wrapper<F>(f)) {}
```

```
    float_function(float_function const& rhs)
      : pimpl(rhs.pimpl->clone()) {}

    float_function& operator=(float_function const& rhs)
    {
        this->pimpl.reset(rhs.pimpl->clone());
        return *this;
    }

    float operator()(float x) const
    {
        return (*this->pimpl)(x);
    }
 private:
    std::auto_ptr<impl> pimpl;
};
```

Now we have a class that can "capture" the functionality of *any* type that's callable with a `float` and whose return type can be converted to a `float`. This basic pattern is at the core of the Boost Function library—another library represented in TR1—where it is generalized to support arbitrary arguments and return types. Our entire definition of `float_function` could, in fact, be replaced with this typedef:

```
typedef boost::function<float (float x)> float_function;
```

The template argument to `boost::function` is a function type that specifies the argument and return types of the resulting function object.

9.8 The Curiously Recurring Template Pattern

The pattern named in this section's title was first identified by James Coplien [Cop96] as "curiously recurring" because it seems to arise so often. Without further ado, here it is.

The Curiously Recurring Template Pattern (CRTP)

A class X has, as a base class, a template specialization taking X itself as an argument:

```
class X
  : public base<X>
{
   ...
};
```

Because of the way X is derived from a class that "knows about" X itself, the pattern is sometimes also called "curiously recursive."

CRTP is powerful because of the way template instantiation works: Although *declarations* in the base class template are instantiated when the derived class is declared (or instantiated, if it too is templated), the *bodies* of member functions of the base class template are only instantiated after the entire declaration of the derived class is known to the compiler. As a result, these member functions can use details of the derived class.

9.8.1 Generating Functions

The following example shows how CRTP can be used to generate an `operator>` for any class that supports prefix `operator<`:

```
#include <cassert>

template <class T>
struct ordered
{
    bool operator>(T const& rhs) const
    {
        // locate full derived object
        T const& self = static_cast<T const&>(*this);
        return rhs < self;
    }
};

class Int
  : public ordered<Int>
{
```

```
public:
    explicit Int(int x)
      : value(x) {}

    bool operator<(Int const& rhs) const
    {
        return this->value < rhs.value;
    }

    int value;
};

int main()
{
    assert(Int(4) < Int(6));
    assert(Int(9) > Int(6));
}
```

The technique of using a `static_cast` with CRTP to reach the derived object is sometimes called the "Barton and Nackman trick" because it first appeared in John Barton and Lee Nackman's *Scientific and Engineering C++* [BN94]. Though written in 1994, Barton and Nackman's book pioneered generic programming and metaprogramming techniques that are still considered advanced today. We highly recommend this book.

CRTP and Type Safety

Generally speaking, casts open a type safety hole, but in this case it's not a very big one, because the `static_cast` will only compile if T is derived from `ordered<T>`. The only way to get into trouble is to derive two different classes from the *same* specialization of `ordered`:

```
class Int : public ordered<Int> { ... };
class bogus : public ordered<Int> {};
bool crash = bogus() > Int();
```

In this case, because Int is already derived from `ordered<Int>`, the `operator>` compiles but the `static_cast` attempts to cast a pointer that refers to a bogus instance into a pointer to an Int, inducing undefined behavior.

Another variation of the trick can be used to define non-member friend functions in the namespace of the base class:

```
namespace crtp
{
  template <class T>
  struct signed_number
  {
      friend T abs(T x)
      {
          return x < 0 ? -x : x;
      }
  };
}
```

If `signed_number<T>` is used as a base class for any class supporting unary negation and comparison with 0, it automatically acquires a non-member `abs` function:

```
class Float : crtp::signed_number<Float>
{
 public:
    Float(float x)
      : value(x)
    {}

    Float operator-() const
    {
        return Float(-value);
    }

    bool operator<(float x) const
    {
        return value < x;
    }

    float value;
};

Float const minus_pi = -3.14159265;
Float const pi = abs(minus_pi);
```

Here the `abs` function is found in namespace `crtp` by **argument-dependent lookup** (ADL). Only unqualified calls are subject to ADL, which searches the namespaces of function arguments and their bases for viable overloads.

It's a curious property of friend functions defined in the body of a class template that, unless also declared outside the body, they can *only* be found via ADL. Explicit qualification doesn't work:

```
Float const erroneous = crtp::abs(pi); // error
```

Keep that limitation in mind when generating free functions with CRTP.

9.8.2 Managing Overload Resolution

In its simplest form, CRTP is used to establish an inheritance relationship among otherwise unrelated classes for the purpose of overload resolution, and to avoid overly general function template arguments. For example, if we are writing a generic function `drive`, which operates on Vehicles (where Vehicle is a Concept), we could write:

```
template <class Vehicle>
void drive(Vehicle const& v)
{ ... }
```

This definition is perfectly fine until someone writes a generic function called "`drive`" that operates on Screws:

```
template <class Screw>
void drive(Screw const& s)
{ ... }
```

The problem is that while the identifiers `Vehicle` and `Screw` have meaning to us, they are equivalent as far as the compiler is concerned. If the two `drive`s are in the same namespace, both declarations refer to the *same* entity. If both function bodies are visible, we'll get a compilation error, but if only one body is visible, we'll have quietly violated the standard's "One Definition Rule," leading to undefined behavior.

Even if they're not in the same namespace, unqualified calls to `drive` may be ambiguous, or worse, may end up invoking the wrong function. Because of the way that ADL quietly adds distant functions to the overload set, and because unqualified function calls are so natural, writing completely general function templates with parameters that can match all types is extremely dangerous. Consider the following contrived example:

```
#include <list>

namespace utility
{
  // fill the range with zeroes
  template <class Iterator>
  Iterator clear(Iterator const& start, Iterator const& finish);
```

```
    // perform some transformation on the sequence
    template <class Iterator>
    int munge(Iterator start, Iterator finish)
    {
        // ...
        start = clear(start, finish);
        // ...
    }
}

namespace paint
{
  template <class Canvas, class Color>  // generalized template
  void clear(Canvas&, Color const&);

  struct some_canvas {  };
  struct black { };

  std::list<some_canvas> canvases(10);
  int x = utility::munge(canvases.begin(), canvases.end());
}
```

In fact, the instantiation of munge usually won't compile, because the list iterators will be class
templates parameterized on paint::some_canvas. Argument-dependent lookup sees that parameter and finds a definition of clear in namespace paint, which is added to the overload set. Inside
munge, paint::clear happens to be a slightly better match than utility::clear for the arguments passed. Fortunately for us, paint::clear returns void, so the assignment fails—but just
imagine that clear returned a Canvas&. In that case, the code might have compiled "cleanly," but
it would have silently done something completely unintended.

To solve this problem, we can use the curiously recurring template pattern to identify models of
our Vehicle and Screw concepts. We only need to add the requirement that models of each concept
be publicly derived from a corresponding CRTP base class:

```
template <class Derived>
struct vehicle
{};

template <class Derived>
struct screw
{};
```

Now our drive function templates can be rewritten to be more discriminating. The usual
downcasts apply:

```
template <class Vehicle>
void drive(vehicle<Vehicle> const& v)
{
    Vehicle const& v_= static_cast<Vehicle const&>(v);
    ...
};

template <class Screw>
void drive(screw<Screw> const& s)
{
    Screw const& s_= static_cast<Screw const&>(s);
    ...
};
```

9.9   Explicitly Managing the Overload Set

Sometimes, CRTP is inadequate for limiting the reach of generalized function template arguments. For example, we may want our function template to operate on built-in types (which cannot have base classes), or on existing third-party types that we don't want to modify. Fortunately, if we can determine the appropriateness of an argument type at compile time, Boost's `enable_if` family of templates will allow us to manage the overload set non-intrusively.

For example, the following function template applies only to iterators over arithmetic types. The examples in this section use `boost::iterator_value`, a metafunction that retrieves an iterator's `value_type`.

```
#include <iterator>
#include <boost/utility/enable_if.hpp>
#include <boost/type_traits/is_arithmetic.hpp>
#include <boost/iterator/iterator_traits.hpp>

template <class Iterator>
typename boost::enable_if<
    boost::is_arithmetic<                   // enabling condition
        typename boost::iterator_value<Iterator>::type
    >
  , typename                                // return type
      boost::iterator_value<Iterator>::type
>::type
sum(Iterator start, Iterator end)
{
```

```
    typename boost::iterator_value<Iterator>::type x(0);
    for (;start != end; ++start)
        x += *start;
    return x;
}
```

If the `::value` of the enabling condition C is `true`, `enable_if<C,T>::type` will be T, so
`sum` just returns an object of `Iterator`'s `value_type`. Otherwise, `sum` simply disappears from
the overload resolution process! We'll explain *why* it disappears in a moment, but to get a feeling
for what that means, consider this: If we try to call `sum` on iterators over non-arithmetic types, the
compiler will report that no function matches the call. If we had simply written

```
    std::iterator_traits<Iterator>::value_type
```

in place of `enable_if<...>:: type`, calling `sum` on iterators whose `value_type` is `std::`
`vector<int>` would fail inside `sum` where it attempts to use `operator+=`. If the iterators'
`value_type` were `std::string`, it would actually compile cleanly, but possibly with an unde-
sired result.

This technique really becomes interesting when there are function overloads in play. Because `sum`
has been restricted to appropriate arguments, we can now add an overload that will allow us to sum
all the arithmetic elements of `vector<vector<int> >` and other nested containers of arithmetic
types.

```
    // given an Iterator that points to a container, get the
    // value_type of that container's iterators.
    template <class Iterator>
    struct inner_value
      : boost::iterator_value<
          typename boost::iterator_value<Iterator>::type::iterator
      >
    {};

    template <class Iterator>
    typename boost::lazy_disable_if<
        boost::is_arithmetic<                    // disabling condition
          typename boost::iterator_value<Iterator>::type
        >
      , inner_value<Iterator>                     // result metafunction
    >::type
    sum(Iterator start, Iterator end)
    {
```

```
typename inner_value<Iterator>::type x(0);

for (;start != end; ++start)
    x += sum(start->begin(), start->end());

return x;
}
```

The word "disable" in `lazy_disable_if` indicates that the function is removed from the overload set when the condition is *satisfied*. The word "lazy" means that the function's result `::type` is the result of *calling* the second argument as a nullary metafunction.[8]

Note that `inner_value<Iterator>` can only be invoked if `Iterator`'s value type is another iterator. Otherwise, there will be an error when it fails to find the inner (non-)iterator's value type. If we tried to compute the result type greedily, there would be error during overload resolution whenever `Iterator`'s value type turned out to be an arithmetic type and not another iterator.

Now let's take a look at how the magic works. Here's the definition of `enable_if`:

```
template <bool, class T = void>
struct enable_if_c
{
    typedef T type;
};

template <class T>
struct enable_if_c<false, T>
{};

template <class Cond, class T = void>
struct enable_if
  : enable_if_c<Cond::value, T>
{};
```

Notice that when C is `false`, `enable_if_c<C,T>::type` doesn't exist! The C++ standard's overload resolution rules (section 14.8.3) say that when a function template's argument deduction fails, it contributes nothing to the set of candidate functions considered for a given call, and it does *not* cause an error.[9] This principle has been dubbed "Substitution Failure Is Not An Error" (SFINAE) by David Vandevoorde and Nicolai Josuttis [VJ02].

---

8. For completeness, `enable_if.hpp` includes plain `disable_if` and `lazy_enable_if` templates, as well as _c-suffixed versions of all four templates that accept integral constants instead of wrappers as a first argument.

9.10   The "sizeof Trick"

Although values used as function arguments pass into the runtime world permanently, it is possible
to get *some* information at compile time about the result type of a function call by using the `sizeof`
operator. This technique has been the basis of numerous low-level template metafunctions, including
many components of the Boost Type Traits library. For example, given:

```
typedef char yes;        // sizeof(yes) == 1
typedef char (&no)[2];   // sizeof(no)  == 2
```

we can write a trait separating classes and unions from other types, as follows:

```
template <class T>
struct is_class_or_union
{
    // SFINAE eliminates this when the type of arg is invalid
    template <class U>
    static yes tester(int U::*arg);

    // overload resolution prefers anything at all over "..."
    template <class U>
    static no tester(...);

    // see which overload is chosen when U == T
    static bool const value
        = sizeof(is_class_or_union::tester<T>(0)) == sizeof(yes);

    typedef mpl::bool_<value> type;
};

struct X{};
BOOST_STATIC_ASSERT(is_class_or_union<X>::value);
BOOST_STATIC_ASSERT(!is_class_or_union<int>::value);
```

This particular combination of SFINAE with the `sizeof` trick was first discovered by Paul
Mensonides in March 2002. It's a shame that in standard C++ we can only pull the size of an

---

9. You might be wondering why `inner_value` and lazy evaluation were needed, while `enable_if` itself doesn't cause
an error. The template argument deduction rules include a clause (14.8.2, paragraph 2) that enumerates conditions under
which an invalid deduced type in a function template signature will cause deduction to fail. It turns out that the form used by
`enable_if` is in the list, but that errors during instantiation of other templates (such as `iterator_value`) during argument
deduction are not.

expression's type, but not the type itself, back from runtime. For example, it would be nice to be able to write:

```
// generalized addition function object
struct add
{
    template <class T, class U>
    typeof(T+U) operator()(T const& t, U const& u)
    {
        return t+u;
    }
};
```

Though it's not in the standard, many compilers already include a `typeof` operator (sometimes with one of the reserved spellings "`__typeof`" or "`__typeof__`"), and the C++ committee is very seriously discussing how to add this capability to the standard language. The feature is so useful that over the years several library-only implementations of `typeof` have been developed, all of which ultimately rely on the more limited capabilities of `sizeof` [Dew02]. The library implementations aren't fully automatic: User-defined types must be manually associated with unique numbers, usually through specializations of some traits class. You can find code and tests for one such library by Arkadiy Vertleyb in the pre-release materials on this book's companion CD.

9.11   Summary

The techniques presented in this chapter may seem to be a hodgepodge collection of programming tricks, but they all have one thing in common: They connect pure compile-time metaprograms to runtime constructs in powerful ways. There are certainly a few other such mechanisms lurking out there, but those we've covered here should give you enough tools to make your metaprograms' presence felt in the real world of runtime data.

9.12   Exercises

9-0.   Many compilers contain a "single-inheritance" EBO. That is, they will allocate an empty base at the same address as a data member, but they will never allocate two bases at the same address. On these compilers, our `storage` implementation is suboptimal for the case where F and G are both empty. Patch `storage` to avoid this pitfall when `NO_MI_EBO` is defined in the preprocessor.

9-1. What happens to our `compose` template when F and G are the *same* empty class? How would you fix the problem? Write a test that fails with identical empty F and G, then fix `compose_fg` so that the test passes.

9-2. We may not be able to compose *arbitrary* function objects with `compose_fg2`, but we can use it to compose statically initialized function objects. (Hint: Review the list at the beginning of section 9.6 of types that can be passed as template arguments). Compile a small program that does so and, if you can read your compiler's assembly-language output, analyze the efficiency of the resulting code.

9-3*. Write a generalized iterator template that uses type erasure to wrap an arbitrary iterator type and present it with a runtime-polymorphic interface. The template should accept the iterator's `value_type` as its first parameter and its `iterator_category` as the second parameter. (Hint 1: Use Boost's `iterator_facade` template to make writing the iterator easier. Hint 2: You can control whether a given member function is virtual by using structure selection.)

9-4. Change the `sum` overload example in section 9.9 so that it can add the arithmetic innermost elements of arbitrarily nested containers such as `std::list<std::list<std::vector<int> > >`. Test your changes to show that they work.

9-5. Revisit the dimensional analysis code in Chapter 3. Instead of using `BOOST_STATIC_ASSERT` to detect dimension conflicts within `operator+` and `operator-`, apply SFINAE to eliminate inappropriate combinations of parameters from the overload sets for those operators. Compare the error messages you get when misusing `operator+` and `operator-` in both cases.

10

Domain-Specific Embedded Languages

If syntactic sugar didn't count, we'd all be programming in assembly language.

This chapter covers what we believe to be the most important application area for metaprogramming in general and C++ metaprogramming in particular: building *domain-specific embedded languages* (DSELs).

Most of the template metaprogramming techniques we use today were invented in the course of implementing a DSEL. C++ metaprograms first began to be used for DSEL creation sometime in 1995, with impressive results. Interest in metaprogramming has grown steadily ever since, but—maybe because a new way to exploit templates seems to be discovered every week—this excitement is often focused on implementation techniques. As a result, we've tended to overlook the power and beauty of the design principles for which the techniques were invented. In this chapter we'll explore those principles and paint the big picture behind the methodology.

10.1 A Little Language . . .

By now you may be wondering, "What is a domain-specific language, anyway?" Let's start with an example (we'll get to the "embedded" part later).

Consider searching some text for the first occurrence of any hyphenated word, such as "domain-specific." If you've ever used **regular expressions**,[1] we're pretty sure you're not considering writing your own character-by-character search. In fact, we'd be a little surprised if you aren't thinking of using a regular expression like this one:

```
\w+(-\w+)+
```

---

1. For an introduction to regular expressions, you might want to take a half-hour break from this book and grab some fine manual on the topic, for instance *Mastering Regular Expressions,* 2nd Edition, by Jeffrey E. F. Friedl. If you'd like a little theoretical grounding, you might look at *The Theory of Computation,* by Bernard Moret. It also covers finite state machines, which we're going to discuss in the next chapter.

If you're not familiar with regular expressions, the incantation above may look rather cryptic, but if you are, you probably find it concise and expressive. The breakdown is as follows:

- \w means "any character that can be part of a **word**"

- + (positive closure) means "one or more repetitions"

- – simply represents itself, the hyphen character

- Parentheses group subexpressions as in arithmetic, so the final + modifies the whole subexpression -\w+

So the whole pattern matches any string of words separated by single hyphens.

The syntax of regular expressions was specifically designed to allow a short and effective representation of textual patterns. Once you've learned it, you have in your arsenal a little tool—a language, in fact, with its own alphabet, rules, and semantics. Regular expressions are so effective in their particular problem domain that learning to use them is well worth the effort, and we always think twice before abandoning them for an ad hoc solution. It shouldn't be hard to figure out where we are going here—regular expressions are a classic example of a **domain-specific language**, or **DSL** for short.

There are a couple of distinguishing properties here that allow us to characterize something as a DSL. First, of course, it has to be a language. Perhaps surprisingly, though, that property is easy to satisfy—just about anything that has the following features constitutes a formal language.

1. An alphabet (a set of symbols).

2. A well-defined set of rules saying how the alphabet may be used to build well-formed compositions.

3. A well-defined subset of all well-formed compositions that are assigned specific meanings.

Note that the alphabet doesn't even have to be textual. Morse code and UML are well-known languages that use graphical alphabets. Both are not only examples of somewhat unusual yet perfectly valid formal languages, but also happen to be lovely DSLs.

Now, the *domain-specific* part of the language characteristic is more interesting, and gives DSLs their second distinguishing property.

Perhaps the simplest way to interpret "domain-specific" would be "anything that isn't general-purpose." Although admittedly that would make it easy to classify languages ("Is HMTL a general-purpose language? No? Then it's domain-specific!"), that interpretation fails to capture the properties of these little languages that make them so compelling. For instance, it is obvious that the language of regular expressions can't be called "general-purpose" — in fact, you might have been justifiably reluctant to call it a *language* at all, at least until we presented our definition of the word. Still, regular expressions give us something beyond a lack of familiar programming constructs that makes them worthy of being called a DSL.

In particular, by using regular expressions, we trade general-purposeness for *a significantly higher level of abstraction and expressiveness.* The specialized alphabet and notations allow us to express pattern-matching at a level of abstraction that matches our mental model. The elements of regular expressions—characters, repetitions, optionals, subpatterns, and so on—all map directly onto concepts that we'd use if asked to describe a pattern in words.

Making it possible to write code in terms close to the abstractions of the problem domain is *the* characteristic property of, and motivation behind, all DSLs. In the best-case scenario, the abstractions in code are identical to those in the mental model: You simply use the language's domain-specific notation to write down a statement of the problem itself, and the language's semantics take care of generating a solution.

That may sound unrealistic, but in practice it's not as rare as you might think. When the FORTRAN programming language was created, it seemed to some people to herald the end of programming. The original IBM memo [IBM54] about the language said:

> *Since FORTRAN should virtually eliminate coding and debugging, it should be possible to solve problems for less than half the cost that would be required without such a system.*

By the standards of the day, that was true: FORTRAN did "virtually" eliminate coding and debugging. Since the major problems of most programmers at the time were at the level of how to write correct loops and subroutine calls, programming in FORTRAN may have seemed to be nothing more than writing down a description of the problem. Clearly, the emergence of high-level general-purpose languages has raised the bar on what we consider "coding."

The most successful DSLs are often **declarative** languages, providing us with notations to describe **what** rather than **how.** As you will see further on, this declarative nature plays a significant role in their attractiveness and power.

10.2 . . . Goes a Long Way

Jon Bentley, in his excellent article on DSLs, wrote that "programmers deal with microscopic languages every day" [Bent86]. Now that you are aware of their fundamental properties, it's easy to see that little languages are all around us.

In fact, the examples are so numerous that this book can't possibly discuss all of them—we estimate that thousands of DSLs are in common use today—but we can survey a few to present you with some more perspective.

10.2.1 The Make Utility Language

Building software rapidly, reliably, and repeatably is crucial to the daily practice of software development. It also happens to be important to the deployment of reusable software and—increasingly in the age of open-source software—end-user installation. A great many tools have cropped up over the years to address this problem, but they are nearly all variations of a single, powerful, build-description language: Make. As a C++ programmer, you're probably already at least a little familiar with Make, but we're going to go through a mini-review here with a focus on its "DSL-ness" and with an eye toward the design of your own domain-specific languages.

The principal domain abstraction of Make is built around three concepts.

Targets.   Usually files that need to be built or sources that are read as inputs to parts of the build process, but also "fake" targets naming states of the build process that might not be associated with a single file.

Dependencies.   Relationships between targets that allow Make to determine when a target is not up-to-date and therefore needs to be rebuilt.

Commands.   The actions taken in order to build or update a target, typically commands in the native system's shell language.

The central Make language construct is called a **rule,** and is described with the following syntax in a "Makefile":

```
dependent-target : source-targets
        commands
```

So, for example, a Makefile to build a program from C++ sources might look like this:

```
my_program: a.cpp b.cpp c.cpp d.cpp
        c++ -o my_program a.cpp b.cpp c.cpp d.cpp
```

where c++ is the command that invokes the C++ compiler. These two lines demonstrate that Make allows a concise representation of its domain abstractions: **targets** (my_program and the .cpp files), their **dependency** relationships, and the **command** used to create dependent targets from their dependencies.

The designers of Make recognized that such rules include some boilerplate repetition of filenames, so they included support for **variables** as a secondary capability. Using a variable, the above "program" might become:

```
SOURCES = a.cpp b.cpp c.cpp d.cpp
my_program: $(SOURCES)
        c++ -o my_program $(SOURCES)
```

Unfortunately, this is not a very realistic example for most C/C++ programs, which contain dependencies on header files. To ensure minimal and rapid rebuilds once headers enter the picture, it becomes important to build separate object files and represent their individual dependencies on headers. Here's an example based on one from the GNU Make manual:

```
OBJECTS = main.o kbd.o command.o display.o \
          insert.o search.o files.o utils.o

edit : $(OBJECTS)
        c++ -o edit $(OBJECTS)
main.o : main.cpp defs.h
        c++ -c main.cpp
kbd.o : kbd.cpp defs.h command.h
        c++ -c kbd.cpp
command.o : command.cpp defs.h command.h
        c++ -c command.cpp
display.o : display.cpp defs.h buffer.h
        c++ -c display.cpp
insert.o : insert.cpp defs.h buffer.h
        c++ -c insert.cpp
search.o : search.cpp defs.h buffer.h
        c++ -c search.cpp
files.o : files.cpp defs.h buffer.h command.h
        c++ -c files.cpp
utils.o : utils.cpp defs.h
        c++ -c utils.cpp
```

Once again you can see some repeated boilerplate in the commands used to build each object file. That can be addressed with "implicit pattern rules," which describe how to build one kind of target from another:

```
%.o: %.cpp
        c++ -c $(CFLAGS) $< -o $@
```

This rule uses pattern-matching to describe how to construct a `.o` file from a `.cpp` file on which it depends, and the funny symbols $< and $@ represent the results of those matches. In fact, this particular rule is so commonly needed that it's probably built into your Make system, so the Makefile becomes:

```
OBJECTS = main.o kbd.o command.o display.o \
          insert.o search.o files.o utils.o
```

```
edit : $(OBJECTS)
        c++ -o edit $(OBJECTS)

main.o : main.cpp defs.h
kbd.o : kbd.cpp defs.h command.h
command.o : command.cpp defs.h command.h
display.o : display.cpp defs.h buffer.h
insert.o : insert.cpp defs.h buffer.h
search.o : search.cpp defs.h buffer.h
files.o : files.cpp defs.h buffer.h command.h
utils.o : utils.cpp defs.h
```

Enough review! Exploring all the features of Make could easily fill an entire book. The purpose of this exercise is to show that Make begins to approach the domain-specific language ideal of allowing a problem to be solved merely by describing it—in this case, by writing down the names of files and their relationships.

In fact, most of the other features of various Make variants are aimed at getting still closer to the ideal. GNU Make, for example, can automatically discover eligible source files in the working directory, explore their header dependencies, and synthesize the rules to build intermediate targets and the final executable. In a classic example of *creolization* [Veld04], GNU Make has sprouted so many features that it approaches the power of a general-purpose language—but such a clumsy one that for all practical purposes it is still domain-specific.

10.2.2 Backus Naur Form

After all this discussion of meta*programming*, we're going to introduce the idea of a meta*syntax*. That's exactly what Backus Naur Form (BNF) is: a little language for defining the syntax of formal languages.[2] The principal domain abstraction of BNF is called a "context-free grammar," and it is built around two concepts.

Symbols.   Abstract elements of the syntax. Symbols in the grammar for C++ include *identifier, unary-operator, string-literal, new-expression, statement,* and *declaration.* The first three are never composed of other symbols in the grammar and are called **terminal symbols** or **tokens**. The rest can be built from zero or more symbols and are called **nonterminals**

Productions (or "rules").   The legal patterns for combining consecutive symbols to form nonterminal symbols. For example, in C++ a *new-expression* can be formed by combining the new keyword (a token) with a *new-type-id* (a nonterminal).

---

2. BNF was actually first developed to specify the syntax of the programming language Algol-60.

Productions are normally written according to the syntax:

```
nonterminal -> symbols...
```

where the *nonterminal* symbol to the left of the arrow can be matched by any input sequence matching the sequence of *symbols* on the right.

Here is a grammar for simple arithmetic expressions, written in BNF, with terminals shown in **bold** and nonterminals shown in *italics:*

```
expression -> term
expression -> expression + term
expression -> expression - term

term -> factor
term -> term * factor
term -> term / factor

factor -> integer
factor -> group

group -> ( expression )
```

That is, an *expression* is matched by a *term,* or by an *expression* followed by the + token and a *term,* or by an *expression* followed by the - token and a *term.* Similarly, a *term* is matched by a *factor*, or by a *term* followed by the * token and a *factor*, or by a *term* followed by the / token and a *factor*... and so on.

This grammar not only encodes the allowed syntax of an *expression* (ultimately just one or more **integer**s separated by +, -, *, or /), but, by grouping syntactic elements according to the operators' usual associativity and precedence rules, it also represents some important semantic information. For example, the structure of

```
1 + 2 * 3 + 4
```

when parsed according to the above grammar, can be represented as:

```
[1 + [2 * 3]] + 4
```

In other words, the subexpression 2 * 3 will be grouped into a single *term* and then combined with 1 to form a new (sub-) *expression.* There is no way to parse the expression so as to generate an incorrect grouping such as

```
[[1 + 2] * 3] + 4
```

Try it yourself; the grammar simply doesn't allow the *expression* 1 + 2 to be followed by *. BNF is very efficient for encoding both the syntax *and the structure* of formal languages.

A few linguistic refinements are possible: For example, it's customary to group all productions that yield a given nonterminal, so the | symbol is sometimes used to separate the different right-hand-side alternatives without repeating the "*nonterminal* ->" boilerplate:

```
expression -> term
           | term + expression
           | term - expression
```

Extended BNF (**EBNF**), another variant, adds the use of parentheses for grouping, and the Kleene star ("zero-or-more") and positive closure ("one-or-more") operators that you may recognize from regular expressions for repetition. For example, all the rules for *expression* can be combined into the following EBNF:

```
expression -> ( term +  | term - )*  term
```

That is, "an *expression* is matched by a sequence of zero or more repetitions of [a *term* and a + token or a *term* and a - token], followed by a *term*."

All grammars written in EBNF can be transformed into standard BNF with a few simple steps, so the fundamental expressive power is the same no matter which notation is used. It's really a question of emphasis: EBNF tends to clarify the allowable inputs at the cost of making the parse structure somewhat less apparent.

10.2.3 YACC

As we mentioned in Chapter 1, YACC (Yet Another Compiler Compiler) is a tool for building parsers, interpreters, and compilers. YACC is a *translator* whose input language is a form of augmented BNF, and whose output is a C/C++ program that does the specified parsing and interpreting. Among computer language jocks, the process of interpreting some parsed input is known as **semantic evaluation**. YACC supports semantic evaluation by allowing us to associate some data (a **semantic value**) with each symbol and some C/C++ code (a **semantic action**) with the rule. The semantic action, enclosed in braces, computes the semantic value of the rule's left-hand-side nonterminal from those of its constituent symbols. A complete YACC program for parsing and evaluating arithmetic expressions follows:

```
%{ // C++ code to be inserted in the generated source file
   #include <cstdio>
   typedef int YYSTYPE; // the type of all semantic values

   int yylex();                        // forward
   void yyerror(char const* msg);      // forward
%}
```

```
%token INTEGER      /* declare a symbolic multi-character token */
%start lines        /* lines is the start symbol */

%% /* grammar rules and actions */
expression : term
           | expression '+' term { $$ = $1 + $3; }
           | expression '-' term { $$ = $1 - $3; }
           ;
term : factor
     | term '*' factor  { $$ = $1 * $3; }
     | term '/' factor  { $$ = $1 / $3; }
     ;

factor : INTEGER
       | group
       ;

group : '(' expression ')'   { $$ = $2; }
      ;

lines : lines expression
        {
          std::printf("= %d\n", $2);   // after every expression
          std::fflush(stdout);         // print its value
        }
        '\n'
      | /* empty */
      ;

%% /* C++ code to be inserted in the generated source file */
#include <cctype>

int yylex()  // tokenizer function
{
  int c;

  // skip whitespace
  do { c = std::getchar(); }
  while (c == ' ' || c == '\t' || c == '\r');

  if (c == EOF)
    return 0;
```

```
  if (std::isdigit (c))
  {
      std::ungetc(c, stdin);
      std::scanf("%d", &yylval); // store semantic value
      return INTEGER;
  }
  return c;
}
// standard error handler
void yyerror(char const* msg) { std::fprintf(stderr,msg); }

int main() { int yyparse(); return yyparse(); }
```

As you can see, some of the C++ program fragments in curly braces are not quite C++: they contain these funny $$ and n symbols (where n is an integer). When YACC translates these program fragments to C++, it replaces $$ with a reference to the semantic value for the rule's left-hand-side nonterminal, and n with the semantic value for the nth right-hand-side symbol. The semantic actions above come out looking like this in the generated C++:

```
yym = yylen[yyn];
yyval = yyvsp[1-yym];
switch (yyn)
{
case 1:
{ std::printf("= %d \n", yyvsp[0]); std::fflush(stdout); }
break;
case 8:
{ yyval = yyvsp[-2] * yyvsp[0]; }
break;
case 9:
{ yyval = yyvsp[-2] / yyvsp[0]; }
break;
case 11:
{ yyval = yyvsp[-2] + yyvsp[0]; }
break;
case 12:
{ yyval = yyvsp[-2] - yyvsp[0]; }
break;
}
yyssp -= yym;
...
```

This code is just a fragment of a source file full of similar unreadable ugliness; in fact, the BNF part of the grammar is expressed in terms of large arrays of integers known as **parse tables**:

```
const short yylhs[] = {
    -1,
    2,    0,    0,    3,    3,    4,    5,    5,    5,    1,
    1,    1,
};
const short yylen[] = {
    2,
    0,    4,    0,    1,    1,    3,    1,    3,    3,    1,
    3,    3,
};
const short yydefred[] = { ... };
const short yydgoto[] = { ... };
const short yysindex[] = { ... };
const short yyrindex[] = { ... };
const short yygindex[] = { ... };
```

You don't need to understand how to generated code works: It's the job of the DSL to protect us from all of those ugly details, allowing us to express the grammar in high-level terms.

10.2.4   DSL Summary

It should be clear at this point that DSLs can make code more concise and easy-to-write. The benefits of using little languages go well beyond rapid coding, though. Whereas expedient programming shortcuts can often make code harder to understand and maintain, a domain-specific language usually has the opposite effect due to its high-level abstractions. Just imagine trying to maintain the low-level parser program *generated* by YACC for our little expression parser: Unless we had the foresight to maintain a comment containing something very close to the YACC program itself, we'd have to reverse engineer the BNF from the parse tables and match it up to the semantic actions. The maintainability effect becomes more extreme the closer the language gets to the domain abstraction. As we approach the ideal language, it's often possible to tell at a glance whether a program solves the problem it was designed for.

Imagine, for a moment, that you're writing control software for the Acme Clean-Burning Nuclear Fusion Reactor. The following formula from a scientific paper describes how to combine voltage levels from three sensors into a temperature reading:

$$T = (a + 3.1)(b + 4.63)(c + 2 \times 10^8)$$

You need to implement the computation as part of the reactor's failsafe mechanism. Naturally, using operator notation (C++'s domain-specific sublanguage for arithmetic) you'd write:

```
T = ( a + 3.1 ) * ( b + 4.63 ) * ( c + 2E8 );
```

Now compare that to the code you'd have to write if C++ didn't include support for operators:

```
T =  mul(mul(add(a, 3.1), add(b, 4.63)), add(c, 2E8));
```

Which notation do you trust more to help prevent a meltdown? Which one is easier to match up with the formula from the paper? We think the answer is obvious. A quick glance at the code using operator notation shows that it implements the formula correctly. What we have here is a true example of something many claim to have seen, or even to have produced themselves, but that in reality is seldom encountered in the wild: *self-documenting code.*

Arithmetic notation evolved into the standard we use today because it clearly expresses both the intent and the structure of calculations with a minimum of extra syntax. Because mathematics is so important to the foundation of programming, most computer languages have built-in support for standard mathematical notation for operations on their primitive types. Many have sprouted support for operator overloading, allowing users to express calculations on user-defined types like vectors and matrices in a language that is similarly close to the native domain abstraction.

Because the system knows the problem domain, it can generate error reports at the same conceptual level the programmer uses. For example, YACC detects and reports on grammatical ambiguities, describing them in terms of grammar productions rather than dumping the details of its parse tables. Having domain knowledge can even enable some pretty impressive optimizations, as you'll see when we discuss the Blitz++ library later in this chapter.

Before moving on, we'd like to make a last observation about DSLs: It's probably no coincidence that both Make and BNF have a "rule" concept. That's because DSLs tend to be *declarative* rather than *imperative* languages. Informally, declarative languages *describe* rather than *prescribe*. A purely declarative program mentions only entities (e.g., symbols, targets) and their relationships (e.g., parse rules, dependencies); the processing or algorithmic part of the program is entirely encoded in the program that interprets the language. One way to think of a declarative program is as an immutable data structure, to be used by the language's conceptual execution engine.

10.3   DSLs, Inside Out

The original Make program contained a very weak programming language of its own, adequate only for the basic software construction jobs to which it was first applied. Since then, Make variants have extended that language, but they all remain somewhat crippled by their origins, and none approaches the expressivity of what we'd call a general-purpose language. Typical large-scale systems using Make dispatch some of the processing work to Perl scripts or other homebrew add-ons, resulting in a system that's often hard to understand and modify.

The designers of YACC, on the other hand, recognized that the challenge of providing a powerful language for expressing semantic actions was better left to other tools. In some sense, YACC's input language actually contains all the capability of whichever language you use to process its output. You're writing a compiler and you need a symbol table? Great, add `#include <map>` to your initial `%{...%}` block, and you can happily use the STL in your semantic actions. You're parsing XML and you want to send it to a SAX (Simple API for XML) interpreter on-the-fly? It's no problem, because the YACC input language *embeds* C/C++.

However, the YACC approach is not without its shortcomings. First of all, there is the cost of implementing and maintaining a new compiler: in this case, the YACC program itself. Also, a C++ programmer who doesn't already know YACC has to learn the new language's rules. In the case of YACC it mostly amounts to syntax, but in general there may be new rules for all sorts of things—variable binding, scoping, and name lookup, to name a few. If you want to see how bad it can get, consider all the different kinds of rules in C++. Without an additional investment in tools development, there are no pre-existing facilities for testing or debugging the programs written in the DSL at their own level of abstraction, so problems often have to be investigated at the low level of the target language, in machine-generated code.

Lastly, traditional DSLs impose serious constraints on language interoperability. YACC, for example, has little or no access to the *structure* of the C/C++ program fragments it processes. It simply finds nonquoted $ symbols (which are illegal in real C++) and replaces them with the names of corresponding C++ objects—a textual substitution. This simple approach works fine for YACC, because it doesn't need the ability to make deductions about such things as C++ types, values, or control flow. In a DSL where general-purpose language constructs *themselves* are part of the domain abstraction, trivial text manipulations usually don't cut the mustard.

These interoperability problems also prevent DSLs from working together. Imagine that you're unhappy with Make's syntax and limited built-in language, and you want to write a new high-level software construction language. It seems natural to use YACC to express the new language's grammar. Make is still quite useful for expressing and interpreting the low-level build system concepts (targets, dependencies, and build commands), so it would be equally natural to express the language's semantics using Make. YACC actions, however, are written in C or C++. The best we can do is to write C++ program fragments that write Makefiles, adding yet another compilation phase to the process: First YACC code is compiled into C++, then the C++ is compiled and executed to generate a Makefile, and finally Make is invoked to interpret it. Whew! It begins to look as though you'll need our high-level software construction language just to integrate the various phases involved in building and using the language itself!

One way to address all of these weaknesses is to turn the YACC approach inside out: Instead of embedding the general-purpose language in the DSL, embed the domain-specific language in a general-purpose host language. The idea of doing that in C++ may seem a little strange to you, since you're probably aware that C++ doesn't allow us to add arbitrary syntax extensions. How can we embed another language inside C++? Sure, we could write an interpreter in C++ and interpret programs at runtime, but that wouldn't solve the interoperability problems we've been hinting at.

Well, it's not that mysterious, and we hope you'll forgive us for making it seem like it is. After all, every "traditional" library targeting a particular well-defined domain—be it geometry, graphics, or matrix multiplication—can be thought of as a little language: its interface defines the syntax, and its implementation, the semantics. There's a bit more to it, but that's the basic principle. We can already hear you asking, "If this is just about libraries, why have we wasted the whole chapter discussing YACC and Make?" Well, it's not *just* about libraries. Consider the following quote from "Domain-Specific Languages for Software Engineering" by Ian Heering and Marjan Mernick [Heer02]:

> In combination with an application library, any general purpose programming language can act as a DSL, so why were DSLs developed in the first place? Simply because they can offer domain-specificity in better ways:
>
> • Appropriate or established domain-specific notations are usually beyond the limited user-definable operator notation offered by general purpose languages. A DSL offers domain-specific notations from the start. Their importance cannot be overestimated as they are directly related to the suitability for end user programming and, more generally, the programmer productivity improvement associated with the use of DSLs.
>
> • Appropriate domain-specific constructs and abstractions cannot always be mapped in a straightforward way on functions or objects that can be put in a library. This means a general purpose language using an application library can only express these constructs indirectly. Again, a DSL would incorporate domain-specific constructs from the start.

In short:

Definition

A true **DSL** incorporates domain-specific notation, constructs, and abstractions as fundamental design considerations. A domain-specific *embedded* language (**DSEL**) is simply a library that meets the same criteria.

This inside-out approach addresses many of the problems of translators like YACC and interpreters like Make. The job of designing, implementing, and maintaining the DSL itself is reduced to that of producing a library. However, implementation cost isn't the most important factor, since both DSLs and traditional library implementations are long-term investments that we hope will pay off over the many times the code is used. The real payoff lies in the complete elimination of the costs usually associated with crossing a language boundary.

The DSEL's core language rules are dictated by the host language, so the learning curve for an embedded language is considerably flatter than that of its standalone counterpart. All of the programmer's familiar tools for editing, testing, and debugging the host language can be applied to the DSEL. By definition, the host language compiler itself is also used, so extra translation phases are eliminated, dramatically reducing the complexity of software construction. Finally, while library interoperability presents occasional issues in any software system, when compared with the problems of composing ordinary DSLs, integrating multiple DSELs is almost effortless. A programmer can make seamless transitions between the general-purpose host language and any of several domain-specific embedded languages without giving it a second thought.

10.4   C++ as the Host Language

Fortunately for us, C++ turns out to be a one-of-a-kind language for implementing DSELs. Its multiparadigm heritage has left C++ bristling with tools we can use to build libraries that combine syntactic expressivity with runtime efficiency. In particular, C++ provides

- A static type system

- The ability to achieve near-zero abstraction penalty[3]

- Powerful optimizers

- A template system that can be used to

    - generate new types and functions
    - perform arbitrary computations at compile time
    - dissect existing program components (e.g., using the type categorization metafunctions of the Boost Type Traits library)

- A macro preprocessor providing (textual) code generation capability orthogonal to that of templates (see Appendix A)

- A rich set of built-in symbolic operators (48!)—many of which have several possible spellings—that can be overloaded with practically no limitations on their semantics

Table 10.1 lists the syntactic constructs provided by operator overloading in C++. Table entries with several lines show some little-known alternative spellings for the same tokens.

---

3. With current compilers, avoiding abstraction penalties sometimes requires a great deal of attention from the programmer. Todd Veldhuizen has described a technique called "guaranteed optimization," in which various kinds of abstraction can be applied at will, with no chance of hurting performance [Veld04].

Table 10.1 C++ Overloadable Operator Syntaxes

$+a$	$-a$	$a + b$	$a - b$
$++a$	$--a$	$a++$	$a--$
$a * b$	a / b	$a \% b$	a , b
$a \& b$ a bitand b	$a \mid b$ a bitor b	$a \wedge b$ a ??' b a xor b	$\sim a$??-a compl a
$a \&\& b$ a and b	$a \mid\mid b$ a or b	$a >> b$	$a << b$
$a > b$	$a < b$	$a >= b$	$a <= b$
$a == b$	$a != b$ a not_eq b	! a not a	$a = b$
$a += b$	$a -= b$	$a *= b$	$a /= b$
$a \%= b$	$a \&= b$ a and_eq b	$a \mid= b$ a or_eq b	$a \wedge= b$ a xor_eq b
$a >>= b$	$a <<= b$	$*a$	$\&a$
a->$name$	a->$*name$	$a[b]$ a??(b??) a<:b:>	$a(arguments)$
new $ctor$-$expr$	delete a		

The unique combination of these features in C++ has made possible a category of domain-specific libraries that are both efficient and syntactically close to languages one might build from scratch.[4] Moreover, these libraries can be written in pure C++, giving them important advantages over standalone DSLs, which require special compilers, editors, and other tools. In the following sections we'll discuss some examples, in each case focusing on the DSL's *design* rather than its implementation.

Namespace Names

Until now, we've been fairly disciplined about always prefixing names from namespace boost with boost:: and names from boost::mpl with mpl:: to avoid confusion. In this chapter only, to emphasize the "sugary" aspects of DSL syntax, we're going to omit namespace names from library identifiers, and trust you to guess where the names come from.

---

4. Haskell is another language that certainly deserves mention when considering platforms for building DSELs. Haskell's strengths for DSEL construction overlap considerably with those of C++, and go even further in some areas. For example, Haskell programmers can define new operators with which to extend the built-in language syntax. Haskell's compilation model, however, tends to limit peak performance.

10.5   Blitz++ and Expression Templates

Blitz++ [Veld95a], a library for high-performance array math, pioneered so many of the techniques and ideas used in this book that it would be hard to overestimate its influence on the world of C++ metaprogramming. It was the first C++ library to use explicit metaprogramming,[5] and the first to implement a domain-specific embedded language. We can't possibly touch on all aspects of Blitz++, so we're going to look at the central innovation: *expression templates* [Veld95b].

10.5.1   The Problem

If we had to boil the problem solved by Blitz++ down to a single sentence, we'd say, "A naive implementation of array math is horribly inefficient for any interesting computation." To see what we mean, take the boring statement

```
x = a + b + c;
```

where x, a, b, and c are all two-dimensional Arrays. The canonical implementation of Array's addition operator is:

```
Array operator+(Array const& a, Array const& b)
{
    std::size_t const n = a.size();
    Array result;

    for (std::size_t row = 0; row != n; ++row)
        for (std::size_t col = 0; col != n; ++col)
            result[row][col] = a[row][col] + b[row][col];

    return result;
}
```

To evaluate the expression a + b + c using that operator, we first compute a + b, resulting in a temporary Array (call it t), and then we evaluate t + c to produce the final result.

The problem is that temporary, t. The efficient way to perform this computation is to step through each position in *all three* input arrays at once, adding the three elements at that position and placing their sum in the result:

---

5. By "explicit metaprogramming" we mean treating template instantiations as first-class compile-time programs. Explicit metaprogramming goes well beyond the sort of trivial type manipulations required for most generic programming, such as accessing the value_type of an iterator through std::iterator_traits. Although that could technically be seen as a metafunction invocation, most generic programmers don't think of it that way, and it's one's *relationship* to the code, as much as anything else, that defines metaprogramming.

```
for (std::size_t row = 0; row != n; ++row)
   for (std::size_t col = 0; col != n; ++col)
      result[row][col] = a[row][col] + b[row][col] + c[row][col];
```

The temporary not only costs an extra dynamic memory allocation for its element storage, but causes the CPU to make *two* complete traversals of that storage: one to write the result of a + b, and another to read the input for t + c. As anyone who has done high-performance numerics knows, these two traversals are the real killer, because they destroy cache locality. If all four of the named arrays nearly fill the cache, introducing t effectively pushes one of them out.

The problem here is that the operator+ signature above is just too greedy: It tries to evaluate a + b just as soon as it can, rather than waiting until the whole expression, including the addition of c, is available.

10.5.2   Expression Templates

In the expression's parse tree, evaluation starts at the leaves and proceeds upwards to the root. What's needed here is some way of delaying evaluation until the library has all of the expression's parts: that is, until the assignment operator is executed. The stratagem taken by Blitz++ is to build a replica of the compiler's parse tree for the whole expression, allowing it to manage evaluation from the top down (see Figure 10.1).

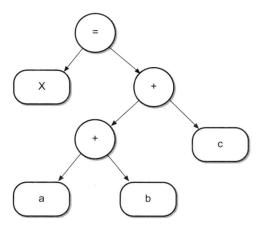

Figure 10.1 Parse tree for x = a + b + c

This can't be any ordinary parse tree, though: Since array expressions may involve other operations like multiplication, which require their own evaluation strategies, and since expressions can be arbitrarily large and nested, a parse tree built with nodes and pointers would have to be traversed at runtime by the Blitz++ evaluation engine to discover its structure, thereby limiting performance. Furthermore, Blitz++ would have to use some kind of runtime dispatching to handle the different combinations of operation types, again limiting performance.

Instead, Blitz++ builds a *compile-time* parse tree out of *expression templates*. Here's how it works in a nutshell: Instead of returning a newly computed `Array`, operators just package up references to their arguments in an `Expression` instance, labeled with the operation:

```
// operation tags
struct plus; struct minus;

// expression tree node
template <class L, class OpTag, class R>
struct Expression
{
    Expression(L const& l, R const& r)
      : l(l), r(r) {}

    float operator[](unsigned index) const;

    L const& l;
    R const& r;
};

// addition operator
template <class L, class R>
Expression<L,plus,R> operator+(L const& l, R const& r)
{
    return Expression<L,plus,R>(l, r);
}
```

Notice that when we write a + b, we still have all the information needed to do the computation— it's encoded in the type `Expression<Array,plus,Array>`—and the data is accessible through the expression's stored references. When we write a + b + c, we get a result of type:

```
Expression<Expression<Array,plus,Array>,plus,Array>
```

and the data is still accessible through the nested references. The interesting thing about the `Expression` class template is that, just like an `Array`, it supports indexing via `operator[]`. But wait! Didn't we just tell you that `operator+` computes nothing, and `Expression` just stores references to its arguments? Yes, we did. If the result of the operation isn't stored in the `Expression`, it must be computed lazily by `operator[]`.

To see how it works, check out this simplified implementation for one-dimensional `Array`s of
`float`s. First, to associate the elementwise arithmetic logic with the operation tags, we'll nest some
static member functions:

```
// operation tags implement elementwise arithmetic
struct plus
{
  static float apply(float a, float b)
    { return a + b; }
};

struct minus
{
  static float apply(float a, float b)
    { return a - b; }
};
```

Next, we'll give the `Expression` an indexing operator that calls its tag's `apply` function to
compute the appropriate element value:

```
// expression tree node
template <class L, class OpTag, class R>
struct Expression
{
    Expression(L const& l, R const& r)
      : l(l), r(r) {}

    float operator[](unsigned index) const
    {
      return OpTag::apply(l[index], r[index]);
    }

    L const& l;
    R const& r;
};
```

This seems almost too simple, right? Amazingly, we now have fully lazy expression evaluation.
To see it at work, let's walk through the evaluation of `(a + b)[1]`. Since the type of `a + b` is
`Expression<Array,plus,Array>`, we have:

```
(a + b)[1]
  == plus::apply(a[1], b[1])
  == a[1] + b[1]
```

Now consider what we'd go through to evaluate the same expression with a greedy strategy. That's right, we'd have to compute a temporary array, (a + b), only to throw out all but one element! The contrast in efficiency couldn't be more striking.

Naturally, (a + b + c)[1] is also computed without any temporary Arrays:

```
(a + b + c)[1]
  == ((a + b) + c)[1]
  == plus::apply((a + b)[1], c[1])
  == plus::apply(plus::apply(a[1], b[1]), c[1])
  == plus::apply(a[1] + b[1], c[1])
  == (a[1] + b[1]) + c[1]
```

All that remains now is to implement Array's assignment operator. Since we can access any single element of the result Expression without ever creating a temporary Array, we can compute the *whole* result by accessing *every* element of the expression:

```
template <class Expr>
Array& Array::operator=(Expr const& x)
{
    for (unsigned i = 0; i < this->size(); ++i)
        (*this)[i] = x[i];
    return *this;
}
```

That's it! Naturally, there's a lot more to array math than addition and subtraction, and Blitz++ has to consider all kinds of things that are not handled by our simple example, from operations like multiplication to "tiling" large array operations so that they stay within the cache. The basic technique of delaying expression evaluation, however, is the tool that allows the library to do all these things with near-optimal efficiency.[6]

As a DSL, this part of Blitz++ is deceptive in its smoothness: The syntax looks exactly as you'd expect it to in a naive implementation, but you can see that behind the syntax lives a highly specialized evaluation engine, tuned for the Blitz++ domain.

---

6. If it seems to you that we've just demonstrated a way to abuse C++ operator overloading, we plead guilty! In fact, we're going to spend much of this chapter looking at creative ways to "abuse" the operators. We hope that by the end, you'll see these techniques as legitimate and well-founded programming paradigms.

Intermediate Results

One drawback of expression templates is that they tend to encourage writing large, complicated expressions, because evaluation is only delayed until the assignment operator is invoked. If a programmer wants to reuse some intermediate result without evaluating it early, she may be forced to declare a complicated type like:

```
Expression<
    Expression<Array,plus,Array>
  , plus
  , Expression<Array,minus,Array>
> intermediate = a + b + (c - d);
```

(or worse). Notice how this type not only exactly and redundantly reflects the structure of the computation—and so would need to be maintained as the formula changes—but also overwhelms it? This is a long-standing problem for C++ DSELs. The usual workaround is to capture the expression using type erasure (see Chapter 9), but in that case one pays for dynamic dispatching.

There has been much discussion recently, spearheaded by Bjarne Stroustrup himself, about reusing the vestigial `auto` keyword to get type deduction in variable declarations, so that the above could be rewritten as:

```
auto intermediate = a + b + (c - d);
```

This feature would be a huge advantage to C++ DSEL authors and users alike.

10.5.3   More Blitz++ Magic

Just in case you find it hard to see the domain-specific language in what we've already covered, here are just a couple more of Blitz++'s syntactic innovations that we think you'll find more striking.

10.5.3.1   Array Initialization

Because Blitz++ `Arrays` are not what the C++ standard calls an "aggregate" (see section 8.5.1 of the Standard), we can't use the convenient syntax of listing initializers within braces, as we can with ordinary built-in arrays. Instead, Blitz++ overloads the comma operator to make a similar syntax possible:

```
Array<float,2> A(3,3);
A = 1, 2, 3,
    4, 5, 6,
    7, 8, 9;
```

10.5.3.2 SubArray Syntax

Blitz++ has a `Range` class that encapsulates a sequence of indices. When an `Array` is indexed using a `Range`, a lazy SubArray view is produced without copying any elements:[7]

```
// add the first two rows and columns of A to B
B += A(Range(0,2), Range(0,2))
```

The exciting thing about Blitz++'s `Range` objects is that you can also perform arithmetic on them directly, resulting in expressions that look remarkably like the body of a multiply-nested loop, using a technique pioneered by the Math.h++ library [KV89]. This example is taken from the online Blitz++ manual:

```
// a three-dimensional stencil (used in solving PDEs)
Range I(1,6), J(1,6), K(1,6);
B = (A(I,J,K) + A(I+1,J,K) + A(I-1,J,K) + A(I,J+1,K)
 + A(I,J-1,K) + A(I,J+1,K) + A(I,J,K+1) + A(I,J,K-1)) / 7.0;
```

This sort of notational simplification has proven itself to be more than mere syntactic sugar. Similar techniques have been used to reduce the evaluation of complex tensor equations from unreadable and error-prone code resembling FORTRAN (called "C++tran" by Scott Haney) to one-liners resembling the equations in the original theory [Land01]. Projects that would be practically impossible to complete correctly using C++tran suddenly become tractable with a DSEL.

10.6 General-Purpose DSELs

One of the nicest features of DSELs is that we can apply them in the domain of general-purpose programming idioms. In other words, a DSEL can function as a kind of extension to the general-purpose host language. Although it may seem contradictory to use the terms "general-purpose" and "domain-specific" when discussing the same library, it makes sense when you consider the domain to be the specific programming idiom enabled by the DSEL.

---

7. Note that Blitz++, like most array packages, uses `operator()` instead of `operator[]` for indexing, because `operator()` allows multiple arguments whereas `operator[]` does not.

10.6.1   Named Parameters

Named parameters is a feature of many languages that allows arguments to be passed by name rather than by position. We'd love to see it supported directly in C++. For example, in an imaginary C++ that supports named parameters, given the declaration:

```
void f(int score = 0, char const* name = "x", float slew = .1);
```

we might call f this way:

```
f(slew = .799, name = "z");
```

Note that the role of each actual argument is now perfectly clear at the call site, and defaults can be used for any parameter without regard to its position or the other parameters being passed. A similar principle can of course be applied to template parameters. As you can imagine, named parameters really begin to pay off in interfaces that accept several independent arguments, each of which has a nontrivial default. Many such functions can be found in the algorithms of the Boost Graph library.

The Graph library's original named parameter DSL used a technique called "member function chaining" to aggregate parameter values into a single function argument, essentially forming a tuple of tagged values. The usage in our example would look something like:

```
f(slew(.799).name("z"));
```

Here, the expression slew(.799) would build a instance of class named_params<slew_tag, float, nil_t> having the empty class nil_t as its only base class, and containing the value .799 as a single data member. Then, its name member function would be called with "z" to produce an instance of:

```
named_params<
    name_tag, char const [2]      // .name("z")
  , named_params<
        slew_tag, double const    // slew(.799)
      , nil_t
    >
>
```

having a copy of the instance just described as its only base, and containing a reference to "z" as its only data member. We could go into detail about how each tagged value can be extracted from such a structure, but at this point in the book we're sure your brain is already working that out for itself, so we leave it as an exercise. Instead, we'd like to focus on the chosen syntax of the DSL, and what's required to make it work.

If you think for a moment about it, you'll see that not only do we need a top-level function for each parameter name (to generate the initial `named_params` instance in a chain), but `named_params` must also contain a member function for *each* of the parameter names we might want to follow it with. After all, we might just as well have written:

```
f(slew(.799).score(55));
```

Since the named parameter interface pays off best when there are many optional parameters, and because there will probably be some overlap in the parameter names used by various functions in a given library, we're going to end up with a lot of *coupling* in the design. There will be a single, central `named_params` definition used for all functions in the library that use named parameter interfaces. Adding a new parameter name to a function declared in one header will mean going back and modifying the definition of `named_params`, which in turn will cause the recompilation of every translation unit that uses our named parameter interface.

While writing this book, we reconsidered the interface used for named function parameter support. With a little experimentation we discovered that it's possible to provide the ideal syntax by using keyword objects with overloaded assignment operators:

```
f(slew = .799, name = "z");
```

Not only is this syntax nicer for users, but adding a new parameter name is easy for the writer of the library containing `f`, and it doesn't cause any coupling. We're not going to get into the implementation details of this named parameter library here; it's straightforward enough that we suggest you try implementing it yourself as an exercise.

Before moving on, we should also mention that it's possible to introduce similar support for named *class template* parameters [AS01a, AS01b], though we don't know of a way to create such nice syntax. The best usage we've been able to come up with looks like this:

```
some_class_template<
    slew_type_is<float>        // slew_type = float
  , name_type_is<char const*>  // slew_type = char const*
>
```

Maybe you can discover some improvement we haven't considered.

10.6.2   Building Anonymous Functions

For another example of "library-based language extension," consider the problem of building function objects for STL algorithms. We looked briefly at runtime lambda expressions in Chapter 6. Many computer languages have incorporated features for generating function objects on-the-fly, the lack of which in C++ is often cited as a weakness. As of this writing, there have been no fewer than *four* major DSL efforts targeted at function object construction.

10.6.2.1 The Boost Bind Library

The simplest one of these, the Boost Bind library [Dimov02], is limited in scope to three features, a couple of which should be familiar to you from your experience with MPL's lambda expressions. To understand the analogy you'll need to know that, just as MPL has placeholder *types* that can be passed as template arguments, the Bind library has placeholder *objects* that can be passed as function arguments.

The first feature of Boost.Bind is **partial function (object) application**, that is, binding argument values to a function (object), yielding a new function object with fewer parameters. For example, to produce a function object that prepends `"hello, "` to a string, we could write:

```
bind(std::plus<std::string>(), "hello, ", _1)
```

The resulting function object can be called this way:

```
std:: cout << bind(                       // prints "hello, world"
            std::plus<std::string>()
          , "hello, ", _1
        )("world");
```

Note that it's not very realistic to see the outer function argument (`"world"`) right next to the `bind` invocation. In real code we'll usually pass the result of calling `bind` to some algorithm that will proceed to invoke it multiple times.

The second feature of Boost.Bind is **function composition.** For example, the following expression produces a function object that computes $y = x(x - 0.5)$:

```
bind(
    std::multiplies<float>()
  , _1
  , bind(std::minus<float>(), _1, 0.5))
```

To us, it seems so natural that `bind` should operate this way that we have to think hard to imagine the alternative: If the inner `bind` expression were not given special treatment by the library, the function object it produces would be passed as the first argument to the `std::multiplies<float>` instance, causing an error.

Lastly, Boost.Bind allows us to invoke member functions with ordinary function call syntax. The basic idea—that member functions—can be seen as free functions accepting an initial class argument is supported by languages such as Dylan, but once again, not by native C++. This is more than an aesthetic concern, though: The different syntax for invoking free and member functions can be a serious problem for generic code that may need to work with both.

Using the Bind library, we can transform a member function `X::foo` declared as

```
struct X { float foo(float) const; } obj;
```

into a function object, and invoke it as follows:

```
bind(&X::foo, _1, _2)(obj, pi)
```

One of the most popular ways to use `bind` is to partially apply a member function to a class instance. For example, the following calls `v.visit(x)` on each element x in [`first, last`):

```
std::for_each(first, last, bind(&Visitor::visit, v, _1));
```

This limited use of partial application is so important in event-based software that Borland implemented a C++ language extension **closures** to support it directly in their compiler.

Before moving on, let's briefly compare the syntax of the `bind` expressions used above with what we'd get using the STL binders and composers:[8]

```
// partial application
bind1st(std::plus<std::string>(), "hello, ")

// function composition
compose2(
    std::multiplies<float>()
  , bind2nd(std::minus<float>(), 1)
  , identity<float>())

// invoking a member function with function call syntax
mem_fun_ref(&X::foo)(obj, pi)

std::for_each(
    first
  , last
  , bind1st(mem_fun_ref(&Visitor::visit), v));
```

We think there's a good argument that even the small amount of syntactic sugar provided by Boost.Bind begins to look like a domain-specific language by comparison.

---

8. `compose1`, `compose2`, and `identity` were included in the original STL design, but never made it into the C++ standard library. You can still find them implemented as extensions in the SGI STL, STLPort, and other standard library implementations.

10.6.2.2   The Boost Lambda Library

The Boost Lambda library, by Jaakko Järvi and Gary Powell, was the original inspiration for Boost.Bind, and for the design of MPL's compile time lambda expressions. The Lambda Library extends the basic facilities of Boost Bind with syntax so sweet that some of the examples we've covered become almost transparent. For example:

```
"hello, " + _1      // x -> "hello, " + x

_1 * (_1 - 0.5)     // x -> x * (x - 0.5)
```

What's interesting about this code is that `operator*` doesn't multiply, and `operator+` doesn't add or even concatenate! Instead, the operators construct function objects that can be called later. The result of `"hello, " + _1` is a function object accepting one argument—call it x—and returning the result of `"hello, " + x`. If this is beginning to sound familiar, that's good: Function objects built on-the-fly are just another example of the "expression templates" idiom first introduced by Blitz++.

The goals of the Lambda library are much more ambitious than those of Boost.Bind. Even if you found it hard to see the syntax of Boost.Bind as a DSL, we think it's clear that Boost.Lambda syntax is a little language unto itself. Its features go way beyond support for operators by implementing control structures and even exception handling! Here are just a few examples.

1. Halve each element of a two-dimensional array.

```
float a[5][10];
int i;
std::for_each(a, a+5,
  for_loop(var(i)=0, var(i)<10, ++var(i),
    _1[var(i)] /= 2
  )
);
```

2. Print a sequence, replacing odd elements with periods.

```
std::for_each(a.begin(), a.end(),
  if_then_else(_1 % 2 != 0,
      std::cout << _1
    , std::cout << constant('.')
  )
);
```

3. Print "zero," "one" or "other: *n*" for each element *n* of v.

```
std::for_each(v.begin(), v.end(),
  (
    switch_statement(
      _1,
      case_statement<0>(std::cout << constant("zero")),
      case_statement<1>(std::cout << constant("one")),
      default_statement(std::cout << constant("other: ") << _1)
    ),
    std::cout << constant("\n")
  )
);
```

In the examples above, `var` and `constant` each wraps its argument in a special class template that prevents it from being evaluated greedily. For example, if we had written `std::cout << "\n"` in the last example, it would have been evaluated once, outside the `for_each` invocation. That's just how C++ works. The result of `constant("\n")`, however, is a nullary function object that returns `"\n"`. The standard library doesn't provide a stream inserter (`operator<<(ostream&, T)`) for T, the type of that function object, but the Lambda library *does* provide an overloaded `operator<<` that works on T. Rather than performing stream insertion, the Lambda library's `operator<<` just produces another nullary function object: This one evaluates `std::cout << "\n"` when it's called.

The need for `var` and `constant`, and the need to use such functions as `for_loop` in place of C++'s built-in `for`, are compromises forced on us by the limitations of the C++ language. Still, the expressivity of Boost Lambda, combined with the fact that the function objects it builds are typically about as efficient as hand-coded functions, is impressive.

10.6.2.3   The Phoenix Library

Never satisfied, C++ library designers continue to search for more expressive ways to program. Before moving on to other domains, we'd like to touch on some of the innovations of two other functional programming libraries. The first is Phoenix, which was developed as part of the Boost.Spirit parser framework [Guz04], discussed later in this chapter. Besides adding some valuable new functionality, the authors of Phoenix invented new syntax for some of the same control structures supported by Boost.Lambda. For example, in Phoenix, the `if_then_else` example above might be written as follows (note that in Phoenix placeholders are called "arg1," "arg2", ...):

```
for_each(a.begin(), a.end(),
        if_(arg1 % 2 != 0)
        [
            std::cout << arg1
        ]
```

```
        .else_
        [
            std::cout << val('.')
        ]
    );
```

The authors of the Boost Lambda library found this syntax so attractive that they have incorporated it as an alternative to if_then_else. As you can see, there is a great deal of cross-pollination between these designs.

10.6.2.4 The FC++ Library

FC++ [MS00b]—short for "Functional C++"—enables C++ programmers to use the idioms of hardcore functional programming languages like Haskell, including lazy sequences, partial function application, and higher-order polymorphic functions.[9] These paradigms are so general-purpose, and so different from those most C++ programmers are used to, that using FC++ almost amounts to using a whole new programming language. We don't have space here to do justice to FC++, but we can present a few examples to give you a sense of it.

First, a look at FC++ lambda expressions. As in most traditional functional programming languages, but unlike C++ lambda expressions you've seen so far, FC++ supports the use of named parameters to improve readability in lambda expressions. For example:[10]

```
lambda_var<1> X;
lambda_var<2> Fun;

g = lambda(Fun,X)[ Fun[Fun[X]] ]   // g(fun,x) -> fun(fun(x))
```

Now, this is really mind-bending! The names Fun and X have both a meaning at the level of the C++ program, *and* a meaning in the program (function object) generated by the lambda expression. In fact, it's not very different from what Boost's Bind and Lambda libraries do with their placeholders. Placeholders implement a mapping from input argument positions to the position of arguments passed to the function being "bound." You could almost think of X as _1 and Fun as _2. All lambda(Fun,X)[...] does is to add another layer of indirection that exchanges the positions represented by the placeholders.

FC++ doesn't stop with named lambda arguments, though. The next example shows a lambda expression with what are essentially *named local constants:*

---

9. We covered the meaning of the term "higher-order function" when we introduced metafunctions—it's just a fancy term for functions that operate on other functions. In this context, "polymorphic" simply means that the function can operate on different types of arguments, like a function template does.
10. FC++ uses square brackets for function calls inside lambda expressions to explicitly delay function evaluation.

```
// f(x) -> 2*(x+3)
lambda(X)[
    let[
        Fun == multiplies[2] // Fun = 2*_1
      , Y == X %plus% 3       // Y = X+3
    ].in[
        Fun[Y]                // fun(Y), i.e. 2*(X+3)
    ]
]
```

The example above shows a few other features of the FC++ DSL. First, you can see partial application at work in the expression `multiplies[2]`, which yields a unary function object that computes `multiplies[2,x]` for its argument x. Next, the % operator is overloaded to make the expression x `%f%` y equivalent to `f[x,y]`, so any FC++ binary function object (e.g., `plus`) can act as a kind of "named infix operator."

The (domain-specific) language designers of FC++ made another interesting choice as well: They decided they didn't like the way that, in certain contexts, libraries like Boost.Lambda demand the use of `constant(...)` or `variable(...)` to prevent greedy evaluation of any expression that doesn't involve a placeholder. They reasoned that having to remember that only one of the two expressions below will work as expected is too error-prone:

```
std::cout << _1 << "world"    // OK; builds a function object
std::cout << "hello, " << _1  // wrong: immediate streaming
```

Instead, they chose a simple rule: Function invocations using round parentheses are evaluated immediately, and those using square brackets are evaluated lazily:

```
plus(2,x) // immediate
plus[2,X] // delayed
```

Likewise, FC++ has a separate syntax for immediate infix evaluation:

```
2 ^plus^ x // immediate
2 %plus% X // delayed
```

As a result, the syntax used to delay evaluation is at once terser than what the Lambda and Phoenix libraries use, and more explicit.

It may seem odd to see `%plus%` used to name the good old infix + operator. In fact, it has some clear drawbacks, as we can see by comparing these two roughly equivalent expressions:

```
// Boost Lambda:
-(3 * _1) + _2

// FC++:
lambda(X,Y)[ negate[ 3 %multiplies% X ] %plus% Y ]
```

The first one is shorter, simpler, and for anyone working in a problem domain that normally uses operator notation, clearer. Within the context of the FC++ language design, though, there are good reasons to use plus instead of +. To understand them, we have to consider the kind of C++ entity that plus refers to. What will allow us to write both plus[2,X] and plus(2,x)? Not a function, or a function pointer, or an array. Only a class instance can support that: plus must be a global class instance in the FC++ library.

Now, recalling that FC++ is all about *higher order* functional programming, it becomes clear that + isn't a name for addition that can be used in all contexts. How do you pass + to a function? If you mean the + operator that adds two ints, well, you can't even name it. If you try to pass the address of operator+, and it's overloaded, your C++ compiler will ask you which one you mean. If you mean a particular *templated* operator+, once again, there's no way to pass a function template as a runtime function argument. Further recalling that FC++ supports higher-order *polymorphic* functions, it's easy to see that if we want to pass an entity that actually represents the abstract + operation, it *has* to be a class instance, something like

```
struct plus
{
    template <class T, class U>
    typename plus_result<T,U>::type[11]
    operator()(T t, U u) const
    {
        return t + u;
    }
};
```

In fact, just about every special feature of FC++, from implicit partial application to explicit lazy notation, is only possible in C++ with function objects. To meet the goals of its designers, it was much more important for FC++ to use function objects than for mathematical expressions to use operator notation. The point of all this is not to say that one of these domain-specific languages is better than another, but to illustrate the wide range of syntactic and semantic choices available to *you*, the DSEL designer.

---

11. The subject of how to implement plus_result is an interesting one that's been tackled in a different way by almost every C++ DSEL framework. In the current C++ language, you can't build that metafunction so that it always returns the right type. There's been much talk in the C++ committee about adding an operator that will make it a simple matter of writing decltype(t+u).

10.7   The Boost Spirit Library

Like YACC, Spirit is a framework for defining parsers. The main difference is that rather than compiling to intermediate C/C++ code, Spirit uses an *embedded* domain-specific language. Here's the meat of the expression grammar we implemented with YACC, using Boost.Spirit's embedded DSL syntax:

```
group       = '(' >> expression >> ')';
factor      = integer | group;
term        = factor >> *(('*' >> factor) | ('/' >> factor));
expression  = term >> *(('+' >> term) | ('-' >> term));
```

You'll notice that there are some differences from traditional EBNF. The most obvious is probably that, because sequences of consecutive values like

```
'(' expression ')'
```

don't fit into the C++ grammar, the author of Spirit had to choose some operator to join consecutive grammar symbols. Following the example of the standard stream extractors (which do, after all, perform a crude kind of parsing), he chose `operator>>`. The next difference worth noting is that the Kleene star (*) and positive closure (+) operators, which are normally written *after* the expressions they modify, must be written as prefix operators instead, again because of limitations of the C++ grammar. These minor concessions aside, the Spirit grammar syntax comes remarkably close to the usual notation of the domain.

Spirit is actually a great example of the power of DSELs to interoperate with one another, because it really consists of a *collection* of little embedded languages. For example, the following complete program brings the above grammar together with semantic actions written between [...] using the Phoenix functional programming DSEL, and another DSEL idiom Spirit calls **closures**:

```
#include <boost/spirit/core.hpp>
#include <boost/spirit/attribute.hpp>
#include <iostream>
#include <string>

using namespace boost::spirit;
using namespace phoenix;
```

```cpp
// provides one named variable of type int...
struct vars : boost::spirit::closure<vars, int>      // CRTP
{
    member1 value; // ...called "value" in lazy expressions
};

// calculator is a grammar with attached int called "value"
struct calculator
  : public grammar<calculator, vars::context_t>      // CRTP
{
    template <class Tokenizer>
    struct definition
    {
      // all our rules have an attached int called "value," too...
        rule<Tokenizer, vars::context_t>
          expression, term, factor, group, integer;

      // ...except the top rule
        rule<Tokenizer> top;

      // build the grammar
        definition(calculator const& self)
        {
            top = expression[self.value = arg1];

            group = '(' >> expression[group.value = arg1] >> ')';

            factor = integer[factor.value = arg1]
                | group[factor.value = arg1]
                ;

            term = factor[term.value = arg1]
                    >> *(   ('*' >> factor[term.value *= arg1])
                          | ('/' >> factor[term.value /= arg1])
                        )
                ;

            expression = term[expression.value = arg1]
                    >> *(   ('+' >> term[expression.value += arg1])
                          | ('-' >> term[expression.value -= arg1])
                        )
                ;

            integer = int_p[integer.value = arg1];
        }
```

```
        // tell Spirit to start parsing with "top"
          rule<Tokenizer> const& start() const { return top; }
    };
};

int main()
{
    calculator calc;      //  our grammar

    std::string str;
    while (std::getline(std::cin, str))
    {
        int n = 0;
        parse(str.c_str(), calc[var(n) = arg1], space_p);
        std::cout << "result = " << n << std::endl;
    }
}
```

10.7.1   Closures

We're going to describe closures at two levels: First we'll examine them from the point of view of
the DSL user, asking you to put aside any consideration of how the magic works, and then we'll look
at the implementation techniques.

10.7.1.1   The Abstraction

To understand the use of closures, it's important to know that Spirit grammars and rules are all—you
guessed it—function objects. When invoked with an appropriate pair of iterators over the input, rules
and grammars attempt to parse it. This leads to *top down* or *recursive descent* parsing. For example,
in order to parse its first symbol, the expression rule in turn invokes the term rule.

Closures provide a set of variables associated with each rule invocation, accessed as members of
the rule itself. The value of the first member of the closure (in our example there is only one: value)
becomes the rule's "return value" and when the rule is used on the right-hand-side of another rule,
may be accessed in semantic actions attached to the rule by using the Phoenix placeholder arg1. So,
for example, in

```
term = factor[term.value = arg1]
        >> *(   ('*' >> factor[term.value *= arg1])
            | ('/' >> factor[term.value /= arg1])
          )
    ;
```

the value associated with the first factor invocation is first moved into the value associated with the current term invocation. Then, as each member of the Kleene star repetition is parsed, the value associated with the current term invocation is modified accordingly.

The really interesting thing about closures is the way they enable yet another programming paradigm: **dynamic scoping.** In C++, unqualified names (those without a "::" prefix) usually refer to the innermost enclosing scope in which they're defined:

```
#include <iostream>

namespace foo
{
  int x = 76;

  int g()
  {
     return x + 1;           // refers to foo::x
  }
}
int main()
{
   int x = 42;
   std::cout << foo::g();    // prints 77
}
```

In dynamic scoping systems, though, names refer to the nearest scope *on the call stack* in which they're defined. Therefore, in the same code, foo::g would see the value of x that was established in main(), and the program would print 43.

The fully qualified names of closure variables (*rulename . membername*) are dynamically scoped. That means, for example, that *any* semantic action in our grammar can refer to expression.value, and in doing so, can reach up the call stack to the value associated with the nearest invocation of the expression rule.

10.7.1.2 Implementation Details

Take a look at the declaration of our closure:

```
struct vars : closure<vars, int>
{
   member1 value;
};
```

The first thing you'll probably notice is that `closure` uses the "Curiously Recurring Template Pattern" (covered in Chapter 9), so that it has access to the type of `vars`. More interesting, though, is the use of the special type `member1` for `value`.

Clearly, if the library lets you write *rulename.closure-variable,* rules must contain public data members with the same names as closure variables. Actually, the limitations of the C++ language give us a big hint as to what's going on here: The only way to automatically allow the closure data members to be addressed as rule data members of the same name is to make the closure a public base of the rule class itself. There's simply no other way to generate identically named public data members in the rule.

Just as clearly, if something like `expression.value += 1` is to work as expected, `expression.value` can't be of type `int`: that would cause an integer addition immediately, as our grammar is defined, instead of later, when its rules are invoked. Sound like a familiar issue? In fact, it is solved in a familiar way, with expression templates. Instead of performing an addition, `expression.value += 1` creates an object that, when suitably invoked by the parser, adds `1` to the `int` variable created for `value` in the stack frame of the nearest enclosing `expression` invocation.

We're not going to go into the nitty-gritty details of how the dynamic scoping mechanism is implemented, as it's not directly related to the "DSEL-ness" of closures—we suggest you look at the Spirit and Phoenix source code if you're curious. The important thing to recognize is that, once again, expression templates and delayed evaluation have allowed us to use a programming paradigm not directly available in native C++.

10.7.2 Subrules

If you look closely at our calculator grammar, you can see that there must be some *type erasure* at work.[12]   Since the expression on the right side of each rule assignment builds an efficient function object, we can expect the types of these function objects to represent the structure of the expression. For example, leaving out the effect of the semantic actions, which further complicate things, the type of the right-hand-side of the `factor` rule is something like:

```
alternative<
    rule<Tokenizer, vars::context_t>  // for integer rule
  , rule<Tokenizer, vars::context_t>  // for group rule
>
```

and the right-hand-side of the `group` rule has a type something like this one:

---

12. See Chapter 9 for more information on type erasure.

```
sequence<
    sequence<
        ch_p                                      // for '(' parser
        , rule<Tokenizer, vars::context_t>        // expression rule
    >
    , ch_p                                        // for ')' parser
>
```

The `factor` and `group` rules themselves, though, have the same type. Clearly the compile time polymorphism generated by the expression templates is being transformed into runtime polymorphism: Rule objects of the same type must contain some function pointer, or virtual function, or *something* that allows one of them to parse `group`s and another to parse `factor`s. Of course, making that choice of behavior at runtime comes with an attendant loss of efficiency. In a simple grammar like this one, the cost of dynamically dispatching for every rule invocation can really add up.

Joel de Guzman, the primary author of Spirit, has written [Guz03]:

> ... the virtual function is a totally opaque wall that blocks all meta type information from passing through. We can never get any of the type information of the RHS or a rule, to, say, re-factor the expression template tree to something else (e.g., do automatic left factoring, static node-type-traversal, static first-follow analysis, etc.).

Those operations are all specialized issues related to parsers, but the point is still universal: Type erasure is a kind of "lossy compression," and valuable information may disappear forever.

The Spirit designers could tell us to simply write out the full type of each rule's right-hand-side, but that idea is basically a DSEL-killer. As you can imagine, writing down a complicated type for each rule, and rewriting those types each time the rules change, would quickly become unmanageable. More importantly, we'd have to fill our grammars with information about rule types, which from a DSEL perspective is just noise: It has nothing to do with the underlying domain abstraction.

It's worth noting that even the `auto` language extension described earlier in this chapter wouldn't completely solve this problem for Spirit, since the grammar rules all reference one another, so the types on the right-hand-side of the first `auto` initialization can never be known to the compiler.

Spirit resolves this tension between efficiency and expressivity in a familiar way: by putting off work until the last possible moment. Just as Blitz++ achieves efficiency by delaying matrix arithmetic until the entire expression is available, Spirit uses *subrules* to delay the erasure of static type information until the entire grammar is available. The following rewrite of `calculator`'s definition uses subrules to achieve near-optimal parsing efficiency:

```
template <class Tokenizer>
struct definition
```

```
{
    subrule<0, vars::context_t> expression;
    subrule<1, vars::context_t> group;
    subrule<2, vars::context_t> factor;
    subrule<3, vars::context_t> term;
    subrule<4, vars::context_t> integer;

    rule<Tokenizer> top;

    definition(calculator const& self)
    {
        top = (
            expression =
                term[expression.value = arg1]
                >> *(  ('+' >> term[expression.value += arg1])
                     |('-' >> term[expression.value -= arg1]) )

            , group =
                '(' >> expression[group.value = arg1] >> ')'

            , factor =
                integer[factor.value = arg1]
              | group   [factor.value = arg1]

            , term =
                factor[term.value = arg1]
                >> *(  ('*' >> factor[term.value *= arg1])
                     |('/' >> factor[term.value /= arg1]) )

            , integer =
                int_p[integer.value = arg1]

        )[ self.value = arg1 ];
    }
    // tell Spirit to start parsing with "top"
    rule<Tokenizer> const& start() const { return top; }
};
```

Two things are particularly worth noticing in this example. First, to achieve this delay without forcing users to write out messy types, the definition of all the subrules has to be done in a single expression. Type erasure doesn't occur until the assignment to top, the only full rule, occurs. At that point, a type even messier than that of any of the right-hand-sides, and containing the definition of all the subrules, is captured in a single virtual function. Once that single dynamic dispatch occurs, the parsing of an expression involves only normal static function calls, many of which can be inlined. The second item of note is that the transformation from dynamically dispatched `rule`s to statically dispatched `subrule`s hardly changed the grammar's representation at all. It is a particularly beautiful feature of Spirit that it offers us the ability to tune our position in the compile-time/runtime continuum so easily, and while staying so close to the fundamental EBNF domain language.

10.8   Summary

We hope this chapter has brought you a new perspective on library design. The most effective libraries provide users with a new level of expressiveness, one that allows them to program in terms appropriate to their problem domain. Although historically the introduction of new idioms and syntax to any programming environment has been viewed with (sometimes justifiable) suspicion, the practice has also been shown to have immense power to simplify programs and speed their development.

Thinking in terms of domain-specific languages provides a foundation for library design choices, and helps us to judge which kinds of new programming idioms and syntax will be effective. By relying on those that are most evocative of *existing* domain abstractions and notation, we can write programs that seem to directly express our intentions.

A unique combination of features—among them flexible operator overloading syntax, a high level of abstraction with little or no performance penalty, and the power of template metaprogramming—gives C++ programmers unmatched power to build efficient, expressive DSELs. Moreover, because DSELs are libraries, users can freely combine DSEL capabilities in the same application without ever leaving a familiar programming environment.

The purely compile-time MPL constructs that occupy most of this book and the techniques we covered in Chapter 9 for interfacing compile-time and runtime code are an effective toolbox for DSEL construction. In the next chapter, we'll go through an example to see just how that can be done.

10.9   Exercises

10-0. Consider the possibility of using operators other than >> in Spirit to separate consecutive grammar symbols. Would any other operator be better? Why or why not? Hint: Consider C++ grammar rules in addition to readability.

10-1. Are you beginning to notice a common theme in which limitations of the host language drive many DSEL design decisions? Consider how you might design a language that allows open-ended DSEL syntax and do a cost/benefit analysis comparing the use of the hypothetical language to what you've seen in C++. You might look at the history and use of macros in LISP for inspiration.

10-2. Use any of the Boost DSEL libraries discussed in this chapter to solve a small problem. Evaluate the user experience: What worked about the library? What was cumbersome about it?

10-3. Build a small DSEL for handling named function parameters using a protocol similar to the one described in this chapter. Compare your design with that of the Boost named parameters library, by David Abrahams and Daniel Wallin, in the prerelease materials on this book's companion CD.

11

A DSEL Design Walkthrough

In this chapter we'll walk through the process of designing and implementing a domain-specific embedded language and a metaprogram that operates on it. First we'll explore a domain and identify its principal abstractions; using a specific example, we'll get a sense of what they mean in the real world. Then we'll design a DSEL to express those abstractions, with our example as a proof-of-concept. Finally, we'll apply the tools and techniques you've learned in this book to write a metaprogram that processes the language to generate useful and efficient runtime components.

11.1 Finite State Machines

Every software engineer should be familiar with finite state machines (FSMs). The concept is so useful that you could expect to find it almost anywhere, from hardware device controllers to pattern-matching and parsing engines such as the one used by YACC. Developers of such diverse applications have embraced the use of FSMs because they make it possible to transform a tangled web of complex program logic into a comprehensible expression of well-understood formalism. We can credit this power to two things: the fundamental simplicity of the FSM abstraction and its declarative form.

Few general-purpose languages have built-in support for constructing FSMs, and C++ is no exception. If they aren't a regular part of every C++ programmer's vocabulary, maybe it's just for want of a tool that makes them as easy and fun to build as they should be. In this chapter we aim to design and build just such a tool: a finite state machine construction framework.

11.1.1 The Domain Abstraction

The domain abstraction of finite state machines consists of three simple elements.

States. An FSM must always be in one of several well-defined states. For example, the states of a simple CD player might be called *Open, Empty, Stopped* (with a CD in the drawer), *Paused,* and *Playing.* The only persistent data associated with a pure FSM is encoded in its state, though FSMs are seldom used alone in any system. For example, the parsers generated by YACC are built around a *stack* of state machines; the state of the whole system includes that of the stack and of each FSM in the stack.

Events.   State changes are triggered by events. In our CD player example, most events would correspond to button presses on its front panel: *play, stop, pause,* and *open/close* (the button that opens and closes the drawer). Events aren't necessarily "pushed" into a state machine from the outside, though. For example, in YACC parsers, each event represents a different token, and is "pulled" from the input stream by the parsing process. In some systems, events contain associated data. For instance, an *identifier* token in a C++ parser might carry the text of the identifier, while an *integer-literal* token might carry the value of the integer.

Transitions.   Each state can have any number of transitions to other states. Each transition is labeled with an event. To process an event, the FSM follows the transition that starts from the current state and is marked with that event. For example, a CD player has a transition from *Playing* to *Stopped* labeled with the *stop* event. Usually, transitions also have some associated **action**, such as *stop playback* in the case of our CD player. In the case of YACC, following transitions means manipulating the stack of FMSs and/or executing the user's semantic actions.

11.1.2   Notations

There are several common ways to describe a state machine on paper, but perhaps the most user-friendly notation is a graphical one. Figure 11.1 represents the CD player we've been using as an example. In the picture, states are shown as circles and transitions are shown as arrows, labeled with the events that trigger them.

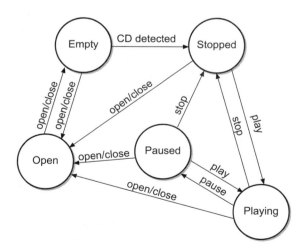

Figure 11.1 CD player FSM in graphical form

Note the transition from *Empty* to *Stopped*. Remember that we said not all events need to be "pushed" on the system from the outside? To model real CD players, the FSM will begin a CD detection process when the drawer is closed; when it detects a CD in the drawer, the system sends itself a *cd-detected* event. To make this work, the transition from *Open* to *Empty* must have an associated action that begins the CD detection process. When a new disc is detected, most CD players collect information about the number of tracks and the total playing time of each one; our *cd-detected* event should contain that information so that the transition's action can store it somewhere and show the number of tracks on the player's front panel.

The graphical representation shows everything that can happen in an FSM at a glance, with no wasted syntactic elements. One popular strategy for FSM construction, in fact, is to draw the state machine using a graphical user interface with a code-generating back end. If only C++ allowed pictures in its input syntax—they could be a perfect DSEL notation!

Since C++ can't parse pictures, we're going to use a different notation called a **State Transition Table** (STT), which is essentially just a vertical list of the FSM's transitions. Table 11.1 shows the **STT** for the CD player.

Table 11.1 CD Player State Transition Table

Current State	Event	Next State	Transition Action
Stopped	*play*	*Playing*	start playback
Stopped	*open/close*	*Open*	open drawer
Open	*open/close*	*Empty*	close drawer; collect CD information
Empty	*open/close*	*Open*	open drawer
Empty	*cd-detected*	*Stopped*	store CD information
Playing	*stop*	*Stopped*	stop playback
Playing	*pause*	*Paused*	pause playback
Playing	*open/close*	*Open*	stop playback; open drawer
Paused	*play*	*Playing*	resume playback
Paused	*stop*	*Stopped*	stop playback
Paused	*open/close*	*Open*	stop playback; open drawer

Although the structure of the FSM is less apparent than it was in the graphical form, it's still fairly easy to follow. To process an event, the state machine finds a row that contains its current state in the first column and the event in the second column; the third and fourth columns of that row indicate the new state and the action to take upon making the transition. Note that while we left transition actions out of the FSM's graphical representation to minimize clutter, in the STT they cause little or no interference.

11.2   Framework Design Goals

Okay, so what do we want from our state machine framework?

1. **Interoperability**. State machines are typically just an abstraction for describing the logic of a system targeted at some problem domain(s) other than FSM construction. We'd like to be able to use libraries built for those domains in the implementation of our FSMs, so we want to be sure we can comfortably interoperate with other DSELs.

2. **Declarativeness**. State machine authors should have the experience of *describing* the structure of FSMs rather than *implementing* their logic. Ideally, building a new state machine should involve little more than transcribing its STT into a C++ program. As framework providers, we should be able to seamlessly change the implementation of a state machine's logic without affecting the author's description.

3. **Expressiveness**. It should be easy both to represent and to recognize the domain abstraction in a program. In our case, an STT in code should look very much as it does when we design a state machine on paper.

4. **Efficiency**. A simple FSM like our CD player should ideally compile down to extremely tight code that can be optimized into something appropriate even for a tiny embedded system. Perhaps more importantly, concerns about the efficiency of our framework should never give programmers an excuse for using ad hoc logic where the sound abstraction of a finite state machine might otherwise apply.

5. **Static Type Safety**. It's important to catch as many problems as possible at compile time. A typical weakness of many traditional FSM designs [LaFre00] is that they do most of their checking at runtime. In particular, there should be no need for unsafe downcasts to access the different datatypes contained by various events.

6. **Maintainability**. Simple changes to the state machine design should result in only simple changes to its implementation. This may seem like an obvious goal, but it's nontrivial to attain—experts have tried and failed to achieve it. For example, when using the State design pattern [Mart98], a single change such as adding a transition can lead to refactoring multiple classes.

7. **Scalability**. FSMs can grow to be far more complex than our simple example above, incorporating such features as per-state entry and exit actions, conditional transition guards, default and triggerless transitions and even sub-states. If the framework doesn't support these features today, it should be reasonably extensible to do so tomorrow.

11.3   Framework Interface Basics

We can make some easy choices right away. Because of goal 1 above—and, of course, because of the name of this chapter—we're going to design an *embedded* DSL. That means taking the library approach rather than building a translator (like YACC) or an interpreter (like Make).

Though it may not be obvious from our CD player example, we might in general want to create multiple instances of any finite state machine, each with a separate state. Therefore, it makes sense to encapsulate FSM logic in a reusable package. Since C++'s unit of data encapsulation is a class, our framework is going to help us build FSM *classes*. Because the whole FSM will be represented as a class, it seems reasonable to represent transition actions like *start playback* as member functions of that class.

We'd like to be able to use readable names like `Playing` and `open_close` to indicate states and events. At this point we can't say much about what *kind* of C++ entity (type, integer value, function object, and so on) to use for state names like `Playing`. Events are a different story, though: In the CD player, only the *cd-detected* event contains data, but in general every distinct kind of event might need to transmit a different data type. Therefore, event names should denote types. To embed arbitrary data in an event, the FSM author can just declare an event class with corresponding data members.

Given that finite state machines will be classes, and that events will be implemented as types, we can imagine that a state machine built with our framework might be used as follows:

```
int main()
{
    player p;                        // an instance of the FSM

    p.process_event(open_close()); // user opens CD player
    p.process_event(open_close()); // inserts CD and closes
    p.process_event(              // CD is detected
        cd_detected(
            "louie, louie"
          , std::vector<std::clock_t>( /* track lengths */ )
        )
    );
    p.process_event(play());       // etc.
    p.process_event(pause());
    p.process_event(play());
    p.process_event(stop());
    return 0;
}
```

11.4   Choosing a DSL

Our next challenge is to design a domain-specific language that allows a programmer to *describe* a finite state machine like the one implemented by player. Later, we'll write metaprogram code that processes the FSM description to *generate* a class like player. As hinted earlier, the state machine author is going to deliver the description in the form of a state transition table, so let's start looking at possible syntaxes for representing it.

11.4.1   The Transition Table

Deciding on a representation for transitions (the rows of our STT) is where things really start to get interesting. We have many options! Let's go through a few of the possible ways of writing just the first two rows of our table, and analyze each one to get a sense of the range of choices at our disposal. At this stage, we're not going to worry too much about how to use these syntaxes to build FSMs; the point is just to consider how STTs might map onto C++ syntax:

```
// Current  Event          Next       Action
//  State                  State
 [ Stopped, play,          Playing, &fsm::start_playback ]
 [ Stopped, open_close, Open,      &fsm::open_drawer      ]
```

Our first attempt is sufficiently table-like to make the state machine's structure clear. What would it take to make this syntax work? To make the brackets legal, there would have to be a class, say transition_table, with an overloaded operator[]. Because the C++ compiler doesn't allow us to write bracketed expressions in isolation, users would have to precede the table with an instance of that class, something like:

```
transition_table STT; // provided by the FSM framework
...

   // Current  Event          Next       Action
   //  State                  State
STT[ Stopped, play,          Playing, &fsm::start_playback ]
   [ Stopped, open_close, Open,      &fsm::open_drawer      ]
```

Next, because operator[] is only allowed to have one argument, there would have to be at least one overloaded comma operator to consolidate the items in between the brackets. Having noticed that, we can make the syntax even more table-like by replacing the comma operator with operator|:

```
// Current  Event          Next         Action
//  State                  State
```

```
STT[ Stopped | play        | Playing  | &fsm::start_playback ]
   [ Stopped | open_close  | Open     | &fsm::open_drawer    ]
```

Given that our event names will denote types, however, both of the syntaxes we've explored present a problem: We can't just use a type in a runtime expression as though it were an object. Instead, we have to pass an *instance* of that type, so our table might end up looking more like this:

```
// Current   Event          Next        Action
// State                    State
STT[ Stopped | play()        | Playing | &fsm::start_playback ]
   [ Stopped | open_close()  | Open    | &fsm::open_drawer    ]
```

A couple of parentheses per row don't compromise the syntax too badly, though we appear to be requiring that events can be default-constructed. Default-constructibility requirements are a red flag to any experienced library designer: In this case, events won't necessarily all be lightweight types, and constructing instances just so we can build the transition table might not be appropriate.

Applying the Fundamental Theorem of Software Engineering,[1] we might get around that problem by asking users to transmit the event's type information to the framework indirectly, in a little wrapper template:

```
// provided by the FSM framework
template <class Event>
struct on
{
    typedef Event type;
};
...

// Current   Event           Next      Action
// State                     State
STT[ Stopped |on<play>()        | Playing |&fsm::start_playback ]
   [ Stopped |on<open_close>()| Open    |&fsm::open_drawer    ]
```

That works in principle, but the syntax is starting to get a little bit heavy, obscuring event names with syntactic "noise." We might recover some of the readability by writing:

```
on<play>       play_;
on<stop>       stop_;
```

---

1. *"We can solve any problem by introducing an extra level of indirection."* See section 2.1.2 for the origin of this idea.

```
on<open_close> open_close_;
...

    // Current    Event              Next        Action
    //  State                        State
STT[ Stopped  | play_          | Playing | &fsm::start_playback ]
   [ Stopped  | open_close_    | Open    | &fsm::open_drawer      ]
```

That's not bad at all. Unfortunately, there's one problem that is going to kill this lovely scheme. Remember our fourth design goal, "Efficiency?" The problem with all of the designs we've seen so far is that they are going to hurt the efficiency of our state machine in two ways:

1.   We're passing pointers to the transition actions as arguments to some operator| function. That means we're going to have to store them in data members somewhere, and later call through the stored pointers when the FSM actually follows the transitions. As a result, even the simplest transition functions won't be inlined. These costs are not significant in all designs. For example, when Boost.Bind[2] is used to build a comparison function object for use with std::sort, the cost of moving sequence elements during sorting will usually swamp the small overhead of repeatedly calling through a single function pointer.   In the case of a finite state machine, however, the code executed to change states is often so trivial that an added indirection really does count.

2.   We're also building the whole transition table at runtime. That's not an efficiency problem in itself: Construction of the table can probably be inlined, and, as we've seen from Blitz++, it's possible to build super-efficient computational engines at runtime using expression templates. Unfortunately, the number of operators used in building such an engine is directly proportional to the complexity of its type structure. After building up a type complicated enough to represent a fairly large STT, there's no way we can ask the user to write that type down. If we want to hold the state machine in a variable, the table either needs to be passed off immediately to a function template or we have to resort to some sort of type erasure,[3] which always results in another level of function-pointer indirection.

We can avoid the cost of indirection through a function pointer on transition actions by passing the action member pointers as template arguments, as described in Chapter 9:

```
//            Current  Event          Next        Action
//             State                  State
transition< Stopped, play,        Playing, &fsm::start_playback >,
transition< Stopped, open_close, Open,    &fsm::open_drawer      >,
```

---

2. See Chapter 10 for more on the Boost Bind library.
3. See Chapter 9 for more on type erasure.

This syntax is not nearly so sweet, but we think it still looks sufficiently tabular. We can go a bit further in that direction just by moving the commas and adding comments:

```
//    Current  Event        Next       Action
//    State                 State
//   +--------+-----------+--------+----------------------+
row < Stopped , play       , Playing , &fsm::start_playback >,
row < Stopped , open_close , Open    , &fsm::open_drawer    >,
//   +--------+-----------+--------+----------------------+
row < Paused  , play       , Playing , &fsm::resume_playback >,
row < Paused  , stop       , Stopped , &fsm::stop_playback   >,
row < Paused  , open_close , Open    , &fsm::stop_and_open   >,
//   +--------+-----------+--------+----------------------+
```

Although we had to replace `transition` with the less meaningful identifier `row` (so the example would fit on the page), the new format is more readable to our eye.

This approach has two important practical advantages over previous attempts, no matter what layout you choose. First, it can be implemented using only type expressions, so there's no loss of efficiency due to a premature crossing of the compile-time/runtime boundary. Since the action function pointer is a template parameter, it is known at compile time and can be completely inlined. Second, because each `row<...>` instantiation is a type, we can pass a comma-separated list of them as parameters to an MPL sequence, and all the MPL tools for manipulating type sequences will be at our disposal.

Now that we know the format we'd like to use for our transition table, we might as well choose the kind of C++ entity to which state names will refer. State machines are, well, stateful. In other words, they don't fit into the compile-time world of *pure* template metaprogramming very well. We need to be able to pass state names as template parameters to `row<...>`, but we also need to be able to store something representing any of the FSM's various states in a single data member. Integral constants meet both those constraints. Luckily, C++ gives us a convenient way to define collections of named integral constants with unique values:

```
enum states {
   Stopped, Open, Empty, Playing, Paused
 , initial_state = Empty
};
```

As you can see, we've defined an additional constant `initial_state`. We're endowing that particular identifier with special meaning: The framework will use it to decide the initial state of default-constructed FSM instances.

11.4.2   Putting It All Together

Except for a couple of small details, we've now explored all the syntactic aspects of the DSEL and are ready to show a complete example of how it might be used to describe a FSM:

```cpp
// concrete FSM implementation
class player : public state_machine<player>
{
 private:
    // the list of FSM states
    enum states {
        Empty, Open, Stopped, Playing, Paused
      , initial_state = Empty
    };

    // transition actions
    void start_playback(play const&);
    void open_drawer(open_close const&);
    void close_drawer(open_ close const&);
    void store_cd_info(cd_detected const&);
    void stop_playback(stop const&);
    void pause_playback(pause const&);
    void resume_playback(play const&);
    void stop_and_open(open_close const&);

    friend class state_machine<player>;
    typedef player p; // makes transition table cleaner

    // transition table
    struct transition_table : mpl::vector11<

    //      Start       Event        Next       Action
    //   +---------+------------+---------+--------------------+
    row < Stopped , play        , Playing , &p::start_playback >,
    row < Stopped , open_close  , Open    , &p::open_drawer    >,
    //   +---------+------------+---------+--------------------+
    row < Open    , open_close  , Empty   , &p::close_drawer   >,
    //   +---------+------------+---------+--------------------+
    row < Empty   , open_close  , Open    , &p::open_drawer    >,
    row < Empty   , cd_detected , Stopped , &p::store_cd_info  >,
    //   +---------+------------+---------+--------------------+
    row < Playing , stop        , Stopped , &p::stop_playback  >,
```

```
        row < Playing , pause       , Paused  , &p::pause_playback  >,
        row < Playing , open_close  , Open     , &p::stop_and_open   >,
        // +---------+------------+--------+--------------------+
        row < Paused  , play       , Playing , &p::resume_playback >,
        row < Paused  , stop       , Stopped , &p::stop_playback   >,
        row < Paused  , open_close  , Open    , &p::stop_and_open   >
        // +---------+------------+--------+--------------------+
      > {};
    };
```

One new detail above is that `player`'s base class is being granted friendship. Because all of `player`'s nested definitions—its states, transition table, and actions—are exclusively for use by the state machine framework, and not for public consumption, we've marked them `private`. Aside from its default constructor, the state machine's public interface consists solely of the `process_event` member function that will be supplied by its base class.

The other detail we ought to discuss is the use of the Curiously Recurring Template Pattern (CRTP), in which `player` is derived from `state_machine<player>`.[4] Like many of our other DSEL design choices, this one is driven by C++ language constraints. Consider how `row` might be declared so that it can accept a pointer-to-member-function of `player` as a template argument. It would have to be something like:

```
template <
    int CurrentState
  , class Event
  , int NextState
  , void (player::*)(Event const&)
>
struct row
{ ... };
```

In other words, `row` needs to know the type of `player`. We could ask the author of `player` to supply the FSM type herself, as an initial template parameter:

```
template<
    class Fsm    // explicit FSM specification
  , int CurrentState
```

---

4. See section 9.8 for more on CRTP.

```
    , class Event
    , int NextState
    , void (Fsm::*action)(Event const&)
  >
  struct row
  { ... };
```

That approach would add an extra column to the transition table—a column full of nothing more than redundant copies of the same class name. Since C++ already requires the state machine author to qualify all member function pointers with the FSM class name, we'd just be adding insult to injury. With CRTP, however, the FSM author passes the class name *once,* to the base class template `state_machine`. Since `state_machine` has full access to the derived class name, it can supply a convenient nested `row` template for that particular `Derived` state machine:

```
  template<class Derived>
  class state_machine
  {
      ...
   protected:
      template<
          int CurrentState
        , class Event
        , int NextState
        , void (Derived::*action)(Event const&)
      >
      struct row
      {
          // for later use by our metaprogram
          static int const current_state = CurrentState;
          static int const next_state = NextState;
          typedef Event event;
          typedef Derived fsm_t;

          // do the transition action
          static void execute(Derived& fsm, Event const& e)
          {
              (fsm.*action)(e);
          }
      };
  };
```

Notice that we've filled in the body of row above. The nested definitions serve only one purpose: They allow convenient access to the values of row's template parameters. It may seem a little strange that the action parameter is accessed through an execute function that calls it; unfortunately, in C++ a nested constant member pointer can never be a compile-time constant. Had action been assigned to a static const member like the other template parameters, calls through it would not be inlined.

11.5 Implementation

Now that we've begun to touch on the details of state_machine's implementation, we may as well dive in head first. You're probably asking yourself, "How the heck are we going to make this thing work?" Mostly the answer comes down to implementing process_event, which after all is entirely responsible for the FSM's runtime behavior (aside from the transition actions, supplied by the derived FSM's author).

The process_event member function presents a classic "double dispatch" problem: Given a start state *and* an event, we need to select a target state and a transition action to perform. In general, implementing double dispatch can be quite challenging, but in our case we have a distinct advantage: We know the event type at compile time, which allows us to capitalize on the compiler's overload resolution capability. If we were going to write an FSM implementation by hand instead of letting the library generate it, we'd have a separate overloaded implementation of process_event for each event type, looking something like this:

```
// "play" event processor
void process_event(play const& e)
{
    switch (this->state)
    {
     case Stopped:
        this->start_playback(e);
        this->state = Playing;
        break;
     case Paused:
        this->resume_playback(e);
        this->state = Playing;
        break;
     default:
        this->state = no_transition(this->state, e);
    }
}
```

```
// "stop" event processor
void process_event(stop const& e)
{
    ...
}

// etc...
```

Ideally, to do the same thing automatically, we'd just instantiate some templates parameterized on the current states, actions, and target states involved, and containing switch statements. Just looking at the *play* event processor, we can already see a problem. There may be an arbitrary number of cases in that switch statement, one for each transition on the event, and C++ doesn't give us a way to generate such an arbitrarily sized switch statement directly. To create one from the information in our transition table, which will be processed row by row, we need to build up the switch semantics from similar-looking bite-sized pieces. The smallest unit of code that we can generate with C++ templates is a function call, so these pieces will have to be functions. Breaking each case into a separate function yields something more like this for the *play* event processor:

```
// "play" event processor
void process_event(play const& e)
{
    this->state = case_Stopped(e);
}

int case_Stopped(play const& e)
{
    if (this->state == Stopped)
    {
        this->start_playback(e);
        return Playing;
    }
    else return this->case_Paused(e);
}

int case_Paused(play const& e)
{
    if (this->state == Paused)
    {
        this->resume_playback(e);
        return Playing;
    }
    else return this->case_default(e);
}
```

```
int case_default(play const& e)
{
    return this->no_transition(this->state, e);
}
```

Here, `process_event(play const&)` forwards its implementation to `case_Stopped`. `case_Stopped` first checks to see if the current state is `Stopped`, and if so, takes the corresponding transition action (`start_playback`) and returns `Playing` as the new state. Otherwise, `case_Paused` checks to see if the state is `Paused`, and if so, resumes playback and again returns `Playing`. Otherwise, `case_default` calls `no_transition` to handle the states that have no outgoing transition on a `play` event.[5]

As you can see, these semantics are identical to those of the `switch` statement above. If we can generate a `case_State` function for each transition on a given event, we can build the right behavior incrementally, by traversing the rows of the transition table. Of course, we're not home free yet, because we *can't* generate `case_State` functions, the problem being the variable part of the name, represented by *State*. A template metaprogram simply can't generate new identifiers. We can, however, associate a separate function with each state as follows:

```
template <int State>
struct case_
{
    static int dispatch(player& fsm, int state, play const& e)
    { ... }
};
```

Provided that we could fill the braces appropriately, `case_<Stopped>::dispatch` would be equivalent to `case_Stopped`, and `case<Paused>::dispatch` would be equivalent to `case_Paused`. To generate bodies for these functions, we'll need `State` (to check against), a transition action (to execute), and a next state (to move to). We *could* pass each of these in a separate template parameter, but it's probably simpler to pass an entire `row` of the transition table, since the members of `row` provide access to all of that information and more. If `case_` isn't taking a state value as its sole template argument, though, it seems badly named. Let's call it `event_dispatcher` instead:

```
template<class Transition> // a row of the transition table
struct event_dispatcher
```

---

5. We don't expect this version of `process_event` to incur the cost of four function calls; we're relying on the compiler's inlining and optimization capabilities to make it efficient.

```
{
    typedef typename Transition::fsm_t fsm_t;
    typedef typename Transition::event event;

    static int dispatch(
        fsm_t& fsm, int state, event const& e)
    {
        if (state == Transition::current_state)
        {
            Transition::execute(fsm, e);
            return Transition::next_state;
        }
        else { ... }
    }
};
```

Conveniently, each row provides us with the identity of the state machine (::fsm_t) and of the event being dispatched (::event). That allows event_dispatcher to be more generic than case_, which was tied to a specific state machine and event.

To complete event_dispatcher we must fill in its else clause, which, in the usual case, just needs to call the next case's dispatch function. That's easy enough if the event_dispatcher for the next case is a template parameter:

```
template<
    class Transition
  , class Next
>
struct event_dispatcher
{
    typedef typename Transition::fsm_t fsm_t;
    typedef typename Transition::event event;

    static int dispatch(
        fsm_t& fsm, int state, event const& e)
    {
        if (state == Transition::current_state)
        {
            Transition::execute(fsm, e);
            return Transition::next_state;
        }
```

```
        else // move on to the next node in the chain.
        {
            return Next::dispatch(fsm, state, e);
        }
    }
};
```

To handle the default case, we'll introduce a default_event_dispatcher with a dispatch function that invokes the FSM's no_transition handler. Because the derived FSM class is only granting friendship to state_machine<FSM> and not to default_event_dispatcher, the handler must be called indirectly through a member of state_machine:

```
struct default_event_dispatcher
{
    template<class FSM, class Event>
    static int dispatch(
        state_machine<FSM>& m, int state, Event const& e)
    {
        return m.call_no_transition(state, e);
    }
};

template <class Derived>
class state_machine
{
    ...
    template <class Event>
    int call_no_transition(int state, Event const& e)
    {
        return static_cast<Derived*>(this)  // CRTP downcast
                    ->no_transition(state, e);
    }
    ...
};
```

Now, to process the play event, we just have to assemble the following type and call its dispatch function:

```
event_dispatcher<
    row<Stopped, play, Playing, &player::start_playback>
  , event_dispatcher<
```

```
        row<Paused, play, Playing, &player::resume_playback>
      , default_event_dispatcher
    >
  >
```

If you look carefully at the structure of that type, you can see that it mirrors the execution pattern of the fold algorithm, beginning with default_event_dispatcher and "folding" it into successive event_dispatcher specializations. To generate it, we just have to run fold over the rows of our table that contain the event we're dispatching:

```
// get the Event associated with a transition
template <class Transition>
struct transition_event
{
    typedef typename Transition::event type;
};

template<class Table, class Event>
struct generate_dispatcher
  : mpl::fold<
        mpl::filter_view<   // select rows triggered by Event
            Table
          , boost::is_same<Event, transition_event<_1> >
        >
      , default_event_dispatcher
      , event_dispatcher<_2,_1>
    >
{};
```

Finally, we're ready to write state_machine's process_event function! Rather than writing overloads for each event type, we'll use a member function templated on the event type, that merely generates the dispatcher and invokes its ::dispatch member:

```
template<class Event>
int process_event(Event const& evt)
{
    // generate the dispatcher type
    typedef typename generate_dispatcher<
        typename Derived::transition_table, Event
    >::type dispatcher;
```

```
    // dispatch the event
    this->state = dispatcher::dispatch(
        *static_cast<Derived*>(this)              // CRTP downcast
      , this->state
      , evt
    );

    // return the new state
    return this->state;
}
```

Note that once again we are taking advantage of the Curiously Recurring Template Pattern to supply functionality that relies on knowing the full type of the derived class in the member functions of the base class. The `static_cast` above allows the `dispatcher` to apply the `Derived` member function pointers in the `transition_table` to *this.

There's very little else to state_machine. We need a `state` member, and a constructor to initialize it:

```
...
  protected:
    state_machine()
      : state(Derived::initial_state)
    {}

  private:
    int state;
...
```

It would be nice to supply a default `no_transition` handler; after all, a user who wants different behavior can always write a `no_transition` function in her derived class:

```
...
  public:
    template <class Event>
    int no_transition(Event const& e)
    {
        assert(false);
        return state;
    }
...
```

In your Boost installation, `libs/mpl/book/chapter10/player.cpp` contains a complete implementation of what we've explored here.

11.6   Analysis

By now you should have a good sense of the DSEL development process. The steps mirror the ones we used to analyze each of the domain-specific languages in Chapter 10.

1.   Identify the domain abstractions.

2.   Experiment with representing those abstractions in code.

3.   Build a prototype.

4.   Iterate.

So how well did it work out this time? Did we achieve our design goals?

1.   **Interoperability**. Interoperability with other DSLs is achieved because we have created our DSL as a library, that is, a domain-specific *embedded* language. We can embed types from other domain libraries in our events, invoke arbitrary functions in other domains from within the transition actions, or operate the FSM from code written in other DSELs.

2.   **Declarativeness**. Looking back at our `player` implementation, the bulk of the code written by its author is in the transition table itself, and almost everything in the declaration of `player` is essential to its meaning. It does appear to be a very direct translation of the domain language into C++. Furthermore, it is possible to completely replace the framework's implementation without altering the state machine declaration. In the examples directory of the code that accompanies this book, player2.cpp illustrates a `state_machine` that dispatches using O(1) lookup into a static table of function pointers.

3.   **Expressiveness**. The STT as declared in `player` does look very much like a table should be expected to, particularly with the formatting conventions we've used.

4.   **Efficiency**. The code generated for `process_event` avoids all runtime dispatch other than switching on the current state, and that doesn't require any memory accesses or table lookups, since `event_dispatcher` uses compile-time constants for comparison. The design is efficient because we ruthlessly kept everything in the compile-time world of metadata as long as possible.

   The authors analyzed the assembly language output for this example by two different compilers, and the generated code appears to rival that of a hand-coded state machine. That said, if you were going to use this framework in a system where every cycle counts, you'd probably want to throw the example at your target compiler and inspect the results. You'd probably also want to expand the STT with more events and transitions to see whether the efficiency of the code scales well with the size of the state machine.

5. **Static Type Safety**. The framework is fairly typesafe. There are only two `static_cast`s in the whole system (in `process_event` and `call_no_transition`), and the potential for damage is limited because they will only compile if `Derived` is indeed derived from the `state_machine`.

6. **Maintainability**. New events can be added to the system by simply creating a new type. New states can be added similarly, by extending the `states` enum. That enum could even be defined outside `player`, if we cared to do so. It wouldn't do much to reduce coupling, though, since the transition table must contain state names and must be visible from the FSM declaration. Transitions are easy to add by writing new `rows` in the `transition_table`.

   One point that might be of some concern is the cost of maintaining the visual alignment of the table as the FSM evolves. That cost does appear to be inevitable if we want to closely match the domain abstraction. Although we have the flexibility to throw out strict alignment if the cost of maintenance grows too high, experiments appear to show that the table representation makes a big difference in its understandability, so we wouldn't want to take this step lightly.

7. **Scalability**. It's a bit harder to evaluate the framework's extensibility from what we've seen here. One thing we can say at this point is that the design *seems* sufficiently modular to make adding new features reasonably easy. You'll get a chance to explore just how easy it *actually* is if you do some of this chapter's exercises. Due to the DSL's declarativeness, we can at least be fairly sure that features can be added without breaking existing user code.

11.7 Language Directions

Although as of today C++ is the most suitable language for building highly efficient DSELs, there is still a lot of room for improvement. As you've seen, the DSELs you can implement within the current language are amazing, but they also require an amount of work that becomes justifiable only if you are really planning to spend a lot of time working in the DSEL's problem domain. Moreover, despite the richness and flexibility of C++'s operator overloading rules, one often has to settle for less-than-perfect syntax. What seems to be liberal in the domain of general-purpose programming is often not quite liberal enough to conveniently express the syntax of an arbitrary domain.

Things don't have to be that way, of course. While C++ will probably never allow *arbitrary* syntax extensions, a few small changes to the language would improve DSEL writing a great deal. One problem we saw in this chapter is that although the language's runtime syntax is incredibly rich, once we cross the boundary into runtime by passing a constant (in our case, a member function pointer) to a function, it's impossible to get that constant back into the compile-time world as metadata. For example, if we could expand the language's ability to do "constant folding," it could be possible to leverage its rich runtime syntax in contexts that require pure metadata [n1521].

11.8 Exercises

11-0. It might be useful to be able to group transitions by their start state, so that each start state only has to be written once. Design such a grouped representation and modify the FSM framework design to support it. Evaluate the success of your changes in reducing redundancy and boilerplate.

11-1. We didn't really have to give up on expression template-based designs so quickly. How could the efficiency lost by passing function pointers be recaptured? (Hint: They must be passed as template arguments.) Rework your favorite expression template DSEL syntax to use this technique and evaluate its success as a DSEL.

11-2. Implement and test the expression-template-based FSM DSEL we explored but then discarded earlier in section 11.4.1. Evaluate its ease-of-use and efficiency tradeoffs.

11-3. Evaluate the possibility of implementing the following expression-template-based FSM DSEL:

```
player()
{
    Stopped[
        play        => Playing | &player::start_playback
      , open_close => Open    | &player::open_drawer
      ]

  ,
    Open[
        open_close => Empty    | &player::close_drawer
      ]

    // ...
    ;
}
```

Based on your evaluation, explain why this syntax is unachievable, or, if it is viable, implement a prototype that demonstrates it.

11-4. Extend the FSM implementation to support optional state entry and exit actions.

11-5. *Transition guards* are additional predicates that you can assign to certain transitions to suppress/enable them depending on some condition. Although formally redundant,[6] they help to reduce the FSM's size and complexity, sometimes significantly, and therefore are often desired. Design a notation and implement support for optional transition guards in this chapter's example.

11-6. Extend the FSM implementation to support "catch-all" transitions, making any of the following possible:

```
// whatever the current state is, allow "reset_event" to
// trigger a transition to "initial_state"
row< _, reset_event, initial_state, &self::do_reset >

// any event received in "error" state triggers a transition
// to "finished"
row< error, _, finished, &self::do_finish >

// any event received in any state triggers a transition
// to "done"
row< _, _, done, &self::do_nothing >
```

Choose and implement a deterministic scheme for handling transitions with overlapping conditions.

11-7*. Extend the FSM implementation to support nested (composite) states. A sketch of a possible design is provided below:

```
class my_fsm
    : fsm::state_machine< my_fsm >
{
    // ...
    struct ready_to_start_;
    typedef submachine<ready_to_start_> ready_to_start;

    struct transition_table : mpl::vector<
          row< ready_to_start, event1, running, &self::start >
        , row< running,        event2, Stopped, &self::stop >
        // ...
        > {};
};
```

---

6. Any finite state machine that uses transition guards can be always transformed into an equivalent "pure" FSM that doesn't.

```
// somewhere else in the translation unit

template<>
struct my_fsm::submachine<ready_to_start_>
  : state_machine< submachine<ready_to_start_> >
{
    // states
    struct ready;
    struct closed;
    struct recently_closed;

    struct transition_table : mpl::vector<
        row< ready,    event3, closed,          &self::close >
      , row< closed,   event4, recently_closed >
        // ...
      > {};
};
```

11-8. Our dispatching code searches linearly over the states with outgoing transitions on a given event. In the worst case, that takes $O(S)$ time, where S is the total number of states in the FSM. In the examples directory of the code that accompanies this book, player2.cpp illustrates a `state_machine` that dispatches using $O(1)$ lookup into a static table of function pointers. That, however, incurs runtime memory access and function pointer indirection overhead. Implement and test a third dispatching scheme that avoids all of these disadvantages by generating an $O(\log_2 S)$ binary search.

Appendix A

An Introduction to Preprocessor Metaprogramming

A.1 Motivation

Even with the full power of template metaprogramming and the Boost Metaprogramming Library at our disposal, some C++ coding jobs still require a great deal of boilerplate code repetition. We saw one example in Chapter 5, when we implemented `tiny_size`:

```
template <class T0, class T1, class T2>
struct tiny_size
  : mpl::int_<3> {};
```

Aside from the repeated pattern in the parameter list of the primary template above, there are three partial specializations below, which also follow a predictable pattern:

```
template <class T0, class T1>
struct tiny_size<T0,T1,none>
  : mpl::int_<2> {};

template <class T0>
struct tiny_size<T0,none,none>
  : mpl::int_<1> {};

template <>
struct tiny_size<none,none,none>
  : mpl::int_<0> {};
```

In this case there is only a small amount of code with such a "mechanical" flavor, but had we been implementing `large` instead of `tiny`, there might easily have been a great deal more. When the number of instances of a pattern grows beyond two or three, writing them by hand tends to become error-prone. Perhaps more importantly, the code gets hard to read, because the important abstraction in the code is really the pattern, not the individual instances.

A.1.1 Code Generation

Rather than being written out by hand, mechanical-looking code should really be generated mechanically. Having written a program to spit out instances of the code pattern, a library author has two choices: She can either ship pre-generated source code files, or she can ship the generator itself. Either approach has drawbacks. If clients only get the generated source, they are stuck with whatever the library author generated—and experience shows that if they are happy with three instances of a pattern today, someone will need four tomorrow. If clients get the generator program, on the other hand, they also need the resources to execute it (e.g., interpreters), and they must integrate the generator into their build processes...

A.1.2 Enter the Preprocessor

...unless the generator is a preprocessor metaprogram. Though not designed for that purpose, the C and C++ preprocessors can be made to execute sophisticated programs during the preprocessing phase of compilation. Users can control the code generation process with preprocessor #defines in code or -D options on the compiler's command line, making build integration trivial. For example, we might parameterize the primary tiny_size template above as follows:

```
#include <boost/preprocessor/repetition/enum_params.hpp>

#ifndef TINY_MAX_SIZE
#  define TINY_MAX_SIZE 3  // default maximum size is 3
#endif

template <BOOST_PP_ENUM_PARAMS(TINY_MAX_SIZE, class T)>
struct tiny_size
  : mpl::int_<TINY_MAX_SIZE>
{};
```

To test the metaprogram, run your compiler in its "preprocessing" mode (usually the -E option), with the Boost root directory in your #include path. For instance:[1]

```
g++ -P -E -Ipath/to/boost_1_32_0 -I. test.cpp
```

---

1. GCC's -P option inhibits the generation of source file and line number markers in preprocessed output.

Given the appropriate metaprograms, users would be able to adjust not only the number of parameters to `tiny_size`, but the maximum size of the entire `tiny` implementation just by `#define`-ing `TINY_MAX_SIZE`.

The Boost Preprocessor library [MK04] plays a role in preprocessor metaprogramming similar to the one played by the MPL in template metaprogramming: It supplies a framework of high-level components (like `BOOST_PP_ENUM_PARAMS`) that make otherwise-painful metaprogramming jobs approachable. In this appendix we won't attempt to cover nitty-gritty details of how the preprocessor works, nor principles of preprocessor metaprogramming in general, nor even many details of how the Preprocessor *library* works. We *will* show you enough at a high level that you'll be able to use the library productively and learn the rest on your own.

A.2 Fundamental Abstractions of the Preprocessor

We began our discussion of template metaprogramming in Chapter 2 by describing its metadata (potential template arguments) and metafunctions (class templates). On the basis of those two fundamental abstractions, we built up the entire picture of compile-time computation covered in the rest of this book. In this section we'll lay a similar foundation for the preprocessor metaprogrammer. Some of what we cover here may be a review for you, but it's important to identify the basic concepts before going into detail.

A.2.1 Preprocessing Tokens

The fundamental unit of data in the preprocessor is the **preprocessing token**. Preprocessing tokens correspond roughly to the tokens you're used to working with in C++, such as identifiers, operator symbols, and literals. Technically, there are some differences between *preprocessing tokens* and regular *tokens* (see section 2 of the C++ standard for details), but they can be ignored for the purposes of this discussion. In fact, we'll be using the terms interchangeably here.

A.2.2 Macros

Preprocessor macros come in two flavors. **Object-like macros** can be defined this way:

> `#define` *identifier replacement-list*

where the *identifier* names the macro being defined, and *replacement-list* is a sequence of zero or more tokens. Where the *identifier* appears in subsequent program text, it is **expanded** by the preprocessor into its replacement list.

Function-like macros, which act as the "metafunctions of the preprocessing phase," are defined as follows:

#define *identifier*(a_1, a_2, ... a_n) *replacement-list*

where each a_i is an identifier naming a **macro parameter**. When the macro name appears in subsequent program text followed by a suitable argument list, it is expanded into its *replacement-list,* except that each argument is substituted for the corresponding parameter where it appears in the *replacement-list.*[2]

A.2.3   Macro Arguments

> **Definition**
>
> A **macro argument** is a nonempty sequence of:
>
> - Preprocessing tokens other than commas or parentheses, *and/or*
> - Preprocessing tokens surrounded by matched pairs of parentheses.

This definition has consequences for preprocessor metaprogramming that must not be underestimated. Note, first of all, that the following tokens have special status:

,   (   )

As a result, a macro argument can never contain an unmatched parenthesis, or a comma that is not surrounded by matched parentheses. For example, both lines following the definition of FOO below are ill-formed:

```
#define FOO(X) X // unary identity macro
FOO(,)           // un-parenthesized comma or two empty arguments
FOO())           // unmatched parenthesis or missing argument
```

Note also that the following tokens do *not* have special status; the preprocessor knows nothing about matched pairs of braces, brackets, or angle brackets:

{   }   [   ]   <   >

As a result, these lines are also ill-formed:

---

2. We have omitted many details of how macro expansion works. We encourage you to take a few minutes to study section 16.3 of the C++ standard, which describes that process in straightforward terms.

```
FOO(std::pair<int, long>)              // two arguments
FOO({ int x = 1, y = 2; return x+y; })  // two arguments
```

It *is* possible to pass either string of tokens above as part of a single macro argument, provided it is parenthesized:

```
FOO((std::pair<int,int>))              // one argument
FOO(({ int x = 1, y = 2; return x+y; }))  // one argument
```

However, because of the special status of commas, it is impossible to strip parentheses from a macro argument without knowing the number of comma-separated token sequences it contains.[3] If you are writing a macro that needs to be able to accept an argument containing a variable number of commas, your users will either have to parenthesize that argument *and* pass you the number of comma-separated token sequences as an additional argument, or they will have to encode the same information in one of the preprocessor data structures covered later in this appendix.

A.3   Preprocessor Library Structure

Since in-depth coverage of the Boost Preprocessor library is beyond the scope of this book, we'll try to give you the *tools* to gain an in-depth understanding of the library here. To do that, you'll need to use the electronic Preprocessor library documentation, which begins with the index.html file in the `libs/preprocessor/` subdirectory of your Boost installation.

On the left of your browser window you'll see an index, and if you follow the "Headers" link, it will reveal the structure of the `boost/preprocessor/` directory. Most of the library's headers are grouped into subdirectories according to related functionality. The top-level directory contains only a few headers that provide general-purpose macros, along with a header for each subdirectory that simply `#include`s all the headers in that subdirectory. For example, `boost/preprocessor/selection.hpp` does nothing more than to `#include` the `min.hpp` and `max.hpp` headers that comprise the contents of `boost/preprocessor/selection/`. The headers whose names *don't* correspond to subdirectories generally declare a macro whose name is the same as the name of the header, without the extension, and with a BOOST_PP_ prefix. For example, `boost/preprocessor/selection/max.hpp` declares BOOST_PP_MAX.

You'll also notice that often a header will declare an additional macro with a _D, _R, or _Z suffix.[4] For instance, `boost/preprocessor/selection/max.hpp` also declares

---

3. The C99 preprocessor, by virtue of its variadic macros, can do that and more. The C++ standardization committee is likely to adopt C99's preprocessor extensions for the next version of the C++ standard.
4. Macros with _1ST, _2ND, or _3RD suffixes, if they appear, should be ignored for a different reason: They are deprecated and will be removed from the library soon.

BOOST_PP_MAX_D. For the purposes of this appendix, you should ignore those macros. Eventually you will want to understand the reason for their existence and how they can be used to optimize preprocessing speed; consult the Topics section of the library documentation under the subheading "reentrancy" for that information.

A.4   Preprocessor Library Abstractions

In this section we'll discuss the basic abstractions of the Preprocessor library and give some simple examples of each.

A.4.1   Repetition

The repeated generation of class T0, class T1,... class Tn that we achieved using BOOST_PP_ENUM_PARAMS was a specific case of the general concept of **horizontal repetition**. The library also has a concept of vertical repetition, which we'll get to in a moment. Horizontal repetition macros are all found in the library's repetition/ subdirectory.

A.4.1.1   Horizontal Repetition

To generate the tiny_size specializations using horizontal repetition, we might write the following:

```
#include <boost/preprocessor/repetition.hpp>
#include <boost/preprocessor/arithmetic/sub.hpp>
#include <boost/preprocessor/punctuation/comma_if.hpp>

#define TINY_print(z, n, data) data

#define TINY_size(z, n, unused)                                   \
  template <BOOST_PP_ENUM_PARAMS(n, class T)>                     \
  struct tiny_size<                                               \
      BOOST_PP_ENUM_PARAMS(n,T)                                   \
      BOOST_PP_COMMA_IF(n)                                        \
      BOOST_PP_ENUM(                                              \
          BOOST_PP_SUB(TINY_MAX_SIZE,n), TINY_print, none)        \
  >                                                               \
    : mpl::int_<n> {};

BOOST_PP_REPEAT(TINY_MAX_SIZE, TINY_size, ~)

#undef TINY_size
#undef TINY_print
```

The code generation process is kicked off by calling BOOST_PP_REPEAT, a **higher-order macro** that repeatedly invokes the macro named by its second argument (TINY_size). The first argument specifies the number of repeated invocations, and the third one can be any data; it is passed on unchanged to the macro being invoked. In this case, TINY_size doesn't use that data, so the choice to pass ~ was arbitrary.[5]

Each time the TINY_size macro is invoked by BOOST_PP_REPEAT, it generates a different specialization of tiny_size. The macro accepts three parameters.

- z is related to the _Z macro suffix we mentioned earlier. You'll never need to use it except for optimization purposes, and can safely ignore it for now.

- n is the repetition index. In repeated invocations of TINY_size, n will be 0, then 1, then 2, and so on.

- unused, in this case, will be ~ on each repetition. In general, the final argument to a macro invoked by BOOST_PP_REPEAT is always the same as its invoker's final argument.

Because its *replacement-list* covers several lines, all but the last line of TINY_size is continued with a trailing backslash. The first few of those lines just invoke BOOST_PP_ENUM_PARAMS (which we already used in the primary template) to generate comma-separated lists, so each invocation of TINY_size produces something equivalent to:[6]

```
template <class T0, class T1, ... class Tn-1>
struct tiny_size<
    T0, T1, ... Tn-1
    ...more...
>
    : mpl::int_<n> {};
```

BOOST_PP_COMMA_IF generates a comma if its numeric argument is not 0. When n is 0, the list generated by the preceding line will be empty, and a leading comma directly following the < character would be ill-formed.

The next line uses BOOST_PP_ENUM to generate TINY_MAX_SIZE-n comma-separated copies of none. BOOST_PP_ENUM is just like BOOST_PP_REPEAT except that it generates commas between

---

5. ~ is not an *entirely* arbitrary choice. Both @ and $ might have been good choices, except that they are technically not part of the basic character set that C++ implementations are required to support. An identifier like ignored might be subject to macro expansion, leading to unexpected results.

6. Note that the line continuation characters *and* the newlines following them are removed by the preprocessor, so the resulting code actually appears on a single line in the preprocessed output.

repetitions, so its second argument (TINY_print, here) must have the same signature as TINY_size. In this case, TINY_print ignores its repetition index n, and simply yields its third argument, none.

BOOST_PP_SUB implements token subtraction. It's crucial to understand that although the preprocessor *itself* can evaluate ordinary arithmetic expressions:

```
#define X 3
...
#if X - 1 > 0  // OK
  whatever
#endif
```

preprocessor *metaprograms* can only operate on tokens. Normally, when a macro in the Preprocessor library expects a numeric argument, it must be passed as a single token. If we had written TINY_MAX_SIZE-n instead of BOOST_PP_SUB(TINY_MAX_SIZE,n) above, the first argument to BOOST_PP_ENUM would have contained three tokens at each invocation: first 3-0, then 3-1, and finally 3-2. BOOST_PP_SUB, though, generates single-token results: first 3, then 2, and finally 1, in successive repetitions.

Naming Conventions

Note that TINY_print and TINY_size are #undef'd immediately after they're used, with no intervening #includes. They can therefore be thought of as "local" macro definitions. Because the preprocessor doesn't respect scope boundaries, it's important to choose names carefully to prevent clashes. We recommend PREFIXED_lower_case names for local macros and PREFIXED_UPPER_CASE names for global ones. The only exceptions are one-letter lowercase names, which are safe to use for local macros: No other header is likely to #define a global single-letter lowercase macro—that would be *very* bad manners.

A.4.1.2 Vertical Repetition

If you send the previous example through your preprocessor, you'll see one long line containing something like this:

```
template <> struct tiny_size< none , none , none > : mpl::int_<0>
  {}; template < class T0> struct tiny_size< T0 , none , none > :
mpl::int_<1> {}; template < class T0 , class T1> struct tiny_size
< T0 , T1 , none > : mpl::int_<2> {};
```

The distinguishing feature of horizontal repetition is that all instances of the repeated pattern are generated on the same line of preprocessed output. For some jobs, like generating the primary `tiny_size` template, that's perfectly appropriate. In this case, however, there are at least two disadvantages.

1. It's hard to verify that our metaprogram is doing the right thing without reformatting the resulting code by hand.

2. The efficiency of nested horizontal repetitions varies widely across preprocessors. Each specialization generated by means of horizontal repetition contains three other horizontal repetitions: two invocations of BOOST_PP_ENUM_PARAMS and one invocation of BOOST_PP_ ENUM. When TINY_MAX_SIZE is 3, you'll probably never care, but on at least one preprocessor still in use today, compilation begins to slow noticeably when TINY_MAX_SIZE reaches 8.[7]

The solution to these problems, naturally, is **vertical repetition**, which generates instances of a pattern across multiple lines. The Preprocessor library provides two means of vertical repetition: **local iteration** and **file iteration**.

Local Iteration

The most expedient way to demonstrate local iteration in our example is to replace the invocation of BOOST_PP_REPEAT with the following:

```
#include <boost/preprocessor/iteration/local.hpp>

#define BOOST_PP_LOCAL_MACRO(n)    TINY_size(~, n, ~)
#define BOOST_PP_LOCAL_LIMITS      (0, TINY_MAX_SIZE - 1)
#include BOOST_PP_LOCAL_ITERATE()
```

Local iteration repeatedly invokes the user-defined macro with the special name BOOST_PP_ LOCAL_MACRO, whose argument will be an iteration index. Since we already had TINY_size lying around, we've just defined BOOST_PP_LOCAL_MACRO to invoke it. The range of iteration indices are given by another user-defined macro, BOOST_PP_LOCAL_LIMITS, which must expand to a parenthesized pair of integer values representing the *inclusive* range of index values passed to BOOST_PP_LOCAL_MACRO. Note that this is one of the rare places where the library expects a numeric argument that can be an expression consisting of multiple tokens.

Finally, the repetition is initiated by #include-ing the result of invoking BOOST_PP_LOCAL_ ITERATE, which will ultimately be a file in the Preprocessor library itself. You may find it surprising that many preprocessors can handle repeated file inclusion more quickly than nested horizontal repetition, but that is in fact the case.

---

7. That said, other preprocessors can handle 256 * 256 nested repetitions without any speed problems whatsoever.

If we throw the new example at our preprocessor, we'll see the following, on three separate lines in the output:

```
template <> struct tiny_size< none , none , none > : mpl::int_<0>
{};

template < class T0> struct tiny_size< T0 , none , none > : mpl::
int_<1> {};

template < class T0 , class T1> struct tiny_size< T0 , T1 , none
> : mpl::int_<2> {};
```

That represents a great improvement in verifiability, but it's still not ideal. As TINY_MAX_SIZE grows, it gets harder and harder to see that the pattern is generating what we'd like. If we could get some more line breaks into the output it would retain a more recognizable form.

Both repetition methods we've used so far have another drawback, though it doesn't show up in this example. Consider what would happen if tiny_size had a member function that we wanted to debug. If you've ever tried to use a debugger to step through a function generated by a preprocessor macro, you know that it's a frustrating experience at best: The debugger shows you the line from which the macro was ultimately invoked, which usually looks nothing at all like the code that was generated. Worse, as far as the debugger is concerned, *every* statement in that generated function occupies that same line.

File Iteration

Clearly, debuggability depends on preserving the association between generated code and the lines in the source file that describe the code pattern. File iteration generates pattern instances by repeatedly #include-ing the same source file. The effect of file iteration on debuggability is similar to that of templates: Although separate instances appear to occupy the same source lines in the debugger, we do have the experience of stepping through the function's source code.

To apply file iteration in our example, we can replace our earlier local iteration code and the definition of TINY_size, with:

```
#include <boost/preprocessor/iteration/iterate.hpp>
#define BOOST_PP_ITERATION_LIMITS (0, TINY_MAX_SIZE - 1)
#define BOOST_PP_FILENAME_1        "tiny_size_spec.hpp"
#include BOOST_PP_ITERATE()
```

BOOST_PP_ITERATION_LIMITS follows the same pattern as BOOST_PP_LOCAL_LIMITS did, allowing us to specify an inclusive range of iteration indices. BOOST_PP_FILENAME_1 specifies the name of the file to repeatedly #include (we'll show you that file in a moment). The trailing 1 indicates that this is the first nesting level of file iteration—should we need to invoke file iteration again from within `tiny_size_spec.hpp`, we'd need to use `BOOST_PP_FILENAME_2` instead.

The contents of `tiny_size_spec.hpp` should look familiar to you; most of it is the same as `TINY_size`'s *replacement-list,* without the backslashes:

```
#define n BOOST_PP_ITERATION()

template <BOOST_PP_ENUM_PARAMS(n, class T)>
struct tiny_size<
    BOOST_PP_ENUM_PARAMS(n,T)
    BOOST_PP_COMMA_IF(n)
    BOOST_PP_ENUM(BOOST_PP_SUB(TINY_MAX_SIZE,n), TINY_print, none)
>
  : mpl::int_<n> {};

#undef n
```

The library transmits the iteration index to us in the result of `BOOST_PP_ITERATION()`; n is nothing more than a convenient local macro used to reduce syntactic noise. Note that we didn't use `#include` guards because we need `tiny_size_spec.hpp` to be processed multiple times.

The preprocessed result should now preserve the line structure of the pattern and be more verifiable for larger values of `TINY_MAX_SIZE`. For instance, when `TINY_MAX_SIZE` is 8, the following excerpt appears in the output of GCC's preprocessing phase:

```
...
template < class T0 , class T1 , class T2 , class T3>
struct tiny_size<
    T0 , T1 , T2 , T3
    ,
    none , none , none , none
>
  : mpl::int_<4> {};
template < class T0 , class T1 , class T2 , class T3 , class T4>
struct tiny_size<
    T0 , T1 , T2 , T3 , T4
    ,
    none , none , none
>
  : mpl::int_<5> {};
...etc.
```

Self-Iteration

Creating an entirely new file like `tiny_size_spec.hpp` each time we want to express a trivial code pattern for file repetition can be inconvenient. Fortunately, the library provides a macro that allows us to place the pattern right in the file that invokes the iteration. `BOOST_PP_IS_ITERATING` is defined to a nonzero value whenever we're inside an iteration. We can use that value to select between the part of a file that invokes the iteration and the part that provides the repeated pattern. Here's a complete `tiny_size.hpp` file that demonstrates self-iteration. Note in particular the placement and use of the `#include` guard `TINY_SIZE_HPP_INCLUDED`:

```
#ifndef BOOST_PP_IS_ITERATING

#   ifndef TINY_SIZE_HPP_INCLUDED
#     define TINY_SIZE_HPP_INCLUDED

#     include <boost/preprocessor/repetition.hpp>
#     include <boost/preprocessor/arithmetic/sub.hpp>
#     include <boost/preprocessor/punctuation/comma_if.hpp>
#     include <boost/preprocessor/iteration/iterate.hpp>

#     ifndef TINY_MAX_SIZE
#       define TINY_MAX_SIZE 3  // default maximum size is 3
#     endif
// primary template
template <BOOST_PP_ENUM_PARAMS(TINY_MAX_SIZE, class T)>
struct tiny_size
  : mpl::int_<TINY_MAX_SIZE>
{};

// generate specializations
#     define BOOST_PP_ITERATION_LIMITS (0, TINY_MAX_SIZE - 1)
#     define BOOST_PP_FILENAME_1     "tiny_size.hpp" // this file
#     include BOOST_PP_ITERATE()

#   endif // TINY_SIZE_HPP_INCLUDED

#else // BOOST_PP_IS_ITERATING

#   define n BOOST_PP_ITERATION()

#   define TINY_print(z, n, data) data
```

```
// specialization pattern
template <BOOST_PP_ENUM_PARAMS(n, class T)>
struct tiny_size<
    BOOST_PP_ENUM_PARAMS(n,T)
    BOOST_PP_COMMA_IF(n)
    BOOST_PP_ENUM(BOOST_PP_SUB(TINY_MAX_SIZE,n), TINY_print, none)
>
  : mpl::int_<n> {};
#   undef TINY_print
#   undef n

#endif // BOOST_PP_IS_ITERATING
```

More

There's a good deal more to file iteration than what we've been able to show you here. For more details, we encourage you to delve into the library's electronic documentation of BOOST_PP_ITERATE and friends. Also, it's important to note that no single technique for repetition is superior to any other: Your choice may depend on convenience, verifiability, debuggability, compilation speed, and your own sense of "logical coherence."

A.4.2   Arithmetic, Logical, and Comparison Operations

As we mentioned earlier, many of the Preprocessor library interfaces require single-token numeric arguments, and when those numbers need to be computed arithmetically, straightforward arithmetic expressions are inappropriate. We used BOOST_PP_SUB to subtract two numeric tokens in our tiny_size examples. The library contains a suite of operations for non-negative integral token arithmetic in its arithmetic/ subdirectory, as shown in Table A.1

Table A.1 Preprocessor Library Arithmetic Operations

Expression	Value of Single Token Result
BOOST_PP_ADD(x,y)	x + y
BOOST_PP_DEC(x)	x - 1
BOOST_PP_DIV(x,y)	x / y
BOOST_PP_INC(x)	x + 1
BOOST_PP_MOD(x,y)	x % y
BOOST_PP_MUL(x,y)	x * y
BOOST_PP_SUB(x,y)	x - y

The `logical/` subdirectory contains the convenient Boolean token operations shown in Table A.2 and the more efficient operations shown in Table A.3, which require that their operands are either 0 or 1 (a single bit).

Table A.2 Preprocessor Library Integer Logical Operations

Expression	Value of Single Token Result
`BOOST_PP_AND(x,y)`	`x && y`
`BOOST_PP_NOR(x,y)`	`!(x || y)`
`BOOST_PP_OR(x,y)`	`x || y`
`BOOST_PP_XOR(x,y)`	`(bool)x != (bool)y ? 1 : 0`
`BOOST_PP_NOT(x)`	`x ? 0 : 1`
`BOOST_PP_BOOL(x)`	`x ? 1 : 0`

Table A.3 Preprocessor Library Bit Logical Operations

Expression	Value of Single Token Result
`BOOST_PP_BITAND(x,y)`	`x && y`
`BOOST_PP_BITNOR(x,y)`	`!(x || y)`
`BOOST_PP_BITOR(x,y)`	`x || y`
`BOOST_PP_BITXOR(x,y)`	`(bool)x != (bool)y ? 1 : 0`
`BOOST_PP_COMPL(x)`	`x ? 0 : 1`

Finally, the `comparison/` subdirectory provides the token integral comparison operations shown in Table A.4.

Table A.4 Preprocessor Library Comparison Operations

Expression	Value of Single Token Result
`BOOST_PP_EQUAL(x,y)`	`x == y ? 1 : 0`
`BOOST_PP_NOT_EQUAL(x,y)`	`x != y ? 1 : 0`
`BOOST_PP_LESS(x,y)`	`x < y ? 1 : 0`
`BOOST_PP_LESS_EQUAL(x,y)`	`x <= y ? 1 : 0`
`BOOST_PP_GREATER(x,y)`	`x > y ? 1 : 0`
`BOOST_PP_GREATER_EQUAL(x,y)`	`x >= y ? 1 : 0`

Because it's common to have a choice among several workable comparison operators, it may be useful to know that `BOOST_PP_EQUAL` and `BOOST_PP_NOT_EQUAL` are likely to be O(1) while the other comparison operators are generally slower.

A.4.3   Control Structures

In its `control/` directory, the Preprocessor library supplies a macro `BOOST_PP_IF(c,t,f)` that fulfills a similar role to the one filled by `mpl::if_`. To explore the "control" group, we'll generate code for a framework of generic function objects: the Boost Function library.[8]   `boost::function` is partially specialized to match function type arguments of each arity up to the maximum supported by the library:

```
template <class Signature> struct function;    // primary template

template <class R>                              // arity = 0
struct function<R()>
  definition not shown...

template <class R, class A0>                    // arity = 1
struct function<R(A0)>
  definition not shown...

template <class R, class A0, class A1>          // arity = 2
struct function<R(A0,A1)>
  definition not shown...

template <class R, class A0, class A1, class A2>    // arity = 3
struct function<R(A0,A1,A2)>
  definition not shown...

etc.
```

We've already covered a few strategies that can be used to generate the pattern above, so we won't belabor that part of the problem; the file iteration approach we used for `tiny_size` would be fine:

```
#ifndef BOOST_PP_IS_ITERATING

#   ifndef BOOST_FUNCTION_HPP_INCLUDED
#     define BOOST_FUNCTION_HPP_INCLUDED

#     include <boost/preprocessor/repetition.hpp>
#     include <boost/preprocessor/iteration/iterate.hpp>
```

---

8. We touched briefly on the design of Boost Function when we discussed type erasure in Chapter 9. See the Function library documentation at `boost_1_32_0/libs/function/index.html` on the CD that accompanies this book for more information.

```
#    ifndef FUNCTION_MAX_ARITY
#      define FUNCTION_MAX_ARITY 15
#    endif

template <class Signature> struct function;    // primary template

// generate specializations
#    define BOOST_PP_ITERATION_LIMITS (0, FUNCTION_MAX_ARITY)
#    define BOOST_PP_FILENAME_1  "boost/function.hpp" // this file
#    include BOOST_PP_ITERATE()

#  endif // BOOST_FUNCTION_HPP_INCLUDED

#else // BOOST_PP_IS_ITERATING

#  define n BOOST_PP_ITERATION()

// specialization pattern
template <class R BOOST_PP_ENUM_TRAILING_PARAMS(n, class A)>
struct function<R ( BOOST_PP_ENUM_PARAMS(n,A) )>
  definition not shown...

#  undef n

#endif // BOOST_PP_IS_ITERATING
```

BOOST_PP_ENUM_TRAILING_PARAMS, used above, is just like BOOST_PP_ENUM_PARAMS except
that when its first argument is not 0, it generates a leading comma.

A.4.3.1 Argument Selection

For the sake of interoperability with C++ standard library algorithms, it might be nice if functions
of one or two arguments were derived from appropriate specializations of std::unary_function
or std::binary_function, respectively.[9] BOOST_PP_IF is a great tool for dealing with special
cases:

```
#  include <boost/preprocessor/control/if.hpp>
#  include <boost/preprocessor/comparison/equal.hpp>
```

---

9. While derivation from std::unary_function or std::binary_function might be necessary for interoperability
with some older library implementations, it may inhibit the Empty Base Optimization (EBO) from taking effect when two
such derived classes are part of the same object. For more information, see section 9.4. In general, it's better to expose
first_argument_type, second_argument_type, and result_type typedefs directly.

```
// specialization pattern
template <class R BOOST_PP_ENUM_TRAILING_PARAMS(n, class A)>
struct function<R ( BOOST_PP_ENUM_PARAMS(n,A) )>
  BOOST_PP_IF(
      BOOST_PP_EQUAL(n,2), : std::binary_function<A0, A1, R>
    , BOOST_PP_IF(
          BOOST_PP_EQUAL(n,1), : std::unary_function<A0, R>
        , ...empty argument...
      )
  )
{ ...class body omitted... };
```

Well, our first attempt has run into several problems. First off, you're not allowed to pass an empty argument to the preprocessor (see footnote 3, page 285). Secondly, because angle brackets don't get special treatment, the commas in the `std::unary_function` and `std::binary_function` specializations above are treated as macro argument separators, and the preprocessor will complain that we've passed the wrong number of arguments to BOOST_PP_IF in two places.

Because it captures all of the issues, let's focus on the inner BOOST_PP_IF invocation for a moment. The strategy that `mpl::eval_if` uses, of selecting a nullary function to invoke, could work nicely here. The preprocessor doesn't have a direct analogue for `mpl::eval_if`, but it doesn't really need one: We can get the right effect by adding a second set of parentheses to BOOST_PP_IF.

```
#define BOOST_FUNCTION_unary()    : std::unary_function<A0,R>
#define BOOST_FUNCTION_empty()    // nothing

...

    , BOOST_PP_IF(
          BOOST_PP_EQUAL(n,1), BOOST_FUNCTION_unary
        , BOOST_FUNCTION_empty
      )()

#undef BOOST_FUNCTION_empty
#undef BOOST_FUNCTION_unary
```

A nullary macro that generates nothing is so commonly needed that the library's "facilities" group provides one: BOOST_PP_EMPTY. To complete the example we'll need to delay evaluation all the way to the outer BOOST_PP_IF invocation, because `std::binary_function<A0,A1,R>` also has a "comma problem":

```
#   include <boost/preprocessor/facilities/empty.hpp>

#   define BOOST_FUNCTION_binary() : std::binary_function<A0,A1,R>
#   define BOOST_FUNCTION_unary()  : std::unary_function<A0,R>

// specialization pattern
template <class R BOOST_PP_ENUM_TRAILING_PARAMS(n, class A)>
struct function<R ( BOOST_PP_ENUM_PARAMS(n,A) )>
  BOOST_PP_IF(
      BOOST_PP_EQUAL(n,2), BOOST_FUNCTION_binary
    , BOOST_PP_IF(
          BOOST_PP_EQUAL(n,1), BOOST_FUNCTION_unary
        , BOOST_PP_EMPTY
      )
  )()
{
    ...class body omitted...
};

#   undef BOOST_FUNCTION_unary
#   undef BOOST_FUNCTION_binary
#   undef n
```

Note that because we happened to be using file iteration, we could have also used #if on n's value directly:

```
    template <class R BOOST_PP_ENUM_TRAILING_PARAMS(n, class A)>
    struct function<R ( BOOST_PP_ENUM_PARAMS(n,A) )>
#if n == 2
    : std::binary_function<A0, A1, R>
#elif n == 1
    : std::unary_function<A0, R>
#endif
```

BOOST_PP_IF has the advantage of enabling us to encapsulate the logic in a reusable macro, parameterized on n, that is compatible with all repetition constructs:

```
#define BOOST_FUNCTION_BASE(n)                              \
    BOOST_PP_IF(BOOST_PP_EQUAL(n,2), BOOST_FUNCTION_binary  \
      , BOOST_PP_IF(BOOST_PP_EQUAL(n,1), BOOST_FUNCTION_unary \
          , BOOST_PP_EMPTY                                  \
        )                                                   \
    )()
```

A.4.3.2   Other Selection Constructs

BOOST_PP_IDENTITY, also in the "facilities" group, is an interesting cousin of BOOST_PP_ EMPTY:

```
#define BOOST_PP_IDENTITY(tokens) tokens BOOST_PP_EMPTY
```

You can think of it as creating a nullary macro that returns tokens: When empty parentheses are appended, the trailing BOOST_PP_EMPTY is expanded leaving just tokens behind. If we had wanted inheritance from mpl::empty_base when function's arity is not one or two, we could have used BOOST_PP_IDENTITY:

```
// specialization pattern
template <class R BOOST_PP_ENUM_TRAILING_PARAMS(n, class A)>
struct function<R ( BOOST_PP_ENUM_PARAMS(n,A) )>
  BOOST_PP_IF(
      BOOST_PP_EQUAL(n,2), BOOST_FUNCTION_binary
    , BOOST_PP_IF(
          BOOST_PP_EQUAL(n,1), BOOST_FUNCTION_unary
        , BOOST_PP_IDENTITY(: mpl::empty_base)
      )
  )()
{
    ...class body omitted...
};
```

It's also worth knowing about BOOST_PP_EXPR_IF, which generates its second argument or nothing, depending on the Boolean value of its first:

```
#define BOOST_PP_EXPR_IF(c,tokens)                               \
    BOOST_PP_IF(c,BOOST_PP_IDENTITY(tokens),BOOST_PP_EMPTY)()
```

So BOOST_PP_EXPR_IF(1,foo) expands to foo, while BOOST_PP_EXPR_IF(0,foo) expands to nothing.

A.4.4   Token Pasting

It would be nice if there were a generic way to access the return and parameter types of *all* function objects, rather than just the unary and binary ones. A metafunction returning the signature as an MPL sequence would do the trick. We could just specialize signature for each function arity:

```
template <class F> struct signature; // primary template

// partial specializations for boost::function
template <class R>
struct signature<function<R()> >
  : mpl::vector1<R> {};

template <class R, class A0>
struct signature<function<R(A0)> >
  : mpl::vector2<R,A0> {};

template <class R, class A0, class A1>
struct signature<function<R(A0,A1)> >
  : mpl::vector3<R,A0,A1> {};
```

...

To generate these specializations, we might add the following to our pattern:

```
template <class R, BOOST_PP_ENUM_TRAILING_PARAMS(n, class A)>
struct signature<function<R( BOOST_PP_ENUM_PARAMS(n,A) )> >
  : mpl::BOOST_PP_CAT(vector,n)<
      R, BOOST_PP_ENUM_TRAILING_PARAMS(n,A)
  > {};
```

BOOST_PP_CAT implements **token pasting**; its two arguments are "glued" together into a single token. Since this is a general-purpose macro, it sits in `cat.hpp` at the top level of the library's directory tree.

Although the preprocessor has a built-in token-pasting operator, **##**, it only works within a macro definition. If we'd used it here, it wouldn't have taken effect at all:

```
template <class R>
struct signature<function<R()> >
  : mpl::vector##1<R> {};

template <class R, class A0>
struct signature<function<R(A0)> >
  : mpl::vector##2<R,A0> {};

template <class R, class A0, class A1>
struct signature<function<R(A0,A1)> >
  : mpl::vector##3<R,A0,A1> {};
```

...

Also, ## often yields surprising results by taking effect before its arguments have been expanded:

```
#define N            10
#define VEC(i)       vector##i

VEC(N)               // vectorN
```

By contrast, BOOST_PP_CAT delays concatenation until after its arguments have been fully evaluated:

```
#define N            10
#define VEC(i)       BOOST_PP_CAT(vector,i)

VEC(N)               // vector10
```

A.4.5   Data Types

The Preprocessor library also provides **data types**, which you can think of as being analogous to MPL type sequences. Preprocessor data types store *macro arguments* instead of C++ types.

A.4.5.1   Sequences

A **sequence** (or **seq** for short) is any string of nonempty parenthesized *macro arguments*. For instance, here's a three-element sequence:

```
#define MY_SEQ     (f(12))(a + 1)(foo)
```

Here's how we might use a sequence to generate specializations of the is_integral template from the Boost Type Traits library (see Chapter 2):

```
# include <boost/preprocessor/seq.hpp>
template <class T>

struct is_integral : mpl::false_ {};

// a seq of integral types with unsigned counterparts
#define BOOST_TT_basic_ints            (char)(short)(int)(long)

// generate a seq containing "signed t" and "unsigned t"
#define BOOST_TT_int_pair(r,data,t)      (signed t)(unsigned t)
```

```
// a seq of all the integral types
#define BOOST_TT_ints                                              \
   (bool)(char)                                                    \
   BOOST_PP_SEQ_FOR_EACH(BOOST_TT_int_pair, ~, BOOST_TT_basic_ints)

// generate an is_integral specialization for type t
#define BOOST_TT_is_integral_spec(r,data,t) \
   template <>                              \
   struct is_integral<t> : mpl::true_ {};

BOOST_PP_SEQ_FOR_EACH(BOOST_TT_is_integral_spec, ~, BOOST_TT_ints)

#undef BOOST_TT_is_integral_spec
#undef BOOST_TT_ints
#undef BOOST_TT_int_pair
#undef BOOST_TT_basic_ints
```

BOOST_PP_SEQ_FOR_EACH is a higher-order macro, similar to BOOST_PP_REPEAT, that invokes its first argument on each element of its third argument.

Sequences are the most efficient, most flexible, and easiest-to-use of the library's data structures, provided that you never need to make an empty one: An empty sequence would contain no tokens, and so couldn't be passed as a macro argument. The other data structures covered here all have an empty representation.

The facilities for manipulating sequences are all in the library's seq/ subdirectory. They are summarized in Table A.5 where t is the sequence $(t_0)(t_1)\ldots(t_k)$. Where s, r, and d appear they have a similar purpose to the z parameters we discussed earlier (and suggested you ignore for now).

Table A.5 Preprocessor Sequence Operations

Expression	Result
BOOST_PP_SEQ_CAT(t)	$t_0 t_1 \ldots t_k$
BOOST_PP_SEQ_ELEM(n,t)	t_n
BOOST_PP_SEQ_ENUM(t)	$t_0, t_1, \ldots t_k$
BOOST_PP_SEQ_FILTER(pred,data,t)	t without the elements that don't satisfy pred
BOOST_PP_SEQ_FIRST_N(n,t)	$(t_0)(t_1)\ldots(t_{n-1})$
BOOST_PP_SEQ_FOLD_LEFT(op, x, t)	$\ldots op(s,op(s,op(s,x,t_0),t_1),t_2)\ldots$
BOOST_PP_SEQ_FOLD_RIGHT(op, x, t)	$\ldots op(s,op(s,op(s,x,t_k),t_{k-1}),t_{k-2})\ldots$
BOOST_PP_SEQ_FOR_EACH(f, x, t)	$f(r,x,t_0)f(r,x,t_1)\ldots f(r,x,t_k)$
BOOST_PP_SEQ_FOR_EACH_I(g, x, t)	$g(r,x,0,t_0)g(r,x,1,t_1)\ldots g(r,x,k,t_k)$
BOOST_PP_SEQ_FOR_EACH_PRODUCT(h, x, t)	Cartesian product—see online docs

Table A.5 Preprocessor Sequence Operations (continued)

Expression	Result
`BOOST_PP_SEQ_INSERT(t,i,tokens)`	$(t_0)(t_1)...(t_{i-1})$ `(tokens)` $(t_i)(t_{i+1})...(t_k)$
`BOOST_PP_SEQ_POP_BACK(t)`	$(t_0)(t_1)...(t_{k-1})$
`BOOST_PP_SEQ_POP_FRONT(t)`	$(t_1)(t_2)...(t_k)$
`BOOST_PP_SEQ_PUSH_BACK(t,tokens)`	$(t_0)(t_1)...(t_k)$ `(tokens)`
`BOOST_PP_SEQ_PUSH_FRONT(t,tokens)`	`(tokens)` $(t_0)(t_1)...(t_k)$
`BOOST_PP_SEQ_REMOVE(t,i)`	$(t_0)(t_1)...(t_{i-1})(t_{i+1})...(t_k)$
`BOOST_PP_SEQ_REPLACE(t,i,tokens)`	$(t_0)(t_1)...(t_{i-1})$ `(tokens)` $(t_{i+1})...(t_k)$
`BOOST_PP_SEQ_REST_N(n,t)`	$(t_n)(t_{n+1})...(t_k)$
`BOOST_PP_SEQ_REVERSE(t)`	$(t_k)(t_{k-1})...(t_0)$
`BOOST_PP_SEQ_HEAD(t)`	t_0
`BOOST_PP_SEQ_TAIL(t)`	$(t_1)(t_2)...(t_k)$
`BOOST_PP_SEQ_SIZE(t)`	$k+1$
`BOOST_PP_SEQ_SUBSEQ(t,i,m)`	$(t_i)(t_{i+1})...(t_{i+m-1})$
`BOOST_PP_SEQ_TO_ARRAY(t)`	$(k+1,(t_0,t_1,...t_k))$
`BOOST_PP_SEQ_TO_TUPLE(t)`	$(t_0,t_1,...t_k)$
`BOOST_PP_SEQ_TRANSFORM(f, x, t)`	$(f(r,x,t_0))$ $(f(r,x,t_1))...(f(r,x,t_k))$

It's worth noting that while there is no upper limit on the length of a sequence, operations such as `BOOST_PP_SEQ_ELEM` that take numeric arguments will only work with values up to 256.

A.4.5.2 Tuples

A **tuple** is a very simple data structure for which the library provides random access and a few other basic operations. A tuple takes the form of a parenthesized, comma-separated list of *macro arguments*. For example, this is a three-element tuple:

```
#define TUPLE3      (f(12), a + 1, foo)
```

The operations in the library's `tuple/` subdirectory can handle tuples of up to 25 elements. For example, a tuple's Nth element can be accessed via `BOOST_PP_TUPLE_ELEM`, as follows:

```
                   // length  index  tuple
BOOST_PP_TUPLE_ELEM(   3    ,   1  , TUPLE3)  // a + 1
```

Notice we had to pass the tuple's length as the second argument to BOOST_PP_TUPLE_ELEM; in fact, *all* tuple operations require explicit specification of the tuple's length. We're not going to summarize the other four operations in the "tuple" group here—you can consult the Preprocessor library's electronic documentation for more details. We note, however, that sequences can be transformed into tuples with BOOST_PP_SEQ_TO_TUPLE, and nonempty tuples can be transformed back into sequences with BOOST_PP_TUPLE_TO_SEQ.

The greatest strength of tuples is that they conveniently take the same representation as a macro argument list:

```
#define FIRST_OF_THREE(a1,a2,a3)     a1
#define SECOND_OF_THREE(a1,a2,a3)    a2
#define THIRD_OF_THREE(a1,a2,a3)     a3

// uses tuple as an argument list
# define SELECT(selector, tuple)     selector tuple

SELECT(THIRD_OF_THREE, TUPLE3)    // foo
```

A.4.5.3   Arrays

An **array** is just a tuple containing a non-negative integer and a tuple of that length:

```
#define ARRAY3    ( 3, TUPLE3 )
```

Because an array carries its length around with it, the library's interface for operating on arrays is much more convenient than the one used for tuples:

```
BOOST_PP_ARRAY_ELEM(1, ARRAY3)      // a + 1
```

The facilities for manipulating arrays of up to 25 elements are all in the library's array/ subdirectory. They are summarized in Table A.6, where a is the array $(k, (a_0, a_1, \ldots a_{k-1}))$.

Table A.6 Preprocessor Array Operations

Expression	Result
BOOST_PP_ARRAY_DATA(a)	$(a_0, a_1, \ldots a_{k-1})$
BOOST_PP_ARRAY_ELEM(i,a)	a_i
BOOST_PP_ARRAY_INSERT(a, i, tokens)	$(k+1, (a_0, a_1, \ldots a_{i-1}, \texttt{tokens},$ $a_i, a_{i+1}, \ldots a_{k-1}))$
BOOST_PP_ARRAY_POP_BACK(a)	$(k-1, (a_0, a_1, \ldots a_{k-2}))$
BOOST_PP_ARRAY_POP_FRONT(a)	$(k-1, (a_1, a_2, \ldots a_{k-1}))$

Table A.6 Preprocessor Array Operations (continued)

Expression	Result
BOOST_PP_ARRAY_PUSH_BACK(a, tokens)	$(k+1, (a_0, a_1, ...a_{k-1}, \texttt{tokens}))$
BOOST_PP_ARRAY_PUSH_FRONT(a, tokens)	$(k+1, (\texttt{tokens}, a_1, a_2, ...a_{k-1}))$
BOOST_PP_ARRAY_REMOVE(a, i)	$(k-1, (a_0, a_1, ...a_{i-1}, a_{i+1}, ...a_{k-1}))$
BOOST_PP_ARRAY_REPLACE(a, i, tokens)	$(k, (a_0, a_1, ...a_{i-1},$ tokens, $a_{i+1}, ...a_{k-1}))$
BOOST_PP_ARRAY_REVERSE(a)	$(k, (a_{k-1}, a_{k-2}, ...a_1, a_0))$
BOOST_PP_ARRAY_SIZE(a)	k

A.4.5.4 Lists

A **list** is a two-element tuple whose first element is the first element of the list, and whose second element is a list of the remaining elements, or BOOST_PP_NIL if there are no remaining elements. Lists have access characteristics similar to those of a runtime linked list. Here is a three-element list:

```
#define LIST3      (f(12), (a + 1, (foo, BOOST_PP_NIL)))
```

The facilities for manipulating lists are all in the library's list/ subdirectory. Because the operations are a subset of those provided for sequences, we're not going to summarize them here—it should be easy to understand the list operations by reading the documentation on the basis of our coverage of sequences.

Like sequences, lists have no fixed upper length bound. Unlike sequences, lists can also be empty. It's rare to need more than 25 elements in a preprocessor data structure, and lists tend to be slower to manipulate and harder to read than any of the other structures, so they should normally be used only as a last resort.

A.5 Exercise

A-0. Fully preprocessor-ize the tiny type sequence implemented in Chapter 5 so that all boilerplate code is eliminated and the maximum size of a tiny sequence can be adjusted by changing TINY_MAX_SIZE.

Appendix B

The `typename` and `template` Keywords

The `template` keyword is used to introduce template declarations and definitions:

```
template <class T>
class vector;
```

The `typename` keyword is often used in place of `class` to declare template type parameters:[1]

```
template <typename T>
class vector;
```

Both keywords also have a second role in the language. This appendix is about that role, why it is needed, and exactly how to apply `typename` and `template` to fill it. Because the rules are subtle, many people wait until the compiler complains before thinking about the use of `typename` or `template`, but it's worth learning these technical details because:

- You'll spend less time fixing trivial syntax errors.

- You'll understand what you did wrong when the compiler does complain.

- Your code will be more portable—many compilers don't complain *enough* to be strictly standards-conforming, and won't tell you when you missed a `typename` or `template`.

- Your code will be more likely to work as you intend—the compiler can't detect all misuses, and leaving one of these keywords out can cause your program to misbehave silently.

---

1. We'll discuss the reasons why this book uses `class` and not `typename` in a moment.

B.1   The Issue

Template compilation has two phases: The first occurs at the template's **point of definition**, and the second at each of its **points of instantiation**. According to the C++ standard, a template must be completely checked for syntactic correctness at its point of definition,[2] so its author can know that it is well-formed long before it is instantiated:

```
template <class ForwardIterator1, class ForwardIterator2>
void iter_swap(ForwardIterator1 i1, ForwardIterator2 i2)
{
    T tmp = *i1;  // error: unknown identifier T
    *i1 = *i2;
    *i2 = tmp;
}
```

B.1.1   Problem One

During standardization, the committee discovered several cases for which it was impossible to do a full syntactic check at a template's point of definition. For example, consider this translation unit containing a definition of iter_swap:

```
double const pi = 3.14159265359;

template <class T> struct iterator_traits; // declaration only

template <class FwdIterator1, class FwdIterator2>
void iter_swap(FwdIterator1 i, FwdIterator2 j)
{
    iterator_traits<FwdIterator1>::value_type* pi = &*i;
    ...continued...
}
```

The compiler has to check iter_swap for syntax errors, but it hasn't seen a definition of iterator_traits yet. Its ::value_type could be a type, in which case the highlighted line is a valid declaration. However, it could also turn out to be an enum value:

---

2. Not all compilers conform in this regard; many postpone some or all checking until the point of instantiation.

```
template <class T>
struct iterator_traits
{
    enum { value_type = 0 };
};
```

in which case the first line of `iter_swap` is nonsense. It's tempting to think that the compiler should deduce that `value_type` *must* be a type, because there's no way the first line of `iter_swap` could be valid otherwise. Consider this counterexample, though:

```
class number
{
 public:
    template <class U>
    number& operator=(U const&);
    int& operator*() const;
};

number operator*(number, double);

template <class T>
struct iterator_traits
{
    static number value_type;
};
```

In this case, `iter_swap` might still be valid—its first line would *multiply* a `number` by `pi`, and then assign into it:

```
(iterator_traits<FwdIterator1>::value_type * pi) = &*i;
```

but if so the syntactic structure of `iter_swap` would be completely different.

It's also tempting to think that the compiler could syntax-check `iter_swap` if it had already seen the definition of `iterator_traits`, but specializations scuttle that possibility: any given instance of `iterator_traits` could be defined differently:

```
template <>
struct iterator_traits<int*>
{
    static void* value_type;
};
```

The problem is that iterator_traits<FwdIterator1>::value_type is a **dependent name**. The syntactic role it plays *depends* on what FwdIterator1 turns out to be, and can never be known at iter_swap's point of definition.

B.1.2 Disambiguating Types

The typename keyword tells the compiler that a dependent name denotes a **dependent type**:

```
template <class FwdIterator1, class FwdIterator2>
void iter_swap(FwdIterator1 i, FwdIterator2 j)
{
    typename iterator_traits<FwdIterator1>::value_type* pi = &*i;
    ...continued...
}
```

Now the syntactic role of iterator_traits<FwdIterator1>::value_type is clear, and the compiler knows that pi denotes a pointer for the rest of the body of iter_swap. If we *don't* write **typename**, the compiler assumes that value_type denotes a non-type, and pi denotes a const double in iter_swap.

B.1.3 Using class Versus typename

As we mentioned earlier, the following two declarations are equivalent:

```
template <class T>
class vector;
```

```
template <typename T>
class vector;
```

The argument in favor of using typename is that it's conceptually accurate: class seems to indicate that the argument must be a class type, when in fact any type will do. There's certainly nothing wrong with vector<int>!

To understand the argument in favor of using class, consider the use of typename in the following declaration:

```
template <typename T, typename T::value_type>
struct sqrt_impl;
```

You may have missed this, but only the first use of `typename` is declaring a type parameter: The second `typename` is declaring that `T::value_type` is a type. Therefore, the second parameter to `sqrt` is a *value* of type `T::value_type`.

If that seems confusing, we can't blame you. Maybe this equivalent declaration will help clarify it:

```
template <class T, typename T::value_type n>
struct sqrt_impl;
```

If so, you understand the argument for using `class` to declare template type parameters: It's less confusing if `typename` is only used to mean one thing (syntax disambiguation) in template parameter lists.

We're not going to tell you which practice you should use; people of goodwill can disagree about whether conceptual accuracy is more important than avoiding confusion in the rare cases where `typename` is used in non-type parameter declarations. In fact, the authors of this book disagreed, which is why you'll see `class` here and `typename` in the MPL reference manual.

B.1.4 Problem Two

The same kind of issue arises with template members:

```
double const pi = 3.14159265359;

template <class T>
int f(T& x)
{
    return x.convert<3>(pi);
}
```

`T::convert` might be a member function template, in which case the highlighted code passes `pi` to a specialization of `convert<3>`. It could also turn out to be a data member, in which case `f` returns `(x.convert < 3 ) > pi`. That isn't a very useful calculation, but the compiler doesn't know it.

B.1.5 Disambiguating Templates

The `template` keyword tells the compiler that a dependent name is a member template:

```
template <class T>
int f(T& x)
```

```
{
    return x.template convert<3>(pi);
}
```

If we omit template, the compiler assumes that x.convert does not name a template, and the < that follows it is parsed as the less-than operator.

B.2 The Rules

In this section we'll cover the standard's rules for the use of template and typename and walk through some illustrative examples.

B.2.1 typename

The relevant standard language comes from section 14.6 [temp.res], paragraph 5:

> The keyword typename shall only be used in template declarations and definitions, including in the return type of a function template or member function template, in the return type for the definition of a member function of a class template or of a class nested within a class template, and in the *type-specifier* for the definition of a static member of a class template or of a class nested within a class template. The keyword typename shall only be applied to qualified names, but those names need not be dependent. The keyword typename is not permitted in a *base-specifier* or in a *mem-initializer;* in these contexts a *qualified-name* that depends on a *template-parameter* (14.6.2) is implicitly assumed to be a type name.

B.2.1.1 typename Required

The typename keyword is required anywhere in templates on *qualified* dependent names that denote types.

Identifying Dependent Type Names

In the following example, the type C::value_type is dependent on the template parameter C.

```
// member data declarations
template <class C>
struct something
```

```
{
    typename C::value_type x;
};
```

The property of being a dependent type is transitive. In the following example, C::value_type is dependent on C and value_type::is_const is dependent on value_type (and therefore also on C).

```
// member type declarations
template <class C>
struct something
{
    typedef typename C::value_type value_type;
    typedef typename value_type::is_const is_const;
};
```

In the following example, the ::type member of the add_const metafunction is dependent on the template parameter T.

```
template <class T>
struct input_iterator_part_impl
{
    typedef typename boost::add_const<T>::type const_T;
};
```

Contexts for Application

You've seen how typename is applied within class template bodies. It is also required within parameter lists, including in default argument expressions:

```
template <
    class T
  , typename non_type_parameter<T>::type value
      = typename non_type_parameter<T>::type()
>
struct initialized
{};
```

and in function templates, including their bodies:

```
template <class Sequence>
typename Sequence::iterator              // in return type
find(
    Sequence seq
  , typename Sequence::value_type x  // in parameter types
)
{
    typename Sequence::iterator it   // inside function body
      = seq.begin();
    ...etc...
}
```

Since the rule is "one typename per dependent name," there might be *several* typenames required within a single declaration.

```
template <class Sequence>
struct key_iterator_generator
{
    typedef typename projection_iterator_gen<
        select1st<typename Sequence::value_type>
      , typename Sequence::const_iterator
    >::type type;
};
```

Subtleties

A type can be dependent for subtle reasons. In the following example, index<1>::type is dependent because one can specialize the index member template for a given Iterator type.

```
template <class Iterator>
struct category_index
{
    template <long N> struct index
    {
        typedef char(&type)[N];
    };
```

```cpp
    int category(std::input_iterator_tag)
    {
        return sizeof(typename index<1>::type);
    }
    int category(std::forward_iterator_tag)
    {
        return sizeof(typename index<2>::type);
    }
};
template <>
template <long N>
struct category_index<int*>::index
{
    typedef char(&type)[N + 1];
};
```

In other words, for the purpose of syntax disambiguation, the primary `category_index` template is equivalent to:

```cpp
template <class Iterator, long N> struct index
{
    typedef char(&type)[N];
};

template <class Iterator>
struct category_index
{
};
```

B.2.1.2   typename Allowed (But Not Required)

The `typename` keyword is optional on qualified *non-dependent* names inside a template. In the following example, `std::unary_function<T,T*>` is not dependent because it is always a class, no matter what T turns out to be.

```cpp
template <class T>
struct something
{
    // OK
    std::unary_function<T,T*> f2;
    std::unary_function<int,int>::result_type x2;
```

```
        // also OK
        typename std::unary_function<T,T*> f1;
        typename std::unary_function<int,int>::result_type x1;
};
```

B.2.1.3   typename Forbidden

typename cannot be used anywhere outside of templates:

```
struct int_iterator
{
    typedef typename int value_type; // error
};
```

It is also forbidden on non-qualified names (those not preceded by ::), even if they are dependent.

```
template <class T>
struct vector
{
    typedef typename int value_type;          // error
    typedef typename pair<int,T> pair_type;   // error
    typedef typename T* pointer;              // error
};
```

typename is forbidden on the name of a base class, even if it is dependent:

```
template <class T> struct base_gen;

template <class T>
struct derived
  : typename base_gen<T>::type // error
{};
```

but in the following, typename is required because T::value_type does not name a base class.

```
template <class T>
struct get_value
  : std::unary_function<T, typename T::value_type> // OK
{};
```

Since an explicit (full) specialization is not a template declaration, the following is not currently allowed, though core language issue #183 argues in favor of allowing it in future revisions of the standard.[3]

```
template <class T> struct vector;

template <class T> struct vector_iterator
  : mpl::identity<T> {};


template <>
struct vector<void*>
{
    typedef typename                                 // error
      vector_iterator<void*>::type iterator;
};
```

B.2.1.4   Miscellaneous Notes

*   The C++ standard (section 14.6.1) allows us to use a class template's own name without arguments as a synonym for the specialization being instantiated, which means we can use a template's name to qualify members of dependent bases. For instance, instead of:

    ```
    template <class T> class base;

    template <class T>
    struct derived
      : base<typename whatever<T>::type> // repeated below
    {
        typedef base<typename whatever<T>::type> base_;
        typedef typename base_::value_type value_type;
    };
    ```

    we can simply write:

    ```
    template <class T> struct base;

    template <class T>
    ```

---

3. See http://www.open-std.org/jtcl/sc22/wg21/docs/cwg_defects.html#183.

```
struct derived
  : base<typename whatever<T>::type> // not repeated
{
    typedef typename derived::value_type value_type;
};
```

- with the acceptance of core language issue #11, [4]

```
template class T> struct base;

template <class T>
struct derived
  : base<T>
{
    using typename base<T>::value_type;
};
```

  is equivalent to

```
template <class T> struct base;

template <class T>
struct derived
  : base<T>
{
    typedef typename base<T>::value_type value_type;
};
```

- core language issue #180 clarifies that `typename` is not allowed in friend declarations,[5] e.g.:

```
template <class T>
class X
{
    friend class typename T::nested; // error
};
```

---

4. See http://www.open-std.org/ jtcl/sc22/wg21/docs/cwg_defects.html#11.
5. See http://www.open-std.org/jtcl/sc22/wg21/docs/cwg_defects.html#180.

B.2.2 `template`

The relevant standardese comes from section 14.2 [temp.names] of the C++ standard, in paragraph 4:

> When the name of a member template specialization appears after `.` or `->` in a *postfix-expression,* or after *nested-name-specifier* in a *qualified-id,* and the *postfix-expression* or *qualified-id* explicitly depends on a *template-parameter* (14.6.2), the member template name must be prefixed by the keyword `template`. Otherwise the name is assumed to name a nontemplate.

and paragraph 5:

> If a name prefixed by the keyword `template` is not the name of a member template, the program is ill-formed. [Note: the keyword `template` may not be applied to nontemplate members of class templates.]

Core language issue #30 adds:[6]

> Furthermore, names of member templates shall not be prefixed by the keyword `template` if the *postfix-expression* or *qualified-id* does not appear in the scope of a template. [Note: just as is the case with the `typename` prefix, the `template` prefix is allowed in cases where it is not strictly necessary; i.e., when the expression on the left of the `->` or `.`, or the *nested-name-specifier* is not dependent on a *template-parameter.*]

B.2.2.1 `template` Required

The `template` keyword is required before dependent names accessing member templates via `.`, `->`, or `::` qualification. In the following example, `convert` and `base` depend on `T`.

```
template <class T> void f(T& x, T* y)
{
    int n = x.template convert<int>();
    int m = y->template convert<int>();
}

template <class T> struct other;
```

---

6. See http://www.open-std.org/jtc1/sc22/wg21/docs/cwg_defects.html#30.

```
template <class T>
struct derived
  : other<T>::template base<int>
{};
```

Note that, unlike the typename keyword, template is required even on class template names that denote base classes.

B.2.2.2 template Allowed (But Not Required)

As long as it actually precedes a member template id, template is optional anywhere in a template. For instance:

```
template <class T>
struct other
{
    template <class U> struct base;
};

template <class T>
struct derived1
  : other<int>::base<T>                  // OK
{};

template <class T>
struct derived2
  : other<int>::template base<T>     // also OK
{};
```

B.2.2.3 template Forbidden

The template keyword is forbidden anywhere outside a template, including explicit (full) template specializations (as per core language issue #30 cited earlier):

```
template <> struct derived<int>
  : other<int>::template base<int> // error
{};
```

template is also forbidden in *using-declaration*s:

```
template <class T>
struct derived
  : base<T>
{
    using base<T>::template apply; // error
};
```

This ban was clarified by core language issue #109 as Not a Defect (NAD).[7]

---

7. See http://www.open-std.org/jtcl/sc22/wg21/docs/cwg_closed.html#109.

Appendix C

Compile-Time Performance

Interpretation of template metaprograms is inherently inefficient. When a class template is instantiated, a C++ compiler must meet all the standard's requirements, including matching against partial specializations, building an internal representation of the class, and recording the specialization in the template's namespace. It may also have to meet requirements imposed by its own design or that of the environment, such as generating mangled symbol names for the linker or recording information for the debugger. None of these activities are directly related to the metaprogram's intended computation.

This inefficiency manifests itself in the time it takes for a program to compile and in the resources used by the compiler. Extensive use of metaprogramming without understanding its costs will magnify these effects. Because your metaprograms will typically be used by other programmers who care more about a quick compile/edit/debug cycle than how your library is implemented, they're not likely to be understanding if compilation gets very slow or stops because resource limits have been exceeded.

Fortunately, problems are not inevitable, and can be avoided if you know how to keep the situation under control. Appendix C gives you the tools to analyze and manage metaprogram efficiency.

C.1 The Computational Model

Can we really say anything useful about a program's compile time costs without examining the implementation of every compiler?

Using the standard techniques for analyzing runtime complexity, we can.[1] When we describe the complexity of runtime programs, we count the number of primitive operations they execute on an **abstract machine**. An abstract machine is a model of the actual hardware that hides such issues as instruction cycle times, cache locality, and register usage. In the case of template metaprograms,

---

1. See http://en.wikipedia.org/wiki/Computational_complexity_theory.

the abstract machine is a model of the compiler implementation that hides such issues as its internal data structures, symbol table lookup efficiency, and the parsing algorithm.

We measure metaprogram complexity in terms of the number of template instantiations required. It's not an entirely arbitrary choice: Compilation times tend to be correlated with the number of template instantiations performed. It's also not a perfect choice, but only by sweeping aside factors that are sometimes relevant can we simplify the abstract machine enough to reason about its performance.

C.1.1 Memoization

Even if we ignore the other factors, thinking about complexity just in terms of template instantiations can be strange, since a particular template specialization is only instantiated once in a translation unit:

```
typedef foo<char>::type t1; // foo<char> instantiated here
...
typedef foo<char>::type t2; // foo<char> is just looked up
```

Unlike the way regular function calls work, when a metafunction is called again with the same arguments, the compiler doesn't have to go through the whole computation again. If you're familiar with the idea of "memoization," you can think of all metafunction results as being memoized. At the first invocation, the instantiated class is stored in a lookup table indexed by the template's arguments. For subsequent invocations with the same arguments, the compiler merely looks up the template instantiation in the table.

C.1.2 An Example

Consider the classic recursive Fibonacci function, with $O(n^2)$ complexity:

```
unsigned fibonacci(unsigned n)
{
    if (n < 2)
        return n;
    else
        return fibonacci(n - 1) + fibonacci(n - 2);
}
```

Invoking fibonacci(3) might cause the following series of calls:

```
fibonacci(3)
  fibonacci(2)
    fibonacci(1)
    fibonacci(0)
  fibonacci(1)
fibonacci(2)
  fibonacci(1)
  fibonacci(0)
```

Now let's do a direct translation into templates:

```
template<unsigned n, bool done = (n < 2)>
struct fibonacci
{
    static unsigned const value
      = fibonacci<n-1>::value + fibonacci<n-2>::value;
};

template<unsigned n>
struct fibonacci<n,true>
{
    static unsigned const value = n;
};
```

In this case, `fibonacci<3>::value` might cause the following sequence of instantiations and lookups, where instantiations are shown in **bold**:

fibonacci<3>
  fibonacci<2>
    fibonacci<1>
    fibonacci<0>
  fibonacci<1>
fibonacci<2>

The complexity of the compile time `fibonacci` function is not $O(n^2)$, but $O(n)$. That's true even if you count lookups: there is at most one instantiation and one lookup per n.

C.1.3   What Are We Hiding?

What's being hidden by this way of describing the abstract machine? Without looking at the compiler's source code, we can't be sure. In the interest of "full disclosure," we'll discuss the things we *know* are being swept under the rug.

As we mentioned earlier, we're hiding implementation details of the compiler. In a moment we'll discuss some ways in which those details can "leak" out of our abstraction and become observable. We're also glossing over a few details of metaprogram implementation. For example, some associative sequences use function overload resolution to implement their lookup strategies.[2] Overload resolution can have a nontrivial cost in the compiler, but we're not considering it.

C.2   Managing Compilation Time

The first and most important thing you can do to improve your metaprograms' execution (compilation) time is to reduce their computational complexity. Use an `mpl::vector` if you need access to arbitrary elements, because each such access will be O(1) instead of O(N), as it would be with an `mpl::list`. Don't search linearly for an element in a sequence when you could use `mpl::lower_bound`, and so forth. There is no substitute for picking the right algorithms and data structures.

Unfortunately, most compilers weren't designed with template metaprogramming in mind, and many use an inferior implementation strategy. For example, an ideal compiler would store all memoized template specializations in a hash table for O(1) lookups. However, as of this writing most implementations use one linked list to store all instantiations of a particular class template. Thus, lookups are technically linear in the number of instantiations of that template that have come before. Usually, this O(N) effect is swamped by the cost of instantiation, but as we shall see, it *can* be observed.

We happen to know this implementation detail of the compilers we've tested, but there are many more individual quirks of specific compilers that we don't know about. By using special-purpose test programs, we can get an idea of the real-world effects of our metaprogram design choices, and which compilers to use when metaprogram speed matters. In this appendix we'll discuss the empirical results of these black-box tests, and we'll reveal some techniques you can use to avoid the trouble spots we've found.

Note that complete details of the tests we describe here can be found on this book's companion CD.

C.3   The Tests

C.3.1   Effectiveness of Memoization

Are template instantiations really being memoized? If they are, how much does memoization save? To find out, we can make some minor changes to the `fibonacci` template:[3]

---

2. There's no runtime execution involved; the function call is wrapped in `sizeof` or `typeof` as described in Chapter 9.
3. The code shown here is a slight simplification of the actual code used to generate the graphs; refer to this book's companion CD for details.

```
template<unsigned n, unsigned m = n, bool done = (n < 2)>
struct fibonacci
{
    static unsigned const v1
      = fibonacci<n-1,m-1>::value;

    static unsigned const value
      = v1 + fibonacci<n-2,m-STEP>::value;
};
template<unsigned n, unsigned m>
struct fibonacci<n,m,true>
{
    static unsigned const value = n;
};
```

When STEP == 2, invoking fibonacci<N> causes the same number of template instantiations as ever. With STEP == 1, though, we ensure that the computation of fibonacci< N-2,...>::value never invokes fibonacci with an argument set that's been used before. The new parameter, m, provides an "additional dimension" for fibonacci specializations, which we exploit to escape memoization.

By subtracting the time it takes to compute fibonacci<N>::value with STEP == 2 from the time it takes with STEP == 1, we can see the savings provided by memoization for increasing values of N (see Figure C.1).

The difference in cost between the two computations rises as N^3 for all compilers tested, so memoization is indeed a big win.

C.3.2   Cost of Memoized Lookups

What's the cost of looking up a previously mentioned template specialization? To measure that, we can use yet another variation on the Fibonacci test:

```
template<unsigned n, bool done = (n < 2)>
struct lookup
{
    static unsigned const v1
      = lookup<n-1>::value;

    static unsigned const value = v1
```

```
#ifndef BASELINE // do memoized lookup
      + lookup<((n%2) ? 0 : n-2)>::value
#endif
        ;
};

template<unsigned n>
struct lookup<n,true>
{
    static unsigned const value = n;
};
```

The difference between the costs of computing `lookup<N>::value` with and without BASELINE defined shows the cost of a memoized lookup when N specializations of the template have already been mentioned. Note that this isn't a Fibonacci computation anymore, though it follows the same instantiation/lookup pattern. We're choosing `lookup<0>` instead of `lookup<n-2>` for the memoized lookup half the time, because specializations tend to be stored in linked lists.

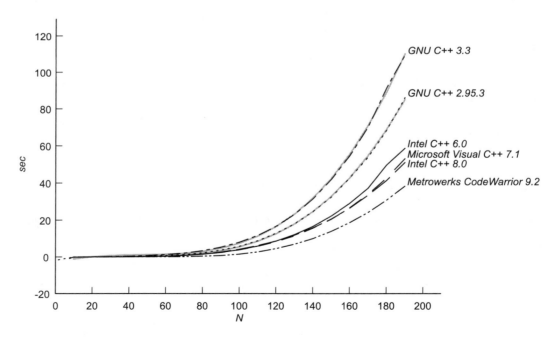

Figure C.1 Performance Savings Due to Memoization

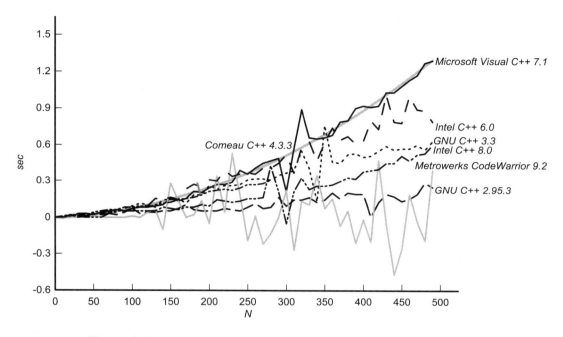

Figure C.2 Cost of Lookups versus Specializations of a Given Template

A compiler that starts looking from the end where the most recently mentioned specializations are stored will always have an advantage with a strict Fibonacci computation. Figure C.2 shows the results.

The first thing to notice is that the numbers are relatively small for all compilers. The time is bounded by that of Microsoft Visual C++ 7.1, which goes as N^2—just what you'd expect if all specializations of a given template were stored in a single linked list. We have no explanation for the erratic performance of Metrowerks' lookups, but we can say that it is at least averaging somewhere near zero cost per memoized lookup.

C.3.3 Mentioning a Specialization

Once a trivial class template specialization has been *mentioned*, instantiating it seems to have no cost. For instance:

```
template <class T> struct trivial { typedef T type; };
typedef mpl::vector<trivial<int> > v; // just a "mention"
trivial<int>::type x;                 // cost-free instantiation
```

This result may surprise you, considering that we are measuring efficiency in terms of template instantiations—it certainly surprised us at first—but we think we now understand the reasons for it.

As you know, `trivial<int>` is a perfectly legitimate type even before it is instantiated. Compilers need some unique identifier for that type so that, for example, they can recognize that two occurrences of `mpl::vector<trivial<int> >` are also the same type. They could identify `trivial<int>` by its human-readable name, but as types get more complicated, matching long names becomes more costly. We believe that most C++ compilers allocate a "memoization record" at the first mention of a template specialization, and leave it in an "empty" state until the moment the specialization is instantiated. The address of a specialization's memoization record can then be used as a unique identifier. The simpler a class template's definition, the closer its memoization record's "empty" and "full" states are to one another, and the less time is taken by instantiation.

You may be asking yourself whether it really makes sense to measure metaprogram efficiency by counting template instantiations, if some instantiations are effectively instantaneous. The answer is yes; it does. Because there is no looping, a metafunction's implementation can only directly mention a constant number of template specializations. What you see is what you get—that is, until the metafunction instantiates one of those templates it mentions. Thus, each metafunction invocation can only directly create a constant number of new memoization records. The only way to "escape" this constant-factor limitation is for the metafunction to instantiate another template.

The graph in Figure C.3 shows the cost of simply *mentioning,* but not instantiating, N distinct specializations of the same template. As you can see, there's quite a spread. The complexity for Comeau and both GCCs is $O(N^3)$.

By eliminating the $O(N^3)$ curves from the graph, (see Figure C.4), we can see that the cost of mentioning N specializations of the same template on the other compilers is $O(N^2)$.

C.3.4 Nested Template Instantiations

Nested template instantiations are the bread-and-butter of compile time programming. Even if you can avoid seeing the recursion by using MPL's algorithms, it's there under the covers. To test the effect of doing recursive template instantiations, we compiled this simple program for increasing values of N:

```
template< int i, int test > struct deep
  : deep<i-1,test>
{};

template< int test> struct deep<0,test>
{
    enum { value = 0 };
};
```

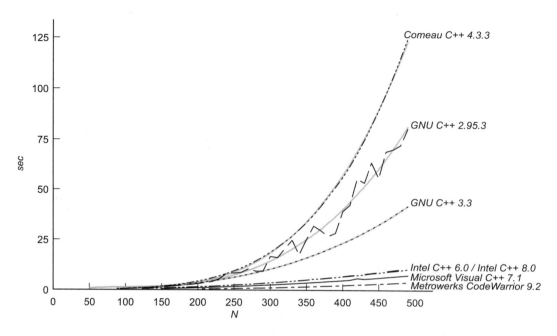

Figure C.3 Cost of Mentioning N Specializations of the Same Template

```
template< int n > struct test
{
    enum { value = deep<N,n>::value };
};

int main()
{
    return test<0>::value + test<1>::value + test<2>::value
        + test<3>::value + test<4>::value + test<5>::value
        + test<6>::value + test<7>::value + test<8>::value
        + test<9>::value;
}
```

As you can see in Figure C.5, for low values of N, all the compilers behave similarly, but when N reaches 100 or so, the EDG-based compilers begin to spend seconds more, and somewhere around 200 their compilation times simply "explode."

If we remove the EDG-based compilers from the graph (see Figure C.6), we can see the behavior of the others, all of which exhibit $O(N^2)$ complexity.

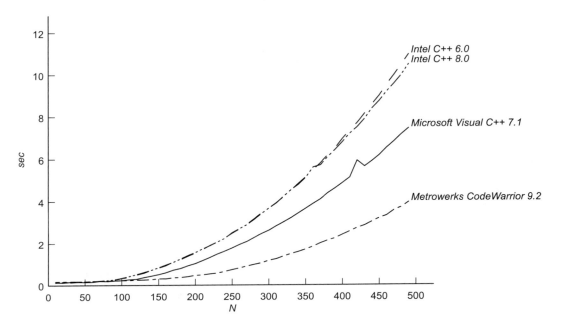

Figure C.4 Cost of Mentioning N Specializations of the Same Template

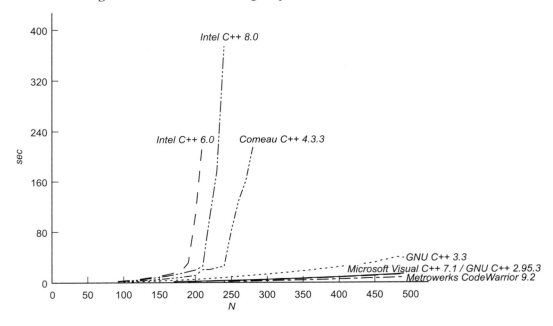

Figure C.5 Time versus Nesting Depth

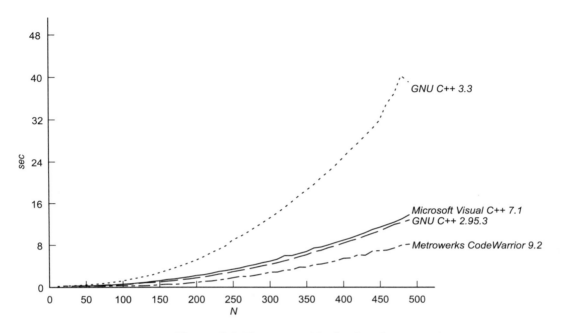

Figure C.6 Time versus Nesting Depth

C.3.4.1   Nested Instantiations Without Forwarding

The following version of the `deep` template, which restates its `::value` at each level rather than inheriting it, reveals that the explosion is triggered by deeply nested metafunction forwarding:

```
template< int i, int test > struct deep
{
    enum { value = deep<i-1,test>::value }; // no forwarding
};

template< int test> struct deep<0,test>
{
    enum { value = 0 };
};
```

As you can see in Figure C.7, EDG's pathological behavior is gone; its times are clustered with most of the other compilers. GNU C++ (GCC) 3.3 also improved its performance somewhat, but its big-O behavior didn't change. It is still $O(N^2)$ like the rest.

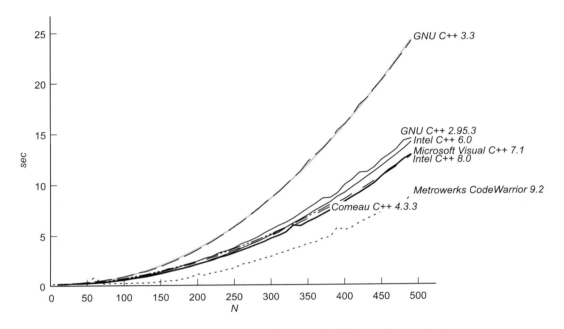

Figure C.7 Time versus Nesting Depth (Without Forwarding)

Metafunction forwarding is so valuable for simplifying programs that we're reluctant to recommend against it, even for EDG users. As far as we know, we've never hit "the EDG wall" in real code;[4] in fact, we only discovered it by writing test cases for this book. That said, if you find your metaprogram is slower to execute on EDG-based compilers than on others, you might want to review it for cases of deep forwarding.

C.3.4.2 Using Recursion Unrolling to Limit Nesting Depth

Even $O(N^2)$ behavior is really unattractive for what should be an $O(N)$ operation. While we can't go in and fix the compiler implementation, we *can* reduce the depth of nested instantiations. Since the time goes as the square of the depth, a factor of two reduction in depth is worth a factor of four in time, and a factor of four reduction in depth will make a recursive metafunction sixteen times as

---

4. We have occasionally seen metaprograms which an EDG-based compiler was slow to compile, but we didn't know about the deep forwarding effect at the time, and the behavior didn't seem to be quite as drastic as our graphs indicate for deep forwarding.

fast, and so on. Furthermore, when a compiler has a pathological behavior like the "EDG wall," or simply a hardcoded depth limit (as some do), reducing the depth can make the difference between throwing in the towel and having a productive day at the office.

Consider this implementation of the guts of `mpl::find`:

```cpp
namespace boost { namespace mpl {

    template <class First, class Last, class T>

    struct find_impl;

    // find_impl on the tail of the sequence
    template <class First, class Last, class T>
    struct find_impl_tail
      : find_impl<
            typename next<First>::type
          , Last
          , T
        >
    {};

    // true if First points at T
    template <class First, class T>
    struct deref_is_same
      : is_same<typename deref<First>::type,T>
    {};

    template <class First, class Last, class T>
    struct find_impl
      : eval_if<
            deref_is_same<First,T>  // found?
          , identity<First>
          , find_impl_tail<First,Last,T>  // search on the tail
        >
    {};

    // terminating case
    template <class Last, class T>
    struct find_impl<Last, Last, T>
    {
        typedef Last type;
    };
}}
```

Right now, `find_impl` incurs one level of recursion for each element of the sequence it traverses. Now let's rewrite it using **recursion unrolling**:

```
// a single step of the find algorithm
template <
    class First, class Last, class T
  , class EvalIfUnmatched = next<First>
>
struct find_step
  : eval_if<
        or_<
            is_same<First,Last>              // sequence empty
          , deref_is_same<First,T>           // or T is found
        >
      , identity<First>
      , EvalIfUnmatched
    >
{};

template <class First, class Last, class T>
struct find_impl
{
    typedef typename find_step<First,Last,T>::type step1;
    typedef typename find_step<step1,Last,T>::type step2;
    typedef typename find_step<step2,Last,T>::type step3;
    typedef typename find_step<
        step3,Last,T, find_impl_tail<step3,Last,T>
    >::type type;
};
```

Now each invocation of `find_impl` does up to four steps of the algorithm, reducing instantiation depth by a factor of four. When the sequence being searched supports random access, it's possible to make this idiom even more efficient by specializing the algorithm for lengths less than the unrolling factor, thereby avoiding iterator identity checks at each step. The MPL's algorithms use these techniques whenever appropriate to the target compiler.

C.3.5 Number of Partial Specializations

The graph in Figure C.8 shows the effect of increasing numbers of partial specializations on the time it takes to instantiate a class template.

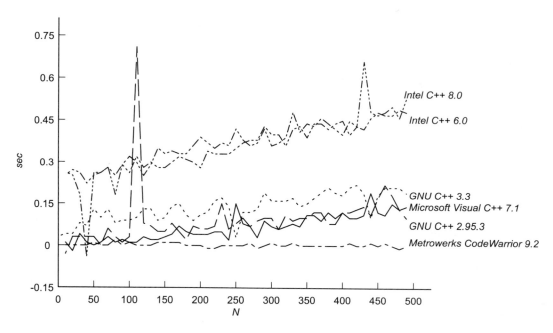

Figure C.8 Instantiation Time versus Number of Partial Specializations

Comeau C++ is omitted from this graph because it was pathologically slow, even at N == 0, for reasons seemingly unrelated to partial specialization. Most other compilers show some effect, but such a small one that you can safely ignore it.

C.3.6   Long Symbols

Symbol name length seems to have no effect on compilation time.[5]   For example, all other things being equal, instantiating either of these two templates incurs the same cost:

```
wee<int>
a_ridiculously_loooooooooooooooooong_class_template_name<int>
```

Also, *passing* long symbol names to templates has no measurable effect on compilation time, so these two are equally expensive to instantiate:

---

5. It's worth noting that we didn't test the effects of long function names, which may have an entirely different impact, because the compiler usually has to mangle them for use by the linker.

```
mpl::vector<a_ridiculously_looooooooooooooooooong_class_name>
mpl::vector<int>
```

C.3.7 Structural Complexity of Metafunction Arguments

We considered three ways of describing the complexity of template specializations that might be passed as metafunction arguments.

1. Its arity (number of template parameters)

2. Its number of "nodes"

3. Its nesting depth

For instance, `mpl::vector30` has arity 30, and we're interested in the cost of passing templates with high arities to a metafunction. For another example, if you think of every unique template specialization as being a "node," the following "list" type has four nodes and a depth of four:

```
node<int, node<long, node<char, node<void, void> > > >
```

while this "DAG" type has four nodes and a depth of three:

```
// 1    2    3 <== Depths              Nodes
   node<                        // #1
      node<                     // #2
         node<void,void>        // #3
       , node<int,void>         // #4
      >
    , node<void, void>          // #3 again
   >
```

C.3.7.1 Structural Complexity Tests

We measured the cost of passing various kinds of complex structures through a chain of recursive metafunction invocations, over and above the cost of passing a simple type like `int`. As you can see in Figure C.9, there is no cost associated with argument arity except on GCC and Comeau, where the cost rises linearly with N.[6]

---

6. Microsoft Visual C++ 7.1 seems to have a hardcoded limit of 63 template parameters. Compilation fails thereafter with "fatal error C1111: too many template parameters."

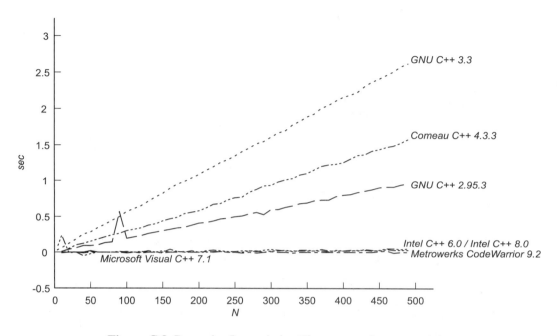

Figure C.9 Recursive Instantiation Time versus Argument Arity

We then passed a balanced binary tree of N unique nodes (and depth $\log_2 N$). The results in Figure C.10 show quite a spread: Comeau takes $O(N^2)$ time, the GCCs are linear with the modern version doing much worse than 2.95.3, and the rest show no cost at all.[7]

Finally, passing a list of N unique nodes with depth N yielded the graph shown in Figure C.11.

This change may have improved the results for GCC slightly, which we're at a loss to explain. The others, except for Comeau, didn't change at all. Comeau's results got noticeably worse, so clearly it responds not only to the number of nodes but also nesting depth. That said, there are no changes in big-O complexity here for any of the compilers.

C.3.7.2 Using Sequence Derivation to Limit Structural Complexity

Sequence derivation, as described in Chapter 5, is a powerful weapon in the fight against the effects of argument complexity on compilation time, especially for vector-like sequences. In large part this is due to the structure of their iterators. Recall the declaration of `tiny_iterator`:

---

7. In fact, GCC 2.95.3 may be exhibiting some $O(N^2)$ behavior here but the coefficient is so low that it's hard to be sure.

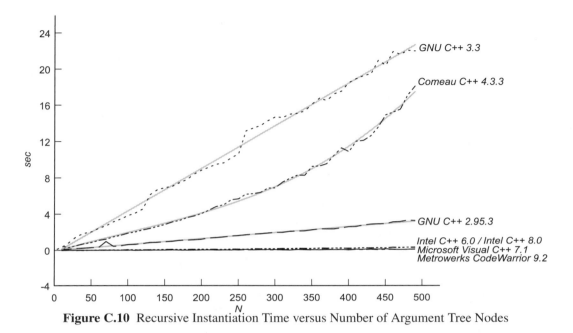

Figure C.10 Recursive Instantiation Time versus Number of Argument Tree Nodes

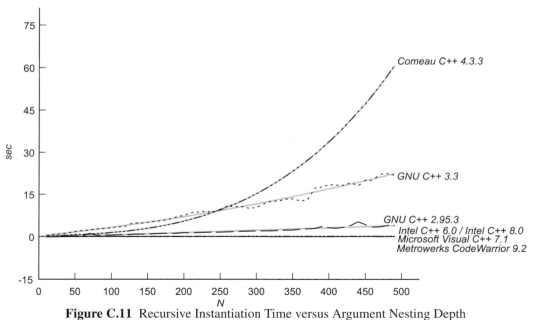

Figure C.11 Recursive Instantiation Time versus Argument Nesting Depth

```
template <class Tiny, class Pos>
struct tiny_iterator;
```

A `tiny_iterator` specialization *mentions* the entire name of the sequence it traverses as a template argument. If we extrapolate to sequences with greater capacity, it's easy to see that:

```
mpl::vector_iterator<my_vector, mpl::int_<3> >
```

may be faster to manipulate than:

```
mpl::vector_iterator<mpl::vector30<int,..., Foo>, mpl::int_<3> >
```

Appendix D

MPL Portability Summary

Most reasonably conforming compilers "just work" with the MPL. We haven't tested every compiler in existence, but Table D.1 lists a few that are known to work as described in the text without any special user intervention. Please keep in mind that this is not a complete list; you can refer to this book's companion CD for more detailed portability reports.

Table D.1 Some Compilers Requiring No User Workarounds

Name	Version
Comeau	4.3.3
GCC	3.2.2
GCC	3.3.1
GCC	3.4
Intel C++	7.1
Intel C++	8.0
Metrowerks CodeWarrior	8.3
Metrowerks CodeWarrior	9.2
Microsoft Visual C++	7.1

The compilers listed in Table D.2 have incomplete support for templates, and so require some help from users, as shown in the last column. See this book's companion CD for specific details of these workarounds.

Table D.2 Compilers That Require User Workarounds

Compiler	Version	Problematic Areas
Borland C++	5.5.1	Lambda expressions, integral constant expressions
Borland C++	5.6.4	Lambda expressions, integral constant expressions
GCC	2.95.3	Lambda expressions
Microsoft Visual C++	6.0 sp5	Lambda expressions, ETI

Table D.2 Compilers That Require User Workarounds (continued)

Compiler	Version	Problematic Areas
Microsoft Visual C++	7.0	Lambda expressions, ETI

Finally, the template machinery in a few compilers has so many problems that even with help from the user we're unable to make the MPL work at all (see Table D.3). The fact that one version of a compiler appears in this list does *not* mean that future versions are also unworkable—some vendors are working hard to correct the problems. . . and, as of this writing, some are not.

Table D.3 Compilers Known Not to Work with MPL

Name	Version
HP aCC	03.55
Sun CC	5.6

Bibliography

[Ale01]   Andrei Alexandrescu. *Modern C++ Design: Generic Programming and Design Patterns Applied.* ISBN: 0201704315, Boston, MA: Addison-Wesley, 2001.

[AS01a]   David Abrahams and Jeremy Seik. "Policy Adaptors and the Boost Iterator Adaptor Library," Second Workshop on C++ Template Programming. October 2001. http://www.boost-consulting.com/writing/iterator_adaptos0.pdf.

[AS01b]   David Abrahams and Jeremy Seik. "Boost Iterator Adaptor Library." November 2001. http://www.boost-consulting.com/writing/iterator_adaptos0.pdf.

[Bent86]   J.L. Bentley. "Programming pearls: Little languages." *Communications of the ACM,* 29(8):711-721, August 1986. http://doi.acm.org/10.1145/6424.315691.

[BMMM98] William J. Brown, Raphael C. Malveau, Hays W. "Skip" McCormick, and Thomas J. Mowbray. *AntiPatterns: Refactoring Software, Architectures, and Projects in Crisis.* ISBN: 0471197130, New York: Wiley, 1998.

[BN94]   John J. Barton and Lee R. Nackman. *Scientific and Engineering C++: An Introduction with Advanced Techniques and Examples.* ISBN: 0201533936, Reading, MA: Addison-Wesley, 1994.

[CDHM01]   Steve Cleary, Beman Dawes, Howard Hinnant, and John Maddock. "Compressed Pair." http://www.boost.org/libs/utility/compressed_pair.htm.

[Cop96]   James O. Coplien. "A Curiosly Recurring Template Pattern." In Stanley B. Lippman, editor, *C++ Gems,* pp. 135–144, New York: Cambridge University Press, 1996.

[Dew02]   Steve Dewhurst, "A Bit-Wise Typeof Operator, Part 1," *Computer User's Journal* 20(8), August 2002.
             "A Bit-Wise Typeof Operator, Part 2," *Computer User's Journal* 20(10), October 2002.
             "A Bit-Wise Typeof Operator, Part 3," *Computer User's Journal* 20(12), December 2002.

[Dimov02]   Peter Dimov. "Boost: bind.hpp documentation." http://www.boost.org/libs/bind.

[GHJV95]   E. Gamma, R. Helm, R. Johnson, and J. Vlissides. *Design Patterns.* ISBN: 0201633612, Reading, MA: Addison-Wesley, 1999.

[GotW50]   Herb Sutter. "Guru of the Week #50: Using Standard Containers." http://www.gotw.ca/gotw/050.htm.

[Guz03]   Joel de Guzman. "MAJOR BREAK-THROUGH !!! Yabadabadoo... Must Read :-)." http://sf.net/mailarchive/forum.php?thread_id=529112&forum_id=1595.

[Guz04]   Joel de Guzman, Hartmut Kaizer, et. al. "The Spirit Parser Framework." http://spirit.sf.net.

[Heer02]   Jan Heering and Marjan Mernik. "Domain-Specific Languages for Software Engineering." Proceedings of the 35th Hawaii International Conference on System Sciences – 2002. http://www.computer.org/proceedings/hicss/1435/volume9/14350279.pdf.

[Hudak89]   Paul Hudak. "Conception, evolution, and application of functional programming languages." ISSN:0360-0300, pp. 359–411, ACM Computing Surveys 21, no. 3, New York: ACM Press, 1989. http://doi.acm.org/10.1145/72551.72554.

[IBM54]   "Preliminary Report: Specifications for the IBM Mathematical FORmula TRANslation System FORTRAN." Programming Research Group, Applied Science Division, IBM Corporation, November 10, 1954.

[ISO98]   ANSI/ISO C++ Committee. *Programming Languages — C++.* ISO/IEC 14882:1998(E). American National Standards Institute, New York, 1998. http://webstore.ansi.org/ansidocstore/find.asp?find_spec=14882

[Joh79]   Stephen C. Johnson. *Yacc: Yet Another Compiler Compiler.* UNIX Programmer's Manual, Vol. 2b, pp. 353–387, Holt, Reinhart, and Winston, 1979.

[KM00]   Andrew Koenig and Barbara E. Moo. *Accelerated C++: Practical Programming by Example.* ISBN: 020170353X, Boston, MA: Addison-Wesley, 2000.

[KV89]   Thomas Keffer and Allan Vermeulen. *Math.h++ Introduction and Reference Manual.* Corvallis, Oregon: Rogue Wave Software, 1989.

[LaFre00]   David Lafreniere. "State Machine Design in C++." *C++ Report,* May 2000. http://www.cuj.com/documents/s=8039/cuj0005lafrenie/.

[Land01]   Walter Landry. "Implementing a High Performance Tensor Library." Second Workshop on C++ Template Programming, 2001. http://citeseer.nj.nec.com/landry01implementing.html.

[Mad00]   John Maddock. "Static Assertions." http://www.boost.org/libs/static_assert.

[Mart98]   Robert Martin. "UML Tutorial: Finite State Machines." *C++ Report,* June 1998.
            http://www.objectmentor.com/resources/articles/umlfsm.pdf.

[MK04]   Paul Mensonides and Vesa Karvonen. "The Boost Preprocessor Library."
            http://www.boost.org/libs/preprocessor.

[MS00a]   Brian McNamara and Yannis Smaragdakis. "Static Intefaces in C++." First Work-
            shop on C++ Template Programming, Erfurt, Germany, October 10, 2000.
            http://oonumerics.org/tmpw00/.

[MS00b]   Brian McNamara and Yannis Smaragdakis. "FC++." 2000–2003.
            http://www.cc.gatech.edu/~yannis/fc++.

[n1185]   Herb Sutter. "vector<bool> Is Nonconforming, and Forces Optimization Choice."
            http://www.gotw.ca/publications/N1185.pdf.

[n1211]   Herb Sutter. "vector<bool>: More Problems, Better Solutions."
            http://www.gotw.ca/publications/N1211.pdf.

[n1424]   John Maddock. "A Proposal to Add Type Traits to the Standard Library."
            http://anubis.dkuug.dk/jtc1/sc22/wg21/docs/papers/2003/n1424.htm.

[n1519]   John Maddock. "Type Traits Issue List."
            http://anubis.dkuug.dk/jtc1/sc22/wg21/docs/papers/2003/n1519.htm.

[n1521]   Gabriel dos Reis. "Generalized Constant Expressions." document number N1521-03-
            0104. http://www.openstd.org/jctl/wg21/docs/papers/2003/nl1521.pdf.

[n1550]   David Abrahams, Jeremy Siek, and Thomas Witt. "New Iterator Concepts."
            http://anubis.dkuug.dk/jtc1/sc22/wg21/docs/papers/2003/n1550.htm.

[Nas03]   Alexander Nasonov. "Re: boost::tuple to MPL sequence."
            http://lists.boost.org/MailArchives/boost/msg46771.php.

[Sey96]   John Seymour, Views—A C++ Standard Template Library Extension.
            http://www.zeta.org/au/~jon/STLviews/doc/views.html.

[SL00]   Jeremy Siek and Andrew Lumsdaine. "Concept Checking: Binding Parametric Poly-
            morphism in C++." First Workshop on C++ Template Programming, Erfurt, Germany,
            October 10, 2000.
            http://oonumerics.org/tmpw00/.

[SS75]   Gerald Sussman and Guy L. Steele Jr. "Scheme: An interpreter for extended lambda calculus." MIT AI Memo 349, Massachusetts Institute of Technology, May 1975.

[Strou03]   Bjarne Stroustrup. *The C++ Standard: Incorporating Technical Corrigendum No. 1.* BS ISO/IEC 14882:2003. ISBN: 0470846747, New York: Wiley, 2003.

[Unruh94]   Erwin Unruh. "Prime number computation." ANSI X3J16-94-0075/ISO WG21-462. 1994.

[Veld95a]   Todd Veldhuizen. "Blitz++." http://www.oonumerics.org/blitz/.

[Veld95b]   Todd Veldhuizen. "Using C++ Template Metaprograms." *C++ Report,* SIGS Publications Inc., ISSN 1040-6042, Vol. 7, No. 4, pp. 36–43, May 1995.

[Veld04]   Todd Veldhuizen. *Active Libraries and Universal Languages.* Doctoral Dissertation, Indiana University, Computer Science, 17 May 2004. http://www.cs.chalmers.se/~tvedhui/papers/2004/dissertation.pdf.

[VJ02]   David Vandervoode and Nicolai M. Josuttis. *C++ Templates: The Complete Guide.* ISBN: 0201734842, Boston, MA: Addison-Wesley, 2002.

[WP99]   Martin Weiser and Gary Powell, The View Template Library. http://www.zib.de/weiser/vtl.

[WP00]   Martin Weiser and Gary Powell, The View Template Library. First Workshop on C++ Template Programming, Erfurt, Germany, October 10, 2000.

Index

The C++ In-Depth Series
Bjarne Stroustrup, Series Editor

Modern C++ Design
Generic Programming and Design
Patterns Applied
By Andrei Alexandrescu
0201704315
Paperback
352 pages
© 2001

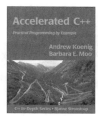

Accelerated C++
Practical Programming by Example
By Andrew Koenig and
Barbara E. Moo
020170353X
Paperback
352 pages
© 2000

Essential C++
By Stanley B. Lippman
0201485184
Paperback
304 pages
© 2000

C++ Network Programming, Volume 1
Mastering Complexity with ACE and
Patterns
By Douglas C. Schmidt and
Stephen D. Huston
0201604647
Paperback
336 pages
© 2002

The Boost Graph Library
User Guide and Reference Manual
By Jeremy G. Siek, Lie-Quan Lee, and
Andrew Lumsdaine
0201729148
Paperback
352 pages
© 2002

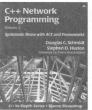

Exceptional C++
47 Engineering Puzzles, Programming
Problems, and Solutions
By Herb Sutter
0201615622
Paperback
240 pages
© 2000

More Exceptional C++
40 New Engineering Puzzles,
Programming Problems, and Solutions
By Herb Sutter
020170434X
Paperback
304 pages
© 2002

C++ Network Programming, Volume 2
Systematic Reuse with ACE and
Frameworks
By Douglas C. Schmidt and
Stephen D. Huston
0201795256
Paperback
384 pages
© 2003

Applied C++
Practical Techniques for
Building Better Software
By Philip Romanik and Amy Muntz
0321108949
Paperback
352 pages
© 2003

Exceptional C++ Style
40 New Engineering Puzzles, Programming
Problems, and Solutions
By Herb Sutter
0201760428
Paperback
352 pages
© 2005

CD-ROM Warranty

Pearson Technology Group warrants the enclosed CD to be free of defects in materials and faulty workmanship under normal use for a period of ninety days after purchase (when purchased new). If a defect is discovered in the CD during this warranty period, a replacement CD can be obtained at no charge by sending the defective CD, postage prepaid, with proof of purchase to:

Disc Exchange
Addison-Wesley Professional/Prentice Hall PTR
Pearson Technology Group
75 Arlington Street, Suite 300
Boston, MA 02116
Email: AWPro@aw.com

Pearson Technology Group makes no warranty or representation, either expressed or implied, with respect to this software, its quality, performance, merchantability, or fitness for a particular purpose. In no event will Pearson Technology Group, its distributors, or dealers be liable for direct, indirect, special, incidental, or consequential damages arising out of the use or inability to use the software. The exclusion of implied warranties is not permitted in some states. Therefore, the above exclusion may not apply to you. This warranty provides you with specific legal rights. There may be other rights that you may have that vary from state to state. The contents of this CD are intended for personal use only.

More information and updates are available at:
www.awprofessional.com/